AMSCO® **Writing for the AP Exam**

English Language
and Composition

Abdon

Freitas

Hall

PERFECTION LEARNING®

Acknowledgments

"Basics of Drug Ads." Center for Drug Evaluation and Research, U.S. Food and Drug Administration, FDA, 19 June 2015.

"Consumers' Experience with and Attitudes toward Direct-to-Consumer Prescription Drug Promotion: A Nationally Representative Survey." by Kathryn J.Aiken, et al, Health Mark Q. 2021 Jan–Mar; 38 (1): 1–11.

"Electric Vehicle Charging Infrastructure Trends from the Alternative Fueling Station Locator: Second Quarter 2020." October 2020, National Renewable Energy Laboratory.

"Explainer: For the Future of Electric Vehicles, One Size Does Not Fit All." by Scott Samuelsen, The Conversation, 19 Jan. 2015. Republished by permission of the author and The Conversation.

"Flamingos with Flu and Hippos in Hurricanes: Emergency Preparedness in Zoos and Aquariums." by Yvette Johnson-Walker. The Conversation, 17 Nov. 2014. Republished by permission of the author and The Conversation.

"Marketing to Families: Why Brands Are Investing in U.S. Zoos & Aquariums" from the Allionce Group, 13 Aug. 2021. Republished by permission of Mark Giovino, CEO of the Allionce Group.

"The Neural Cruelty of Captivity: Keeping Large Mammals in Zoos and Aquariums Damages Their Brains." by Bob Jacobs. The Conversation, 5 July 2023. Republished by permission of the author and The Conversation.

"Perspective: The Problem with Direct-To-Consumer Pharmaceutical Advertising." by Robin Feldman from The Washington Post. © 2 Mar. 2023 The Washington Post. All rights reserved. Used under license.

"Range Anxiety? Today's Electric Cars Can Cover Vast Majority of Daily U.S. Driving Needs." by Jessika E. Trancik, The Conversation, 16 Aug. 2016. Republished by permission of the author and The Conversation.

"Should the Government Restrict Direct-to-Consumer Prescription Drug Advertising? Six Takeaways on Their Effects." by Neeraj Sood, USC Schaeffer, 23 Mar. 2023.

"Trade Agreements and Direct-to-Consumer Advertising of Pharmaceuticals." by Deborah Gleeson and David B Menkes, International Journal of Health Policy and Management, U.S. National Library of Medicine, 1 Feb. 2018.

"The US Is Worried about Its Critical Minerals Supply Chains – Essential for Electric Vehicles, Wind Power and the Nation's Defense." Lee, Jordy, and Morgan Bazilian. The Conversation, 6 Apr. 2021. Republished by permission of the author and The Conversation.

Wildt, Chris. https://www.cartoonstock.com/cartoon?searchID=WJ900238

"Zoos and Aquariums Shift to a New Standard of 'Animal Welfare' That Depends on Deeper Understanding of Animals' Lives." by Michael J. Renner. The Conversation, 13 Sept. 2022. Republished by permission of the author and The Conversation.

Every reasonable effort has been made to properly acknowledge ownership of all material used. Any omissions or mistakes are not intentional and, if brought to the publisher's attention, will be corrected in future editions.

Authors

Brandon Abdon, Senior Author, Doctor of Arts, English Brandon Abdon worked for five years as Director of Curriculum, Instruction, and Assessment for the AP® English courses at The College Board, during which time he collaborated with experts from around the country to develop the Course and Exam Descriptions (CEDs) now in use. This work was a culmination of more than 15 years' experience in high schools and universities, teaching both the AP English Language and Composition and the AP English Literature and Composition courses as well as college composition, literature, and teacher education courses. He has also taught or trained thousands of teachers around the country, served as an AP Exam Reader, led many professional developments, and offered dozens of conference presentations. Currently an affiliate faculty member at Murray State University, he also serves as a professional development consultant for the Advanced Placement® program and works as a Curriculum, Instruction, and Assessment Consultant. He is also the senior author of AMSCO's *Advanced Placement Edition: English Language and Composition* coursebook. He lives with his family in Kentucky.

Timothy Freitas, Master of Arts in Teaching, Secondary English Education A College-Board-endorsed AP English Language and Composition consultant, Timothy has been teaching AP English Language and Composition and AP English Literature and Composition for more than a decade. He has presented at the AP Annual Conference (APAC) and at the NCTE Annual Conference. He has been an AP Reader, sample-selection Table Leader, AP Question Leader, and member of the College Board's Instructional Design Team for the current AP English Language and Composition framework. Timothy is a co-author of the AMSCO's *Advanced Placement Edition: English Language and Composition* coursebook. He has also been a consultant and professional development facilitator for multiple educational initiatives, typically working with underserved populations. Timothy teaches English and theology in Massachusetts at Whitinsville Christian School; before that he was a teacher at Blackstone Valley Regional Vocational Technical High School. In his free time, Timothy oversees The Garden of English—a website and YouTube channel that assists both students and teachers with planning and instruction. All of this happens while he works his real jobs: being a husband and father of five.

Beth Hall, Master of Fine Arts in Creative Writing Beth Hall, a College Board-endorsed AP English Language and Composition consultant and AP reader, has been teaching AP English Language and Composition for nearly a decade. In 2019, she began Coach Hall Writes, a platform providing writing resources for AP English Language and Composition teachers and students. In 2020, the Coach Hall Writes YouTube Channel was listed as one of the resources AP English Language and Composition teachers felt was most helpful in preparing their students for the AP English Language and Composition exam. Beth teaches honors, AP, and concurrent credit classes in Arkansas.

Reviewers

Senior Reviewer
Beverly Ann Chin, Ph.D.
Professor Emeritus of English and former Director of the English Teaching Program,
   the Montana Writing Project, and the Composition Program at the University of Montana
Past President, National Council of Teachers of English
Former Member, Instructional Design Team for AP English

Jerry W. Brown, B.M.E., M.M.E.
College Board Consultant, Reader,
   Table Leader
AP English Language and Literature Teacher
Georgetown, Texas

Erica Griffin, Ed.S.
AP English Content Director
AP English Reader
A+ College Ready
Birmingham, Alabama

Jim Jordan, M.A. Ed.
AP English Language and
   Composition Workshop Consultant
AP Reader/Question Leader
Sacred Heart Cathedral Preparatory
San Francisco, California

Chris Judson, M.S., M.A.
English Content Director
AP Teacher Investment Program
University of Notre Dame
Middlebury, Indiana

Jacqueline N. Stallworth, M.A.
College Board Consultant
AP Literature and AP African American Studies
Founder of Stallworth Educational
   Consulting Team
Washington DC

Introduction

Congratulations.

Advanced Placement courses are not for everyone, but anyone who wants to take them should have the chance. You have chosen to take this course and deserve that congratulations. Accepting the challenge of the Advanced Placement English Language and Composition course provides you opportunities to improve your writing, thinking, and reading for any other course you may take. Also, taking this course and scoring well on the AP English Language and Composition Exam may give you access to course credit or advanced courses at thousands of colleges and universities.

While the exam you take for this course has both multiple-choice questions and free-response (or essay) questions, the free responses combined account for 55% of the overall score. For this reason and others, this book focuses on key aspects of the different essay types on the exam. While writing well involves more than what you do on that exam, your exam writing allows you to show how well you can use fundamental and essential tools for analysis, argument, and general writing taught in this class.

Free-Response Questions

The free-response question (FRQ) section of the exam consists of three prompts you must respond to in 135 minutes. The College Board recommends spending 40 minutes each on two of the free-response questions and 55 minutes, 15 minutes extra, on a third that also requires reading a number of texts and source materials. This book should help you develop a plan to use this time in ways that best suit you.

There are three types of free-response prompts on the exam: Synthesis, Rhetorical Analysis, and Argument. These responses are often called "essays," but they differ from what you may be writing as essays in the actual course or in other classes. The goal of these prompts is to demonstrate your response in a set amount of time, showing that you have all the necessary skills, knowledge, and understanding to produce effective writing. You do not need to worry too much about the style of your writing on these responses. Style does matter, but not nearly as much as your claim, your reasoning, your organization, and your use of evidence and examples. Even introductions and conclusions are not strictly required. While they may help, they also may take away time you need to develop a successful argument.

In short, the prompts ask for a very good first draft of an essay you would expand later if you had the time.

The Three Types of Free-Response Questions (FRQs)

Synthesis: This is the first free-response question on the exam. The synthesis prompt provides you with a topic along with a brief introduction to the rhetorical situation of that topic. You are then also provided six or seven sources from real-world publications. These include two visuals. One will always be quantitative (a graph or chart with numbers, for example) while the other could be quantitative or qualitative (picture, cartoon, poster, for example). You must develop a written argument about the given topic using at least three of the provided sources. You are not expected to be an expert on the topic. You aren't even expected to know much at all about the topic. You can use the sources to inform you and to help you shape your perspective in the argument. However, if you do have some knowledge about the topic, you are welcome to use it as long as you also use three of the provided sources.

Rhetorical Analysis: The second free-response question asks you to read nonfiction (usually an argument of some sort) and then analyze the choices the writer or speaker made in an attempt to convey that argument. As with the synthesis FRQ, you are provided with a brief introduction to the topic and the rhetorical situation of the passage. You are not interpreting the passage or trying to figure out what the writer's or speaker's purpose is. Instead, you are identifying moves the writer or speaker makes in the text and explaining how those moves enhanced the message within the rhetorical situation.

Argument: The third and final free-response question provides you with a topic and very brief introduction to the rhetorical situation. You then are asked to write a response that argues your position on some aspect of the topic provided. This task is very similar to what you are asked to do on the synthesis FRQ, but in this case you are not given sources. Instead, you must draw upon evidence and examples from your experiences with the world around you (via media, personal experience, and history, for example).

FRQ Scores

Scoring the FRQ involves a scoring rubric that evaluates certain aspects of your response to see if you have earned points across three different "rows."

- Row A: Thesis (0–1 point)
- Row B: Evidence and Commentary (0–4 points)
- Row C: Sophistication (0–1 point)
- Total possible points: 6

Though there is a total of 6 points possible, getting a 4 or 5 out of 6 is still a good score. In fact, in most cases, a 4 out of 6 on the essays may be enough to qualify for college credit or advanced placement.

The points get more difficult to earn as you move down the rubric, meaning that the thesis point should be the easiest to get while the sophistication point is the most difficult. In fact, the sophistication point relies on so many different parts of the response working together that it is not only difficult, but *very* difficult to get. Even without it, you could earn a very good score with 1 point in Row A and 4 points in Row B.

You will have a chance to study the rubrics for each question in depth. In all three main sections (Synthesis, Rhetorical Analysis, and Argument), you will find a Thesis Review (Row A), Evidence and Commentary Review (Row B), and Sophistication Review (Row C). You will also be able to use these rubrics to evaluate sample essays, just as exam readers will evaluate yours.

Your exam essays are scored by a teacher or college professor specially trained to score the specific prompts on the exam. The readers are trained to see your essay as a first draft (but not a rough draft). Your spelling and grammatical correctness do not matter as much as your claims, evidence, and reasoning. You could write an essay with perfect spelling and no grammar or punctuation errors and not do as well as someone else who has a few such errors but has a stronger overall argument. As long as those mistakes do not interfere with what you are trying to communicate, you will be fine.

Layout of this Book

You will need a plan for approaching each essay type on exam day. This plan includes using the information the exam gives you for the essays, efficiently planning your responses, and effectively writing them.

Each essay has unique demands. This book follows the order of the essays as presented on the exam (though you do not have to write them in that order). Within each of these sections (Synthesis, Rhetorical Analysis, and Argument), the prompt is clearly explained. Then the lessons follow the rubric used to score the essays, starting with the essentials of a thesis statement, building from thesis to the development of ideas with evidence and commentary, and finally focusing and polishing writing toward the sophistication point.

Within each section of this book, individual lessons focus on very specific aspects of a certain type of essay. These lessons are also organized according to the prompt and rubric, with the first several lessons in each section relating to the prompt and thesis statements, the lessons that follow (and the bulk of the lessons in each section) relating to evidence and commentary, and the final lessons applying to aspects of essays assessed according to the sophistication row. Each section ends with two lessons that provide sample essays for analysis. Additional sample essays are included in the Appendix.

	Section 1: Synthesis	Section 2: Rhetorical Analysis	Section 3: Argument
Prompt	6 Lessons	5 Lessons	4 Lessons
Thesis (Row A)	2 Lessons	3 Lessons	4 Lessons
Evidence and Commentary (Row B)	8 Lessons	7 Lessons	7 Lessons
Sophistication (Row C)	4 Lessons	3 Lessons	4 Lessons
Sample Essays	2 Lessons	2 Lessons	2 Lessons

Each section also has two new and unique prompts (prompts A and B). You use and return to these prompts throughout the lessons. Immediately and independently applying concepts you learn in relation to Prompt A to another prompt (Prompt B) allows you to learn the concepts and skills in the lessons more quickly than if you had to use a new prompt for each lesson.

Each lesson has three main parts: Learn, Practice, and Write. Across these parts, you work with Prompt A and Prompt B at different times. Within each of those parts, you do exactly what the labels indicate:

- The **Learn** section introduces and briefly explains and models the concept of the lesson's focus.
- Next, the **Practice** section takes what was introduced and modeled in the first section and asks you to apply it through activities.
- Finally, the **Write** section extends the new concept and skill into composing.

Several additional features within each lesson make the book even more dynamic:

- **Eyes on the Exam** tells you why the lesson matters to your performance on the exam.
- **Key Point** summarizes the most important ideas to remember from the lesson.
- **Watch** points you to helpful videos for your learning, practice, and review.
- **What's the Point?** asks you to recall and remind yourself of what you learned and how that can help you on the exam.

You will also encounter **Team Up** activities that encourage you to learn with your peers through conversation, analysis, and feedback.

Using This Book

You may use this book in a class with a teacher, on your own, with a group of friends, with a tutor, or in some other setting. Regardless of the setting and regardless of what lesson you use, follow the "Learn, Practice, Write" structure of the lessons, because that is a pattern that reflects and supports how people learn.

There are a few strategies for using this book:

1. If you are using this book in a class, your teacher may decide to use the book when the class needs it, by assigning different parts to different students, or by following it step by step.

2. You do not have to follow this book in order from the first lesson to the last in an essay section. You might instead try building the basics of effective essays first by doing the lessons about the prompt and thesis, then the first several lessons on evidence and commentary. Once you have built a foundation, then you might revisit later lessons in each section on evidence and commentary and on sophistication.

3. You may decide to follow each essay section all the way through. You will certainly learn all you need to know to write well for each essay, though you will absolutely need to review what you've learned in the days and weeks leading up to the actual exam. A **Key Point Review** included for each type of FRQ will help with that.

4. You may choose to look only for those lessons that will be useful as you seek to improve the work you are doing for a class. For example, if a teacher tells you that you need to work on a certain skill, you can find a lesson in this book to help with that.

This book does not replace what a teacher teaches you about the course or about how to approach essays on the exam. Your teacher knows you and the class best. Instead, you can use approaches in this book to help you supplement what your teacher does.

Top Tips

The authors of this book—Brandon, Timm, and Beth—have decades of combined experience teaching the AP English Language and Composition course. They also have collectively trained hundreds of teachers and thousands of students around the country and even the world. With all that experience, they have gathered the following **Top Three Tips** for the exam.

1. **From Brandon:** One trait appears in essays that score well more than it does in essays that earn lower scores. I can't say that this trait makes the difference every time. However, this trait requires a high level of thinking and understanding, and that higher level of thinking finds its way into the essay and says "I am a student who can think about things in advanced and complex ways." This trait is just that: complexity. **Recognizing, including, discussing, and even rebutting or refuting complexities** related to your claim or topic all demonstrate that you are a mature, complex thinker who can use that complex thinking when you write. Try to always think about what bigger ideas underlie topics and claims, and also think about any ideas that may be in conflict or tension with those you identify. People and the world are complicated, so expect and recognize complexity across all your essays.

2. **From Timm:** If you're nervous when taking your AP exam, that's a good thing; being nervous means that you care. But you don't want your nerves to debilitate you as you allow doubt to subdue your abilities on test day. One simple way to stay confident and ready is by remembering to **include cause-and-effect language in your commentary.** The lack of that language—which includes such words as *because, consequently, since, due to the fact that,* and so *that,* for example—commonly prevents students from scoring higher on each of their essays because they don't explain how evidence, examples, or choices create an effect. I can't tell you how many times I've read papers where I've thought to myself, "Oh, if this student had just put the word *because* at the end of that sentence and completed the explanation!" Remembering and using this language in your commentary is essential and helps you more clearly articulate your reasoning. Doing so also helps me—the person scoring your essays—to accurately understand your thinking.

3. **From Beth:** As a student, you've likely examined how writers make rhetorical choices, but you might not have realized that when writing an essay, you **make rhetorical choices** too. Don't be afraid to experiment as you're finding your voice. Add in detailed anecdotes. Pose thought-provoking questions. Repeat meaningful phrases. Incorporate advanced punctuation like colons or dashes. By experimenting with the rhetorical choices you make, you're not only honing your writing skills but also crafting a more engaging argument.

For more from **Brandon Abdon, Timm Freitas, and Beth Hall,** visit the companion website (tinyurl.com/2mrx3r99) for *AMSCO Writing for the AP Exam: English Language and Composition.* There you will find new videos by the authors as well as all the links included in the lessons in this book.

NOTE: The links included in these lessons have been coded to be ad free. Occasionally you may see a message saying that a video is not available. In that case, just refresh your browser and the video will load.

Table of Contents

PART 1: SYNTHESIS

Prompt

Thesis

Evidence and Commentary

Sophistication

Synthesis Sample Essays

©Perfection Learning® • No Reproduction Permitted.

PART 2: RHETORICAL ANALYSIS

PART 3: ARGUMENT

LESSON SYN.1 The Synthesis Prompt

Eyes on the Exam

Exam readers will evaluate your synthesis essay based on how effectively you understand and **respond to the specific task** required by the prompt, especially how you **use sources to support the thinking that justifies your position.** *Justifies* means "shows to be right or reasonable."

LEARN

The goal of the Synthesis Free-Response Question is to demonstrate your understanding of an ongoing conversation on a topic of current interest, read different types of sources that contribute to that conversation, evaluate them as evidence, and then create your own argument that allows you to *synthesize*, or combine, your position with the arguments of others in a way that is well developed, supported, clear, and complex.

Following is a synthesis prompt modeled on the one you will see in the first free-response question of your exam. The parts of the prompt are labeled in the example below, but these parts *are not* labeled on the exam.

[Background]

In 1853, the London Zoo introduced a new showcase: the first public aquarium. Since this time, major municipalities and private companies alike have developed fine-tuned and well-balanced showcases of marine life for people to enjoy. Some of these public and private entities have even developed methods that, in conjunction with safely displaying the diversity of marine life, allow patrons to have personal interactions with animals entrusted to their care. Advocates of the aquatic life industry argue that aquariums and sea-life attractions promote education and conservation, while many others challenge the ethics of holding animals in captivity for any reason, especially if such captivity results in amusement and profit.

[Task 1]

Carefully read the following six sources, including the introductory information for each source. Write an essay that synthesizes material from at least three of the sources and develops your position on the extent to which aquariums and other sea-life attractions fulfill a role in education and wildlife conservation.

—or—

[Task 2]

Carefully read the following six sources, including the introductory information for each source. Write an essay that synthesizes material from at least three of the sources and develops your position on what factors individuals need to consider when choosing to visit an aquarium or other sea-life attraction.

Source A (Jacobs)

Source B (Renner)

Source C ("Marketing to Families")

Source D (Johnson-Walker)

Source E (AZA)

Source F (Tidière)

[Specific directions]

In your response you should do the following:

- Respond to the prompt with a thesis that presents a defensible claim.
- Select and use evidence from at least three of the provided sources to support your line of reasoning. Indicate clearly the sources used through direct quotation, paraphrase, or summary. Sources may be cited as Source A, Source B, etc., or by using the description in parentheses.
- Explain how the evidence supports your line of reasoning.
- Use appropriate grammar and punctuation in communicating your argument.

The first paragraph of the prompt provides the rhetorical background: both the context of the prompt's topic as well as its relevance to today. The first paragraph also usually presents several perspectives and positions to invite you into the conversation. You may choose to agree with one of these, or you may choose to vary your position from those offered and construct an entirely new argument on the topic.

The second paragraph of the prompt contains the overall directions for completing the synthesis task. The task itself contains key words such as *read, write, synthesize,* and *develop.* The second paragraph also provides you a specific focus for your writing.

NOTE: In the example above, you will notice that the task-based section of the prompt is labeled as *TASK 1* and *TASK 2.* This is because there are two different types of synthesis tasks that may show up on the exam. On exam day, you will be asked to respond to *only one* task, but it's good to be prepared for either type of task.

Source information follows the tasks. Six or seven sources, labeled Source A, Source B, Source C, and so on, represent the various voices in the conversation. Each source letter is followed by a name, title, or description inside parentheses, such as Source A (Jacobs). These are the shortened versions you can use to cite the sources in your essay. Two of the sources will always be visuals, and at least one of those visuals will be quantitative—a chart, graph, or other infographic that will require you to accurately read and interpret some type of data.

The final paragraph of the synthesis prompt contains a bulleted list of very specific directions for writing your response and identifies what the exam readers will be expecting to see as they score the essays. Note that you will be expected to *use at least three sources.*

The sources themselves appear below the complete prompt. Their labels (Source A and Source B, for example) appear in a box at the top of the source, which also includes the author of the source, the title of the original source, the date, and any other publication information.

Beneath the source box is a brief sentence about the original source and its author. It provides important information about the validity or authority the source may have. For example, as you can see below, the introductory sentence for Source A states that the author is a professor of neuroscience. An author with those credentials will have more authority than, say, a blogger on a social media site.

Following the brief introduction is the source itself, usually excerpted from a longer work. Take a few minutes to read through the sources for this prompt. On the exam, the directions suggest you take 15 minutes to read the sources.

Source A

Jacobs, Bob. "The neural cruelty of captivity: Keeping large mammals in zoos and aquariums damages their brains." The Conversation, 24 September 2020, theconversation.com/the-neural-cruelty-of-captivity-keeping-large-mammals-in-zoos-and-aquariums-damages-their-brains-142240.

The following is excerpted from an article written by a professor of neuroscience.

Many animals try to cope with captivity by adopting abnormal behaviors. Some develop "stereotypies," which are repetitive, purposeless habits such as constantly bobbing their heads, swaying incessantly or chewing on the bars of their cages. Others, especially big cats, pace their enclosures. Elephants rub or break their tusks.

Changing brain structure

Neuroscientific research indicates that living in an impoverished, stressful captive environment physically damages the brain. These changes have been documented in many species, including rodents, rabbits, cats and humans.

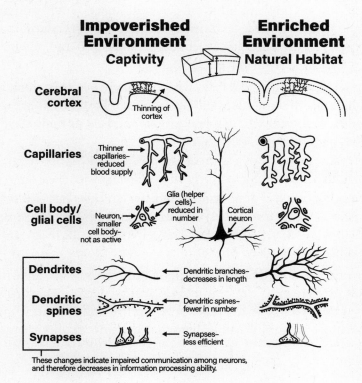

This illustration shows differences in the brain's cerebral cortex in animals held in impoverished (captive) and enriched (natural) environments. Impoverishment results in thinning of the cortex, a decreased blood supply, less support for neurons and decreased connectivity among neurons.
Arnold B. Scheibel, CC BY-ND

Although researchers have directly studied some animal brains, most of what we know comes from observing animal behavior, analyzing stress hormone levels in the blood and applying knowledge gained from a half-century of neuroscience research. Laboratory research also suggests that mammals in a zoo or aquarium have compromised brain function.

Source B

Renner, Michael J. "Zoos and aquariums shift to a new standard of 'animal welfare' that depends on deeper understanding of animals' lives." The Conversation, 13 Sept. 2022, theconversation.com/zoos-and-aquariums-shift-to-a-new-standard-of-animal-welfare-that-depends-on-deeper-understanding-of-animals-lives-164839.

The following is an excerpt taken from an article written by a professor of biology who serves on the board of directors of a zoo accredited by the Association of Zoos and Aquariums (AZA).

Changing standards

Accreditation is a mechanism for maintaining and pioneering best practices. Being accredited by the Association of Zoos and Aquariums is the highest level of professional recognition for North American zoos and aquariums. Fewer than 250 out of approximately 2,800 animal exhibitors licensed by the U.S. Department of Agriculture are AZA accredited.

To earn that accreditation, a zoo or aquarium must demonstrate alignment with its mission, a sound business operation and significant activity in the areas of education, conservation and research. But the centerpiece of accreditation is demonstrating quality of life for animals under human care.

For decades, the focus was on practices that correlate with animal health, like absence of illness, successful reproduction and longevity. The AZA has published objective standards for what it means to provide proper care for a tapir, a tiger or a Japanese spider crab—for example, requirements specifying certain amounts of physical space, environmental temperature ranges and cleaning routines. These extensive and detailed standards were devised by working groups of experts in various species from across the zoo and aquarium community and based on the best available scientific evidence.

A recent revision to accreditation standards in 2018, however, supersedes this model in favor of a new goal—that a zoo or aquarium demonstrate it has achieved animal welfare. Not only must animals be healthy, but they should also display behavior typical of their species. Climbers must climb, diggers must dig and runners must run.

Understanding the lives of animals is central

Over the past 60 years, scientific understanding of animals' cognitive abilities has exploded. A large body of scientific work has shown that a relatively rich or impoverished environment has effects on both brain and behavior. Such awareness has led the zoo and aquarium community to formally embrace a higher standard of care.

Zoo or aquarium personnel can provide such behavioral opportunities only if they know what is normal for that species in the wild. So optimizing animal welfare requires a knowledge base that is both broad and deep. For example, a zoo must understand what is normal behavior for a pygmy marmoset before it can know what behavioral opportunities to provide.

Many zoos and aquariums house hundreds of animal species. Each species exists because it occupies a unique niche in the ecosystem, so the conditions that produce ideal welfare for one species may not be the same as those for a different species.

Developing welfare standards for the wide diversity of zoo species will take time and quite a bit of research. Although AZA-accredited zoos and aquariums contribute over $200 million per year to research in over 100 countries around the world, the need for conservation research always far outstrips the available funding.

How old is an eastern black rhinoceros before it begins to go on adventures away from its mother? If a flamingo chick has a medical issue that is successfully resolved, how can keepers tell if its development has been affected? How can keepers evaluate whether items introduced into the enclosure of a troop of Japanese macaque monkeys, intended to enrich their environment, are actually serving that purpose? Knowing the answers to these questions, and a multitude of other similar ones, will help the zoo community truly optimize the welfare of animals under their care.

Another major factor behind the AZA's new standard is its role in species conservation. Captive animals typically outlive their wild counterparts. Zoos and aquariums are the figurative lifeboat for an increasing number of species that are extinct in the wild. Simply keeping an animal alive is now no longer enough. Zoo-based efforts to save endangered species will succeed only if understanding of the animals' lives is fully integrated with husbandry standards.

Source C

"Marketing to Families: Why Brands Are Investing in U.S. Zoos & Aquariums," Allionce Group, 13 Aug. 2021, www.allioncegroup.com/why-brands-should-invest-in-u-s-zoos-aquariums/.

The following is taken from the website of a marketing company that focuses on marketing to parents and children.

BOSTON (PRWEB) AUGUST 13, 2021

The last few years has given us permission to do things differently. For brands exploring new ways for marketing to families look no further than a market that has recently been catching the attention of marketers looking for a new, fresh and highly efficient approach.

Marketing to Families: Five reasons why brands are investing in U.S. Zoos & Aquariums

1) **Family Audience:** Parents with young children are hard to reach! This market represents the highest concentration of parents with young children 2–12 years old. With an average visit of 3 to 4 hours, families visiting zoos and aquariums are uniquely "in the moment," offering a rare opportunity for brands to engage with kids and their parents at one of their most authentic and connected moments, free from the many distractions that often compete for their attention. A recent independent research study shows that by a factor of almost 3 to 1, the number one reason families visit a zoo or aquarium is to spend uninterrupted time together.

2) **Impressive Scale:** With more than 200 non-profit, accredited zoos and aquariums in the U.S., this market has over 195 million annual visits, more than all four major sports leagues . . . combined! These venues include a balanced, national distribution across 48 of the top 50 media markets.

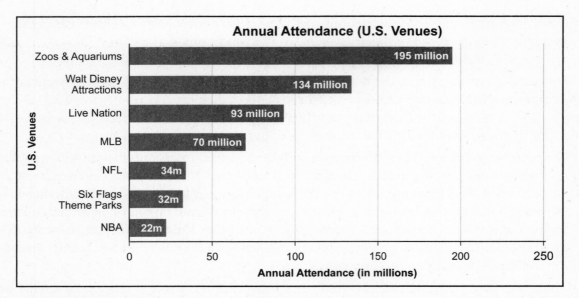

Annual Attendance (U.S. Venues)

3) **Purpose:** Consumers believe that brands have the power to make the world better and research shows that brand actions and partnerships influence their purchase decision. Nine out of ten people feel better about a brand if they focus on an environmental or social cause. Zoos & Aquariums mission is grounded in environmental conservation, contributing more than $1 billion every five years, and directly improving the long-term survival of species in natural ecosystems and habitats. In fact, zoos & aquariums are widely credited with saving several animal species from extinction. Brand partnerships generate financial resources that directly fund and support these critical environmental conservation and educational efforts that zoos and aquariums provide.

4) **Emotional Connection:** Awe, wonder, and childhood joy connect families in a deeper way while enjoying time together at these brand-safe, trusted, community and cultural attractions. For parents, a visit to the zoo or aquarium offers a respite from the chaos of everyday life allowing them to see more clearly through the eyes of their children, often evoking feelings of nostalgia. Additional core themes like discovery, curiosity, health, and wellness validate this market as ideal locations to drive positive brand sentiment.

5) **Uncluttered Environment:** Zoos and aquariums are an oasis, offering an unparalleled share of voice for brands marketing to families. This efficiency is the result of an environment that is free from over-saturation and brand clutter. This pure white space allows brands to extend reach across multiple touch points including experiential, digital/social, hospitality, sponsorship, media, and consumer/retail promotions.

When it comes to marketing to families and building a family-friendly marketing strategy, as compelling as the above five reasons may be, perhaps it's the flexibility, adaptability, efficiency, and minimization of downside risk this market offers that will inspire more brands to consider a partnership investment with U.S. Zoos & Aquariums.

Source D

Johnson-Walker, Yvette. "Flamingos with flu and hippos in hurricanes: Emergency preparedness in zoos and aquariums." The Conversation, 17 Nov. 2014, theconversation. com/flamingos-with-flu-and-hippos-in-hurricanes-emergency-preparedness-in-zoos-and-aquariums-33501.

The following is excerpted from an article by a clinical instructor of veterinary clinical medicine.

You need only look at the papers or television news to see the reports. Infectious disease outbreaks, weather emergencies and disasters both natural and man-made. They're all not just threats to human populations – they have the potential to disrupt the daily operations of zoos and aquariums and the lives of their animal inhabitants.

Past disasters

In 2004 an outbreak of H5N1 avian influenza among tigers and leopards at zoos in Thailand resulted in the deaths of 45 animals. Hurricanes Katrina and Rita damaged the Audubon Zoo in New Orleans in 2005, though the only animals lost were two otters and a raccoon. The New Orleans Aquarium of the Americas did not fare as well after that storm; most of the fish in their collection died when they lost power. The 2007 California wildfires threatened the San Diego Wild Animal Park causing the facility to close and relocate some of the endangered species within its collection. These events can be devastating for the involved facilities.

There are more than 2,800 USDA licensed animal exhibitors in the US, ranging from very large facilities to private individuals with few animals. It's crucial for all the venues in this diverse community to prepare for disasters and have contingency plans in place. The 175 million people who visit zoos or aquariums annually form a unique ecosystem where humans, exotic wildlife, domestic animals and local wildlife interact with each other on a daily basis. As a result, emergency response planning must take the welfare of visitors, staff, first responders, collection animals, agricultural animals, and even local wildlife into consideration.

Get ready

For the past four years, a team of experts from the University of Illinois College of Veterinary Medicine, the US Department of Agriculture Division of Animal Care and the Association of Zoos and Aquariums has encouraged animal facilities to plan for the worst. Our group has been running preparedness exercises at large and small zoological institutions in urban, rural and suburban locations.

The first step for zoos is to figure out where they stand. Have they thought about what they would do if a tornado is headed their way or a contagious disease is affecting wild animals in their vicinity? The goal is to protect the health, safety and welfare of all the animals in their collection. But in the face of an emergency, it may not be possible to relocate all the animals that may be in harm's way. Endangered and threatened species often take priority for relocation – if there is a nearby facility to house the animals, and if they can be moved safely. In other circumstances the best approach may be to shelter-in-place. It should help to have decisions of this kind made before disaster strikes.

Zoo and aquarium personnel have to think through disease control measures as well. These can include isolation and quarantine of exposed animals, closing exhibits, moving animals normally housed outdoors to an indoor facility and using special disinfectants and personal protective equipment for personnel. Preparedness planning includes keeping needed items in stock and identifying emergency suppliers.

[. . .]

Why it matters

Zoos and aquariums play beneficial roles in global conservation efforts and environmental and biomedical teaching and research. In 2010, American zoos and aquariums contributed US$16 billion to the economy and provided in excess of 142,000 jobs. In addition, zoos and aquariums enhance public understanding of wildlife and the conservation of the places animals live.

For these reasons, as well as concern for the welfare of the animals they contain, it's important that substantial progress has been made on the readiness front for zoos and aquariums.

Source E

"About Us." Association of Zoos & Aquariums, www.aza.org/about-us. Accessed 21 Nov. 2023.

The following is from the "About Us" page on the Association of Zoos and Aquariums' website.

The Association of Zoos and Aquariums (AZA) is a 501(c)3 non-profit organization dedicated to the advancement of zoos and aquariums in the areas of conservation, education, science, and recreation. AZA represents more than 235 facilities in the United States and overseas, which collectively draw more than 200 million visitors every year. AZA-accredited zoos and aquariums meet the highest standards in animal care and welfare and provide a fun, safe, and educational family experience. In addition, they dedicate millions of dollars annually to support scientific research, conservation, and education programs.

Leaders in Animal Care and Welfare

AZA is the independent accrediting organization for the best zoos and the best aquariums in America and the world, assuring the public that when they visit an AZA-accredited facility, it meets the highest standards for animal care and welfare. Less than 10 percent of the 2,800 wildlife exhibitors licensed by the United States Department of Agriculture under the Animal Welfare Act meet the more comprehensive standards of AZA accreditation. The highly trained professionals at AZA-accredited zoos and aquariums provide excellent care for more than 800,000 animals, making them the leading experts in animal care and welfare. [. . .]

Leaders in Conservation

Conservation is a priority for AZA-accredited zoos and aquariums and a key part of their mission to save species from extinction. Every year, AZA-accredited zoos and aquariums spend $230 million on field conservation alone, supporting projects benefitting more than 800 species in 130 countries. To date, the AZA Conservation Grants Fund has provided $7.7 million in support for 400+ projects worldwide. [. . .]

AZA-accredited zoos and aquariums are leaders in the protection of threatened and endangered species. Through AZA SAFE: Saving Animals from Extinction, the entire AZA-accredited zoo and aquarium community is focusing our conservation science, wildlife expertise, and outreach to millions of annual visitors on saving species in the wild. The AZA Species Survival Plan® (SSP) program is a cooperative animal management, breeding, and conservation effort that works to ensure genetically diverse, self-sustaining populations of more than 500 species of animals.

Leaders in Conservation Education

As centers for conservation, AZA-accredited zoos and aquariums provide the public with essential connections to the natural world. More than 50 million visitors to AZA-accredited zoos and aquariums are children, making accredited zoos and aquariums essential to science and environmental education. AZA-accredited facilities train 40,000 teachers every year, supporting state science curricula with teaching materials and hands-on opportunities for students who might otherwise have no first-hand experience with wildlife. In fact, there is growing evidence that aquariums and zoos are highly effective at teaching people about science and connecting them to the natural world. [. . .]

Source F

Tidière, Morgane, et al. "Comparative analyses of longevity and senescence reveal variable survival benefits of living in zoos across mammals." *Scientific Reports* 6, 36361 (2016). https://doi.org/10.1038/srep36361.

The graphic below is based on an article in a scientific journal.

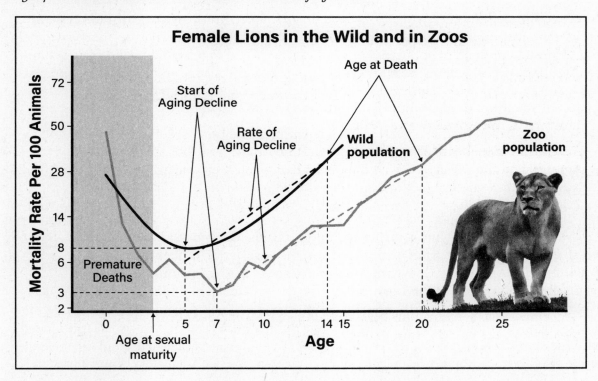

KEY POINT: The synthesis prompt contains **five main parts:** rhetorical background, focused writing task, source and citation information, specific directions for selecting evidence and writing the essay, and the sources themselves.

PRACTICE

You will learn more about each section of the prompt in the lessons that follow. For now, do your best to complete the following activities with the aquarium prompt (pages 1–2).

Part 1 Answer the following questions using the information provided in the **background** section of the prompt.

1. What do you learn about the prompt topic in the background information?
2. What are the differing positions held by individuals already involved in the conversation? What is your position?
3. What is the difference between each of the synthesis task types?
4. In your own words, describe the **task** that you are expected to complete when responding to the prompt in the synthesis question.

Part 2 Describe what the first three bullet points in the **specific directions** ask you to do.

WRITE

A key requirement for the synthesis essay is that you **keep your own arguments central** rather than just summarizing the arguments of the different sources. Future lessons will help you accurately respond to both types of synthesis tasks and to read and include sources in your writing. For now, though, based on just your own knowledge and experience, complete the Task 1 and Task 2 sentences below to express what position you may currently hold on the subject of aquariums and to understand how the two tasks differ.

Task 1 My position on the extent to which aquariums and other sea-life attractions fulfill a role in education and wildlife conservation is . . .

Task 2 My position on what factors individuals need to consider when choosing to visit an aquarium or other sea-life attraction is . . .

Watch this video (tinyurl.com/3ywemdnk) about the Cheyenne Mountain Zoo, which earned a clean report of inspection from the Association of Zoos and Aquariums (AZA). Though Cheyenne Mountain Zoo isn't an aquarium, it gets certified by the same national organization that covers aquariums. This establishment is only the fourth organization to ever earn such a report. After watching the quick video, you may want to consider the rarity of the achievement, the visuals intermixed with the speakers' reflections, the implications of the language and visuals, and the messages of the speakers, and then revise what you have written in response to Task 1 and Task 2.

Watch Timm Freitas go through the two types of synthesis tasks based on the aquariums prompt at the companion website (tinyurl.com/2mrx3r99) for this book. There you will find other videos by the authors as well as all the links included in the lessons in this book.

NOTE: The links included in these lessons have been coded to be ad free. Occasionally you may see a message saying that a video is not available. In that case, just refresh your browser and the video will load.

What's the Point? In one sentence, explain how this lesson can help you on the AP English Language and Composition exam.

_____

_____

_____

TEAM UP

Throughout this book you will see "Team Up" activities. Working in peer groups can be a great way to enhance your understanding and performance in this course. To make the most of your group sessions, here are some guidelines to follow:

- **Be Respectful:** Always listen to your peers and respect their opinions. Remember, everyone has valuable insights to offer.

- **Give Constructive Feedback:** When reviewing each other's work, be specific and helpful. Focus on how to improve the writing in terms of content, structure, and language use.

- **Participate Equally:** Make sure everyone in the group has a chance to speak and contribute. Share the floor and encourage quieter members to voice their thoughts.

- **Set Clear Goals and Deadlines:** To keep your group on track, agree on what you want to achieve in each session and when tasks should be completed.

- **Embrace Different Perspectives:** Be open to various viewpoints and interpretations, especially when analyzing texts and arguments.

- **Support Each Other:** Encourage and motivate your peers. Celebrate improvements and good ideas.

- **Regularly Reflect on Your Learning:** Talk with group members about the most important takeaways from each group session.

- **Practice Together:** Work on practice exams and essays as a group. This is a great way to prepare for the AP exam and get helpful feedback.

For your first group work on synthesis, focus on sources. After reading each source for the **aquariums prompt** carefully on your own, with your teacher's permission, form groups of about six students each. Assign each student in the group one of the sources. The goal is for each student to become an expert on the assigned source. Take about five minutes to reread or closely examine the source you were assigned. Then "present" it to the rest of the group. Include the following in your presentation:

- The credibility of the source as far as you can tell and how you determined that
- The aspect of the topic it covers
- The perspective it brings to the conversation
- How it relates to your own perspective

When everyone has presented a source, briefly discuss how you might use the sources to respond to Task 1 and Task 2.

LESSON SYN.2 Unpacking the Prompt: Join the Conversation

Eyes on the Exam

Exam readers will look for your skill in developing a position and recognizing the points of view of the sources provided.

LEARN

The word *synthesis* means "a combination of different elements that form a cohesive whole." The different elements in the synthesis response are your own views and those of the varied sources.

Reading the prompt and the sources is like stepping into the middle of a conversation whose subject and viewpoints you are just beginning to grasp. Approach the question as an invitation to learn what people are saying on an interesting issue, how they agree and disagree, and where your own views might fit into the conversation.

Look again at the first two paragraphs of the prompt on aquariums. Note the "think-aloud" notes of someone who may be reading it for the first time.

In 1853, the London Zoo introduced a new showcase: the first public aquarium. *< History and context* Since this time, major municipalities and private companies alike have developed fine-tuned and well-balanced showcases of marine life for people to enjoy. Some of these public and private entities have even developed methods that, in conjunction with safely displaying the diversity of marine life, allow patrons to have personal interactions with animals entrusted to their care. *< Sounds like a positive thing* Advocates of the aquatic life industry argue that aquariums and sea-life attractions promote education and conservation, *< This is one view, supportive* while many others challenge the ethics of holding animals in captivity for any reason, especially if such captivity results in amusement and profit. *< This is a different view, challenging the first one. At the moment, I lean more toward this view.*

Carefully read the following six sources, including the introductory information for each source. *< These are the voices in the conversation.* Write an essay that synthesizes material from at least three of the sources and develops your position on the extent to which aquariums and other sea-life attractions fulfill a role in education and wildlife conservation. *So I'm going to see what the different voices have to say and determine how they shape the position I will end up taking.*

KEY POINT: Annotate the synthesis prompt as you read to identify the **context**, the **varying positions**, and what, if any, **perspectives you already have** on the topic.

PRACTICE

Read the synthesis prompt on the next page. Like the aquariums prompt in Lesson SYN.1, this prompt includes labels for each part. Remember, the parts will not be labeled in the exam and there will only be one task. You will be working with this prompt throughout this section.

Part 1 As you read this prompt, which has been printed with **extra space between lines,** make notes on it like the ones above, identifying the context, the different points of view, and your own possible position.

[Background]

Over the past 100+ years, the world has seen significant technological advancements. Each time a particular technology seems to have achieved its pinnacle performance, within a short time period a new version of it appears, and it's often billed as being better than ever before. One enterprise that has seen some of the most significant improvement and growth is the automobile industry. This is because the contemporary world requires automobile companies to explore and produce new avenues of convenience, performance, and efficiency while maintaining an affordable price tag for the average consumer. Since the early 2000s, electric vehicles have become increasingly more common, often being celebrated by many as the most sustainable vehicles for the future. There are critics, however, who have suggested that such technologies overcommit and underdeliver on their promises to meet consumer, cultural, and environmental needs.

[Task 1] Carefully read the following six sources, including the introductory information for each source. Write an essay that synthesizes material from at least three of the sources and develops your position on the extent to which electric vehicles should be embraced as the future of consumer transportation. –or– *[Task 2]* Carefully read the following six sources, including the introductory information for each source. Write an essay that synthesizes material from at least three of the sources and develops your position on what factors an individual should consider when buying an electric vehicle.

[Source information]

Source A (Samuelsen)
Source B (Trancik)
Source C (Lee and Bazilian)
Source D (Getty)
Source E ("Hydrogen in Transportation")
Source F (FOTW)

continued

[Specific directions]

In your response you should do the following:

- Respond to the prompt with a thesis that presents a defensible claim.
- Select and use evidence from at least three of the provided sources to support your line of reasoning. Indicate clearly the sources used through direct quotation, paraphrase, or summary. Sources may be cited as Source A, Source B, etc., or by using the description in parentheses.
- Explain how the evidence supports your line of reasoning.
- Use appropriate grammar and punctuation in communicating your argument.

Part 2 Read the sources on the following pages. You may want to make notes as you read, marking ideas you believe are especially important or revealing of the source's viewpoint. For example, in the prompt on aquariums, you might underline or circle the following part of Source A (page 3) because it so clearly states a position:

From Source A on Aquariums

Changing brain structure

Neuroscientific research indicates that living in an impoverished, stressful captive environment physically damages the brain. These changes have been documented in many species, including rodents, rabbits, cats and humans.

Look for and mark such clear position statements in the sources on electric vehicles.

Source A

Samuelsen, Scott. "Explainer: for the future of electric vehicles, one size does not fit all." The Conversation, 19 Jan. 2015, theconversation.com/ explainer-for-the-future-of-electric-vehicles-one-size-does-not-fit-all-36052.

The following is an excerpt from an article written for an online news source by a professor of mechanical, aerospace, and environmental engineering.

[. . .] Plug-in battery electric vehicles (BEVs), hybrid electric vehicles (HEVs), plug-in hybrid electric vehicles (PHEVs), and hydrogen fuel cell electric vehicles (FCEVs) are all electric vehicles. They're all propelled by an electric motor and have batteries to store or supply electricity as required and absorb energy when braking the vehicle.

Some of these vehicles can also generate electricity on board, either through a gasoline-powered combustion engine or a hydrogen-powered fuel cell.

They all represent a fundamental break from the gasoline combustion vehicles we drive today in three ways: the drivetrain is electric, rather than mechanical; the engine under the hood is electrochemical instead of combustion-based; and the fuel is electricity and hydrogen, rather than gasoline.

[. . .]

Since 1990, three additional forces have emerged to further affirm the decision to target the hydrogen fuel cell vehicle as the product of the future, including climate change, policies that favor fuel independence, and air quality regulations, notably in California.

Battery electric vehicles (BEVs)

In the past five years, though, there's been a resurgence of battery electric vehicles, which rely solely on battery power. Examples include the Nissan Leaf, the GM Spark and the Kia Soul. After 40 to 60 miles, the batteries are depleted and need to be recharged by plugging into a residential circuit or 220-volt, purpose-built charger at a commercial center or workplace. Charging time depends on the voltage, the charger technology and the battery "state of charge" (i.e., how much the battery has been depleted) but generally requires one to six hours to fully charge the vehicle.

A BEV is attractive because its range satisfies the majority of trips taken by the public, recharging at home is convenient, and driving is vibration-free and quiet. The size of the vehicle is relatively small, providing good maneuverability and relatively easy parking, and there are no air pollutants during driving. [. . .]

Working against BEVs is the time required to recharge the vehicle and the range anxiety —that is, concern over limited driving range—experienced by drivers, which effectively reduces the useful range of the vehicle. Also, charging can stress the electric grid and there are cases where there is no charging infrastructure available, particularly for people who live in apartments.

[. . .]

Hybrid electric vehicles (HEVs)

Hybrid electric vehicles are a BEV with a gasoline combustion engine on board to generate electricity and move the car in conjunction with the electric motor. They can provide the same 300-mile range people expect with a conventional gasoline vehicle. And with advanced software controls, the combustion engine interacts with the batteries to achieve high efficiencies and low emission of pollutants.

[. . .]

Plug-in hybrid electric vehicles (PHEVs)

PHEVs are a HEV with added battery capacity that can provide an electric drive range of between ten and 60 miles. The Chevy Volt, for example, can drive nearly 40 miles on battery power before a gasoline generator kicks in. This allows the convenience of recharging the batteries overnight at home and a daily electric range that the majority of the US public does not exceed. And the PHEV provides the 300-mile range which the driving public is accustomed to.

Hydrogen fuel cell electric vehicles (FCEVs)

Fuel cell vehicles are hybrid electric vehicles with two major differences. A fuel cell, an electrochemical device that takes a fuel, such as hydrogen, and oxygen from the air to generate electricity, replaces the gasoline engine under the hood. The fuel cell has remarkably high efficiency (three times that of the conventional gasoline automobile) and zero emission of air pollutants when driving. The product of the reaction is water, which is exhausted through the tailpipe with nitrogen and some oxygen remaining from the air. [. . .] The refueling time of a fuel cell vehicle is comparable to a conventional gasoline automobile and fuel can be sourced domestically.

Some of the challenges associated with fuel cell vehicles are the limited number of hydrogen fueling stations nationally. California has the most hydrogen fueling stations in the US, with 51 projected to be operating by the end of 2015, over 70 by the end of 2017, and 100 by 2020. Sixty eight stations are considered the initial minimum to support acceptance of fuel cell vehicles in the State.

Source B

Trancik, Jessika E. "Range anxiety? Today's electric cars can cover vast majority of daily U.S. driving needs." The Conversation, 16 Aug. 2016, theconversation.com/range-anxiety-todays-electric-cars-can-cover-vast-majority-of-daily-u-s-driving-needs-63909.

The following is an excerpt taken from an article written by an associate professor in energy studies at the Massachusetts Institute of Technology (MIT).

Vehicle range is not a single number

An electric vehicle's range is typically thought of in terms of a fixed number, but the number of miles covered on a single charge changes with factors including driving speed and style, and outdoor temperature. To understand the range of a car, we need to look beyond the car itself to how people are behaving.

Over the last four years in my research group, we've built a model (called "TripEnergy") of the second-by-second driving behavior of people across the United States, how they are likely to use heating and cooling systems in their cars, and how various electric and conventional vehicles would consume energy if driven in this way.

This approach gives us a probabilistic view of electric vehicle range. For example, for the Nissan Leaf, we find that 74 miles is the median range—based on driving patterns, half of the cars on the road in the U.S. would be able to travel this far, and half would not. (A Ford Focus electric performs similarly.) There is a distribution in this range, which demonstrates how widely actual performance can vary. We estimate, for instance, that five percent of 58-mile trips could not be covered on one charge, and five percent of 90-mile trips could.

Evaluating electric vehicle technology against driving behavior

With the TripEnergy model in hand, we asked how many cars on the road could be replaced with a low-cost electric vehicle available today. We considered a case where drivers can charge only once daily: for example, at home overnight. This allowed us to study a situation where only limited changes are needed to existing public charging infrastructure and cars can use power plants that would otherwise sit idle overnight.

We found that, given how people are driving across the U.S., 87 percent of cars on an average day could be replaced with a current-generation, low-cost electric vehicle, with only once-daily charging. This is based on the driving behavior of millions of people across the U.S. across diverse cities and socioeconomic classes.

Switching from conventional to electric vehicles for those cars would cut emissions by an estimated 30 percent, even with today's fossil fuel-based supply mix. In total, the trips taken by those cars represent roughly 60 percent of gasoline consumption in the U.S.

This large daily adoption potential is remarkably similar across both dense and more sprawling U.S. cities, ranging from 84 percent to 93 percent.

While it's true that people behave differently across cities—in how they use public transport, whether they own a car, and how often they drive the cars they own—when they do drive, we found that a similar number of cars in different cities fall within the range provided by a low-cost electric vehicle.

[. . .]

In all, our analysis shows that current electric vehicles can meet most daily driving needs in the U.S. Improved access to shared, long-range transport, alongside further-advanced batteries and cars and decarbonized electricity, provides a pathway to reaching a largely decarbonized personal vehicle fleet.

Source C

Lee, Jordy, and Morgan Bazilian . "The US is worried about its critical minerals supply chains—essential for electric vehicles, wind power and the nation's defense." The Conversation, 6 Apr. 2021, theconversation.com/the-us-is-worried-about-its-critical-minerals-supply-chains-essential-for-electric-vehicles-wind-power-and-the-nations-defense-157465.

The following is an excerpt from an article written by a program manager and director of the Payne Institute at the Colorado School of Mines.

When U.S. companies build military weapons systems, electric vehicle batteries, satellites and wind turbines, they rely heavily on a few dozen "critical minerals"—many of which are mined and refined almost entirely by other countries. Building a single F-35A fighter jet, for example, requires at least 920 pounds of rare earth elements that come primarily from China.

That level of dependence on imports worries the U.S. government.

Natural disasters, civil unrest, trade disputes and company failures can all disrupt a mineral supply chain and the many products that depend on it – making many critical minerals a national security priority.

[. . .]

The question policy experts like ourselves are exploring is how best to provide sustainable and secure critical mineral supply chains in a way that limits environmental damage and promotes good governance.

[. . .]

Getting serious about supply chains

The amounts of lithium, cobalt, graphene, indium and other critical minerals needed for low-carbon technologies alone are expected to increase anywhere from 100% to 1,000% by 2050.

These estimates are concerning on their own, but when combined with military needs, industrial needs and the decline of U.S. mining, it paints a troubling picture for U.S. supply shortages.

Countries like the Democratic Republic of Congo, which made headlines in the past due to mineral sales that financed armed conflict, are not particularly appealing partners for U.S. companies. The DRC is responsible for producing more than 70% of the world's cobalt, used in almost all rechargeable lithium ion batteries that power everything from cellphones and laptops to electric vehicles, and China has invested heavily in the region.

The ability of the United States to drive demand—but hesitation to get involved with "risky" nations or commit to domestic production—means the U.S. is reliant on countries that are more willing to accept those risks. China now controls 80% of the world's lithium-ion battery material refining, 77% of the world's battery cell capacity and 60% of the world's battery component manufacturing.

How to strengthen critical supply chains

[. . .]

Expanding recycling and reuse of critical minerals can also increase sustainability and make minerals more available for U.S. use. One way to encourage recycling programs is to shift responsibility from waste managers to major producers like Apple and Samsung.

International agreements can also be written in ways that require responsible mining. U.S. companies, similarly, can do more to ensure that they aren't purchasing from unsustainable sources or supporting practices that encourage the abuse and exploitation of developing economies.

The U.S. can also expand its exploration for critical minerals. Rio Tinto recently announced plans for a new plant to recover tellurium, a critical mineral used in solar panels, from its copper refining operations in Utah. Lithium mining in the California desert has also started to attract investors, as have rare earth projects in Colorado and Nevada.

[. . .]

Source D

Getty Images. Open Pit of the Greenbushes Mine. Greenbushes WA 6254, Australia.

The photo below is of the Greenbushes Lithium Mine, an open-pit mining operation in Western Australia and the world's largest hard-rock lithium mine. It is located to the south of the town of Greenbushes, Western Australia.

The following is from a guide published by the United States Environmental Protection Agency.

Hydrogen has the potential to meaningfully reduce GHG emissions in the transportation sector. It can offer benefits to the heavy-duty transportation sector applications (i.e., long-haul trucks, locomotives, ships, etc.) where current battery technology might not yet be suitable for certain transportation modes (e.g., the necessary battery weight would be too substantial). Hydrogen can also store energy for long periods of time. As additional renewable electricity from wind and solar technologies is added to the grid, hydrogen could be used to help balance intermittent supply with varying demand . . .

Globally, there is a lot of interest in hydrogen as a low- and zero-carbon fuel option. Hydrogen is abundant in the universe and is a highly versatile energy carrier. It can be produced from many domestic resources and has a high energy content by weight. It is also extremely light, so it needs to be compressed or liquified, which can make it challenging and expensive to transport, store, and use. As hydrogen scales up across the economy, the costs are expected to continue to drop and become more competitive with other sources of energy.

Emissions

[. . .]

While hydrogen is abundant in the universe, it must be separated from other compounds to be used as fuel. This process can be energy intensive. The quantity of emissions associated with producing hydrogen fuels depends on the source of feedstock and method of production. Currently, almost all hydrogen in the U.S. is derived from natural gas by stripping and recombining hydrogen molecules from methane and water in a process called steam methane reforming. This process is well established but also energy intensive and results in carbon dioxide (CO_2) emissions to the atmosphere if they are not captured and sequestered, and methane (CH_4) emissions due to leakage throughout the natural gas supply chain. [. . .]

Another commonly used process for producing hydrogen is electrolysis, which involves running an electrical current through water to split the hydrogen from the oxygen. If this electricity comes from non-emitting source (e.g., solar photovoltaic, wind turbines, or hydropower), there are no upstream GHG emissions. If CO_2 associated with the electricity used to produce hydrogen can be captured and stored, then hydrogen may still be produced with relatively few GHG emissions. [. . .]

Safety

Hydrogen is a small molecule that is flammable and has the potential to leak. However, hydrogen leak detection methods are in place to prevent leaks into the atmosphere. Furthermore, the storage tanks undergo rigorous testing where they must function properly at a rate that is double the pressure of what would be applied during normal use. The carbon fiber material used to make storage tanks is stronger than steel. And to provide even more assurance, all storage tanks must have a backup safety system in place.

Hydrogen Fuel Cell Vehicles in Action

A few examples of hydrogen being used in the real world

1. There are more than 50,000 hydrogen fuel cell electric forklifts already operating across the country. These forklifts can be refueled in minutes and require less maintenance, which is why many major retailers around the country are using them to enhance warehouse productivity.

2. The Alameda-Contra Costa Transit District (AC Transit) is the largest public bus-only transit agency in California. Their Zero Emission Bus Program has expanded from a single hydrogen fuel-cell electric bus to a fleet of thirty-six (36) 40-foot fuel-cell electric transit buses, plus several battery electric buses. . . . Their switch to zero emission buses has generated over 5 million miles and eliminated over 12,800 metric tons of CO2.

As hydrogen fuel cell technologies expand, a sector that could greatly benefit is seaports. Replacing diesel engines across a variety of port applications can significantly reduce air pollutants associated with diesel emissions. Many other fuel cell applications are under development, including for port drayage trucks, yard tractors, cargo handlers (top loaders), switcher locomotives, and marine vessels such as harbor craft.

Source F

National Renewable Energy Laboratory, Electric Vehicle Charging Infrastructure Trends from the Alternative Fueling Station Locator: Second Quarter 2020, October 2020, https://www.energy.gov/eere/vehicles/articles/fotw-1174-february-22-2021-over-20000-new-electric-vehicle-charging-outlets.

The following information comes from the Office of Energy Efficiency & Renewable Energy within the U.S. Department of Energy.

In 2009, there were 245 new electric vehicle (EV) charging outlets installed nationwide, but by 2019 that number had risen to more than 20,000 new installations. From 2017 to 2019, about 5,000 new charging outlets were installed each year. The majority of new charging outlets are Level 2, but the number of DC Fast Charging outlets has been expanding, which helps reduce refueling times. In 2019, there were 4,482 DC Fast Charging outlets installed, representing just over 20% of all new installations. Cumulatively, by 2019 there were more than 78,000 charging outlets at about 26,000 electric vehicle charging stations.

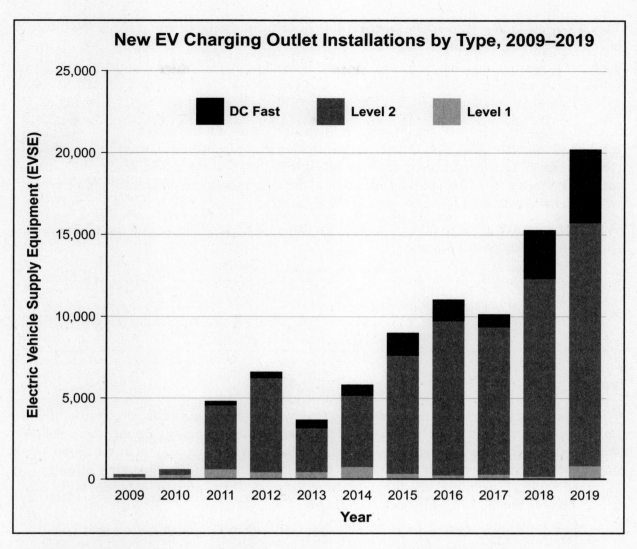

New EV Charging Outlet Installations by Type, 2009–2019

Electric Vehicle Supply Equipment (EVSE) (y-axis)

Legend: ■ DC Fast ■ Level 2 ■ Level 1

y-axis values: 0, 5,000, 10,000, 15,000, 20,000, 25,000

x-axis: **Year** — 2009, 2010, 2011, 2012, 2013, 2014, 2015, 2016, 2017, 2018, 2019

Part 3 Answer the following questions using the prompt on electric vehicles.

1. What do you learn about the prompt topic in the **background information?**
2. What are the **differing positions** held by individuals already involved in the conversation?
3. What is the difference between each of the **synthesis task types?**
4. In your own words, describe the task that you are expected to complete when responding to the prompt in the synthesis question.

WRITE

You will be developing a synthesis essay on electric vehicles from start to finish in the remaining lessons in this section. As you read in Lesson SYN.1, one of the most important requirements for the synthesis essay is that you keep your own arguments central rather than just summarizing the arguments of the different sources. Even though you have read through the prompt and sources on electric vehicles just once, complete the Task 1 and Task 2 sentences on the next page to express what position you may now hold on the subject of electric vehicles and to understand how the two tasks differ.

Task 1 My position on the extent to which electric vehicles should be embraced as the future of consumer transportation is . . .

Task 2 My position on what factors an individual should consider when buying an electric vehicle is . . .

Watch this video (tinyurl.com/3swwx5m5) about the how electric vehicles respond to salt-water flood conditions. After watching the video, you may want to consider the sources listed, the visuals intermixed with the speakers' reflections, the implications of the language and visuals, and the messages of the speakers and then revise what you have written in response to Task 1 and Task 2.

What's the Point? In one sentence, explain how this lesson can help you on the AP English Language and Composition exam.

_____

_____

_____

TEAM UP

With your teacher's permission, repeat the activity you did at the end of the first lesson, this time with the sources for the **electric vehicles prompt** and with new group members. Follow the same steps. Read each source carefully on your own, assign each student in the group one of the sources, and become an expert on your assigned source. Take about five minutes to reread or closely examine the source you were assigned. Then "present" it to the rest of the group. Include the following in your presentation:

- The credibility of the source as far as you can tell and how you determined that
- The aspect of the topic it covers
- The perspective it brings to the conversation
- How it relates to your own perspective

When everyone has presented a source, have a brief discussion on how you might use the sources to respond to Task 1 and Task 2.

LESSON SYN.3 Mining the Prompt for Ideas

Eyes on the Exam

Exam readers will want to see that you create and establish your arguments based on interrelated ideas, not just the topics of the prompts.

LEARN

Use your understanding of the structure of the synthesis prompt to your advantage on exam day. You can use several strategies while reading the prompt to help you better understand the prompt topic and sources so you can produce a more complex argument and essay. Start by locating ideas in the prompt so you can focus on all the requirements of the synthesis task.

Ideas represent things you cannot experience with your senses. *Love, courage, faith, economics,* and *boredom* are all ideas. Look at the chart below to see more examples in a few common categories of ideas.

Human Behavior	Society	Ethics	Identity	Politics	Nature	Pop Culture
Arrogance	Art	Abuse	Adolescence	Authority	Adaptation	American Dream
Benevolence	Commercialism	Arrogance	Alienation	Capitalism	Adventure	Fame
Citizenship	Community	Compassion	Belonging	Colonialism	Adversity	Luxury
Civility	Diversity	Complacency	Certainty	Control	Beauty	Prestige
Consumerism	Dominance	Consequence	Creativity	Democracy	Change	Prosperity
Convenience	Economics	Deception	Doubt	Efficiency	Conservation	Social Trends
Courage	Education	Discrimination	Experience	Globalism	Energy	Success
Delinquency	Equality	Dominance	Failure	Government	Environment	Technology
Empathy	History	Faith	Gratefulness	Leadership	Health	
Enthusiasm	Industry	Greed	Guilt	Liberty	Physiology	
Hypocrisy	Innovation	Honor	Humor	Patriotism	Survival	
Independence	Labor	Hope	Imagination	Peace	Sustainability	
Materialism	Life	Integrity	Individuality	Power		
Obedience	Modernization	Joy	Maturity	Regulation		
Ownership	Opportunity	Judgment	Metacognition	Socialism		
Pacifism	Poverty	Justice	Nostalgia	Tyranny		
Protest	Privilege	Love	Purpose	War		
Rebellion	Progress	Patience	Shame			
Religion	Property	Perseverance	Stress			
Risk	Race	Productivity				
Sympathy	Racism	Responsibility				
Tradition	Reality	Sacrifice				
Violence	Truth	Safety				
Weakness	Victory					
Wonder						
Zeal						

As you read the background and task sections of the synthesis prompt, dissect them for ideas and idea-based language. In other words, look for words and phrases in the prompt that either are ideas themselves (that is, abstract concepts) or that imply some relationships to ideas.

If you look for specific words expressing *ideas* in the aquariums prompt background (reproduced below), you will find the following: *life, public entities, private entities, diversity (of marine life), industry, education, conservation, ethics, captivity,* and *amusement.* Not all synthesis prompts include as many ideas as this one, but you will always be able to locate some. Underline them when you find them.

> In 1853, the London Zoo introduced a new showcase: the first public aquarium. Since this time, major municipalities and private companies alike have developed fine-tuned and well-balanced showcases of marine <u>life</u> for the masses to enjoy. Some of these <u>public and private entities</u> have even developed methods that, in conjunction with safely displaying <u>the diversity of marine life</u>, allow patrons to have personal interactions with animals entrusted to their care. Advocates of the aquatic life <u>industry</u> argue that aquariums and sea-life attractions promote <u>education</u> and <u>conservation</u>, while many others challenge the ethics of holding animals in <u>captivity</u> for any reason, especially if such captivity results in <u>amusement</u> and profit.

You can also try to locate other words in the prompt's background and task areas that relate closely to, or imply, ideas. When you find these words and phrases, highlight or circle them and label them with the ideas they imply. In the case of the aquariums prompt, you will find such language as *well-balanced showcases,* which relates to the idea of entertainment. Or you might identify the phrase *safely displaying,* which reflects the idea of safety or security. You might identify the word *profit,* which is directly tied to the idea of economics.

Once you have found ideas in the synthesis prompt, you'll be able to read the sources and explore how they interrelate with bigger ideas (see Lesson SYN.6). You will also have a greater understanding of how the prompt topic links to ideas in other areas of life. Most important, you will be able to anchor the different sources to one or two main ideas. Suppose, for example, you choose to generate an argument grounded in the ideas of ethics and profits and consider each source in relation to those ideas. The following examples show how you plan a focused argument for each of the two task types.

Using Ideas in Task 1	
Task 1	Write an essay that synthesizes material from at least three of the sources and develops your position on the <u>extent to which aquariums and other sea-life attractions fulfill a role</u> in education and wildlife conservation.
Task 1 Frame	If I were to focus on the idea of [insert idea tied to prompt], I could write an argument that explores how aquariums [**choose one:** *should be/ should not be/could possibly be*] the [**choose one:** *best/worst*] way to [insert an argument connecting the initial idea].
Task 1 Completed Frame	If I were to focus on the idea of ethics, I could write an argument that explores how aquariums and other sea-life attractions should be better regulated to make sure animals in captivity are treated with the highest level of ethical standards.

Using Ideas in Task 2	
Task 2	Write an essay that synthesizes material from at least three of the sources and develops your position on <u>what factors individuals need to consider</u> when choosing to visit an aquarium or other sea-life attraction.
Task 2 Frame	When people choose to visit an aquarium or other sea-life attraction, they should consider how their visit affects [insert two to three ideas tied to aquariums].
Task 2 Completed Frame	When people choose to visit an aquarium or other sea-life attraction, they should consider how their visit affects the ethical treatment of animals and the profits generated by these attractions.

KEY POINT: All synthesis prompts include or imply **multiple ideas.** Identifying these ideas will help you **purposefully read sources, generate idea-based arguments,** and avoid producing a paper that just summarizes sources.

PRACTICE

Based on the background and task sections of the electric vehicles synthesis prompt reproduced below, do your best to complete the activities on the next page.

[Background]

Over the past 100+ years, the world has seen significant technological <u>advancements</u>. Each time a particular technology seems to have achieved its pinnacle performance, within a short time period a new version of it appears, and it's often billed as being better than ever before. One enterprise that has seen some of the most significant improvement and growth is the automobile industry. This is because the contemporary world requires automobile companies to explore and produce new avenues of convenience, performance, and efficiency while maintaining an affordable <u>price tag</u> for the average consumer. Since the early 2000s, electric vehicles have become increasingly more common, often being celebrated by many as the most sustainable vehicles for the future. There are critics, however, who have suggested that such technologies overcommit and underdeliver on their promises to meet consumer, cultural, and environmental needs.

[Task 1]

Carefully read the following six sources, including the introductory information for each source. Write an essay that synthesizes material from at least three of the sources and develops your position on the extent to which electric vehicles should be embraced as the future of consumer transportation.

—or—

[Task 2]

Carefully read the following six sources, including the introductory information for each source. Write an essay that synthesizes material from at least three of the sources and develops your position on what factors an individual should consider when buying an electric vehicle.

Part 1 List the *idea words that are included in the prompt* and connect to the topic. You might want to make a chart like the one below to record your thoughts. One example is done for you.

Language in the Prompt That Specifies Ideas

Prompt Topic	Idea Words
Electric vehicles	• advancements

Part 2 Make an organizer like the one below to record language in the prompt that *relates to or implies ideas,* and then identify the ideas that correlate with that language. One example is done for you.

Language in the Prompt That Implies Ideas

Prompt Language	Implied Idea(s)
price tag	• economics

WRITE

Based on any one of the ideas you have located in the electric vehicles prompt, explain how focusing on that idea could help you generate an argument in response to each of the two task types. Use the text frames for each task on pages 24 and 25 to help you if needed.

Watch this video (tinyurl.com/y74yet29) by AP teacher Timm Freitas in which he models how to break down a synthesis prompt with ideas in mind.

What's the Point? In one sentence, explain how this lesson can help you on the AP English Language and Composition exam.

_____

_____

_____

LESSON SYN.4 Turning the Prompt into a Question

Eyes on the Exam

Exam readers will want to see that your thesis statement effectively responds to the prompt provided.

LEARN

After you have mined the prompt for ideas and idea-based language to help read the sources with focus, you can next turn your attention to what the prompt requires you to do so you can effectively respond to the task and create a well-developed argument.

To effectively respond to the prompt, turn the task section of the prompt into a guiding question or questions. Depending on the type of synthesis task, you may be able to generate more than one question, but do not be worried if you can generate only one question from the task.

Review the task possibilities for the aquarium prompt (see Lesson SYN.1 for the background to the prompt). Remember, you will be given only one of the tasks on exam day.

[Task 1]

Carefully read the following six sources, including the introductory information for each source. Write an essay that synthesizes material from at least three of the sources and develops your position on the extent to which aquariums and other sea-life attractions fulfill a role in education and wildlife conservation.

[Task 2]

Carefully read the following six sources, including the introductory information for each source. Write an essay that synthesizes material from at least three of the sources and develops your position on what factors individuals need to consider when choosing to visit an aquarium or other sea-life attraction.

To turn either of the prompt tasks into a question or questions to be answered in your essay, follow these steps.

Turning a Task into a Question or Questions	
Step 1	**Notice that both of tasks begin the same way:** "Carefully read the following six sources, including the introductory information for each source. Write an essay that synthesizes material from at least three of the sources and develops your position on . . . ." You can save time if you remember that only the last part of the task varies from one prompt task to the other. The phrase *develops your position on* provides a clear directive for what you need to do: You must develop your own position about the topic that follows it. Notice that the language does not direct you to summarize other individuals' positions; rather, you are to write your *own* argument, and this needs to be at the forefront of your mind.

Step 2	Once you have found what you are directed to do (in Step 1), **focus on what follows the phrase "develops your position on."** Notice that the last part of each type of task points back to the subject of the background paragraph: aquariums and other sea-life attractions.
	In Task 1, you focus on this: "develops your position on the extent to which aquariums and other sea-life attractions fulfill a role in education and wildlife conservation." In Task 2, focus on "develops your position on what factors individuals need to consider when choosing to visit an aquarium or other sea-life attraction."
Step 3	Once you've homed in on this specific part of the task directive (from the word *develops* until the end of the sentence), **turn that part of the task into a question**. Create questions that will guide the creation of your thesis and essay. Generate questions that start with *What* or *To what extent* because these questions are easier to answer than questions that begin with *Why* or *How*. You will explain *why* and *how* in the body of the essay itself. Right now, you are just generating questions to guide your reading, thought processes, and creation of your thesis statement.

Example Question for Task 1

This task is directing you to consider the role of these attractions in education and wildlife conservation, so your question would be "To what extent do aquariums and other sea-life attractions fulfill a role in education and wildlife conservation?" As you read the sources, you should be looking for material that is relevant to those two ideas. You may also ask, "What is my position on this issue?"

As you respond to these questions in your essay, make sure you clearly articulate *your* stand on the role aquariums and other sea-life attractions have in education and wildlife conservation. By responding to the first question ("To what extent . . . "), you will also be answering the second, because how you answer the first question is your position in relation to it.

Stop and think through these questions. Do you think these establishments help? Or do you think they hurt? Do you think they predominantly help or hurt, but you can recognize it is not entirely one way or the other? Good. Wherever you stand, once you answer the questions you have created, you will be able to craft a claim in response to the prompt. You will also be able to read your sources so you can consider how each would answer these questions as well. Reading sources with pointed questions in mind will help you synthesize them into your argument later.

Example Question for Task 2

You can create a guiding question in exactly the same way for the other type of task: "What factors should individuals consider when choosing to visit an aquarium or other sea-life attraction?" Here you are asked to identify factors to consider in choosing to visit one of these attractions. This topic is more subjective, as indicated in the last sentence of the background paragraph: What, if any, ethical considerations might someone take into account in deciding whether to patronize one of these attractions?

When you now read your sources and think about your own argument, make sure you clearly identify the factors *you* think someone needs to consider if they choose to visit an aquarium. Should individuals consider prices? Professional accreditation? Handicapped accessibility? New and contemporary exhibits? The establishment's reputation? These are just a few of the factors you might consider.

> **KEY POINT:** All synthesis tasks include the phrase "develops your position on."
> **Generating questions** directly from the words following that phrase will give you a significant advantage when you read your sources and construct your argument.

PRACTICE

Read the tasks for the electric vehicles prompt on page 13. Then, for each task type, on separate paper generate the question(s) that will guide you as you develop the synthesis essay. Remember, the question or questions you create should start with the word *What* or the phrase *To what extent*. Follow Steps 1–3 above.

1. **Synthesis Task 1** Write an essay that synthesizes material from at least three of the sources and develops your position on the extent to which electric vehicles should be embraced as the future of consumer transportation.

   My Question(s):

2. **Synthesis Task 2** Write an essay that synthesizes material from at least three of the sources and develops your position on what factors an individual should consider when buying an electric vehicle.

   My Question(s):

WRITE

Now that you have at least one question for each task in the electric vehicles prompt, write a one-sentence response that indicates your position now.

3. **Synthesis Task 1** Write an essay that synthesizes material from at least three of the sources and develops your position on the extent to which electric vehicles should be embraced as the future of consumer transportation.

   My Position:

4. **Synthesis Task 2** Write an essay that synthesizes material from at least three of the sources and develops your position on what factors an individual should consider when buying an electric vehicle.

   My Position:

Watch this video (tinyurl.com/mr27j4r2) produced by the reputable UK news source *The Guardian*. It focuses on how "green" electric cars are. After watching the video, consider going back and revising the original claims you created for each task in the Write activity of this lesson.

What's the Point? In one sentence, explain how this lesson can help you on the AP English Language and Composition exam.

_____

_____

_____

TEAM UP

Even before you read any sources on marine-life attractions or electric vehicles, you already had a position on those topics, or at least an opinion. You have been forming opinions your whole life, even if you haven't been aware of the experiences and influences that have led you to those opinions. This activity will help you identify the factors that influenced your perspective on the topic of electric vehicles and help you bring it into clearer focus. That perspective, after all, is the backbone of the synthesis essay.

With your teacher's permission, meet in small groups. Begin by each stating your position in response to both Task 1 and Task 2. Then, for each of the following possible influences, take turns discussing how strongly it has influenced you: not at all, somewhat, quite a bit, or very much. For each factor that has had some influence on you, relate a specific example that served as a confirmation or turning point in the way you think about the topic.

- Peer and family opinions
- Media influence
- Practical or personal experience
- Environmental awareness
- Economic considerations
- Regional norms
- Technology interest

Clarifying your position through this activity will help you when you write the synthesis essay because it is the foundation on which you build your argument—the perspective through which you see the sources. Recognizing and articulating your own position will help you evaluate potential biases in your own perspective and the perspectives presented in the sources. This self-awareness can be a critical aspect of academic writing and discourse.

LESSON SYN.5 Reading Source Information

Eyes on the Exam

On exam day, you will have 15 minutes to read the sources for the synthesis free-response prompt. Read the sources as efficiently as possible.

LEARN

Even 15 minutes is not a lot of time to critically read sources and evaluate how to use them, so you need strategies that will help you read your sources in a focused way.

Each source that accompanies any synthesis prompt will be preceded by a box containing citation information about the author and source publication. These boxes are followed by important background information in italics about the source—additional information about the author, the publishing organization, or even the region in which the information was published. Often, students ignore this information because they think that reading the sources themselves is a better use of the limited time they have. However, learning to use the source information can help you increase your exam-day efficiency.

When you read source information, you should look for any clues that will help indicate a source's **perspective, position, biases,** or **limitations.** Identifying any or all these will help you later when you use the sources to develop your argument.

- The **perspective** of a source is the outlook or view the writer takes toward the subject. The writer's background, interests, and experiences all contribute to the writer's perspective. The best way to understand perspective is to ask, "What authority does the person discussing this topic have?" Was the source produced by a politician, doctor, professor, other expert, parent, concerned citizen, a professional organization, or someone (or something) else? Each of these writers would bring a different perspective to a topic.

- A **position** is the source's attitude toward a subject, the argument the author is making. A writer may have a position supporting aquariums because of their educational value or opposing them on ethics, for example.

- **Bias** is a potential prejudice any source may hold toward a topic. For example, the owner of an aquarium would be biased in favor of them because of the money it can make.

- A **limitation** is anything that may weaken the argument of the source itself. Limitations may be tied to a source's perspective, bias, or possibly even the date of publication.

Examine the following source information and the italicized background information below the boxed source for Source A of the aquariums prompt on page 3.

Source A

Jacobs, Bob. "The neural cruelty of captivity: Keeping large mammals in zoos and aquariums damages their brains." The Conversation, 24 Sept. 2020. theconversation.com/ the-neural-cruelty-of-captivity-keeping-large-mammals-in-zoos-and-aquariums-damages-their-brains-142240.

The following is excerpted from an article written by a professor of neuroscience.

The name of the author does not necessarily tell you anything about perspective, position, bias, or limitations. However, once you move past the name and read the title of the piece, you may notice that the wording reveals the position of the piece. Words like *cruelty*, *captivity*, and *damages* all have negative meanings and connotations. Also, notice that the title makes a claim: "Keeping large mammals in zoos and aquariums damages their brains." Though you haven't yet read the entire source, you can infer that this particular source is probably opposed to animal captivity, especially in service of entertainment and amusement.

You should not stop at the title, however. Keep reading and see that the article was published in September of 2020. That date is important because generally more recent sources contain more up-to-date data. A recent date can help add some credibility to the claims of an article, especially if information cited in the source is recent as well. Older sources containing older data may be limited because of new discoveries since the source's publication.

If you read on, you'll notice that the italicized information below the box provides a clue to the author's perspective. The title already indicates the author's position, but the italicized information reveals that the author is a professor of neuroscience. That credential adds credibility to the argument. This particular author has an advanced degree in neuroscience and therefore can be considered a trusted authority to discuss the neuroactivity of large mammals.

As you begin to consider your own argument in response to the prompt, analyzing the source information can help you decide whether you can use this source either to support your position or in opposition to it. Or you may end up changing your mind about your position after fully reading the source. You should also be able to tell whether the source will have any relevance to your argument. If not, you may decide not to read the entire source.

Not all source information will be as helpful as the above example, but you should still evaluate all of your sources because they may be helpful in different ways. Look at the information for Source C of the aquariums prompt below.

Source C

"Marketing to Families: Why Brands Are Investing in U.S. Zoos & Aquariums." Allionce Group, 13 Aug. 2021, www.allioncegroup.com/why-brands-should-invest-in-u-s-zoos-aquariums/.

The following is taken from the website of a marketing company that focuses on marketing to parents and children.

The title of the piece indicates a potential bias to consider: profiting from family experiences. If you continue to read the source information, you'll find that the creators of this source are the Allionce Group, and the URL contains a phrase suggesting that there is a reason why "brands-should-invest" in wildlife encounters. You can infer the potential position of this source: that supporting zoos and aquariums is good for maximizing profits. While other sources might support investing in zoos, the reasons why the Allionce Group supports it are significantly different from those that may focus on conservation, such as Source B, which you can find on page 4.

The perspective of the source is clarified in the italicized information below the box: Allionce Group is a marketing company. Perhaps this source will introduce you to a new position that you can consider engaging with in relation to the prompt. Did you already think about your response to Task 1 or Task 2 in relation to marketing and investment? If not, you now have a new position to consider as you build your own position.

You also may be able to recognize the limitation of the source. If you want to develop your position based on conservation, this source probably will contribute little to your argument.

PRACTICE

Look at the information that precedes each of the sources on pages 14–21 for the electric vehicles prompt. Then make a chart like the one below as an information organizer for each source. If the source doesn't have an author, see if you can find the sponsoring organization.

Synthesis Information Organizer						
	Source A	**Source B**	**Source C**	**Source D**	**Source E**	**Source F**
Author						
Title						
Date of Publication						
Italicized Background Information						

WRITE

Based on the source information you collected in the Practice activity above, make a chart like the one below to evaluate each source's potential perspective(s), position(s), bias(es), or limitation(s).

Synthesis Source Evaluation						
	Source A	**Source B**	**Source C**	**Source D**	**Source E**	**Source F**
Perspective						
Position						
Potential Bias						
Limitation(s)						

Go to this video (tinyurl.com/49nydz75) produced by the Union of Concerned Scientists. Before watching the video, evaluate the video title, the publishing group, date of publication, and other source information you can find in the video's description. Discuss what you can infer about the video's potential perspective(s), position(s), bias(es), or limitation(s) before viewing the content.

What's the Point? In one sentence, explain how this lesson can help you on the AP English Language and Composition exam.

_____

_____

_____

LESSON SYN.6 Reading Sources with Ideas in Mind

Eyes on the Exam

Exam readers will want to see that you create and establish your arguments centered on interrelated ideas, not just the general topic of the prompt.

LEARN

On exam day, you will navigate through a lot of text as you work through all three of the assigned essays in limited time. To make the most of your time, learn to read the sources with focus. In time, you will be able to organize the sources into potential conversation partners as you see connections among ideas.

Every synthesis prompt includes or alludes to ideas, as you saw in Lesson SYN.3. This lesson will help you understand how your sources relate to the ideas suggested by the prompt and ultimately to the development of your position and arguments about the topic.

For example, here are some ideas tied to the aquariums prompt on page 1: marine life, public and private enterprise, diversity (of marine life), industry, education, conservation, ethics, captivity, amusement, entertainment, safety, security, economics. Before reading the sources focusing on these ideas, cut the list down to a manageable number that relate directly to the task you are completing. Three to six ideas are about the right number to help you read your sources. Too few ideas won't provide you with enough to guide your reading, but too many ideas will slow you down as you search the sources.

A good way to cut down your list is to see if any ideas are closely related. For example, the ideas of marine life and diversity (of marine life) can be tied together. Safety and security are similar, so you can choose to focus on either one. Amusement and entertainment are also closely related, so you can choose either of these as well. With just a little consideration, the list of ideas has already been condensed, and even more ideas could be combined.

Task 1 asks you to develop "your position on the extent to which aquariums and other sea-life attractions fulfill a role in education and wildlife conservation," so it would probably be best for you to focus on ideas such as diversity of marine life, ethics, captivity, conservation, education, and entertainment.

Task 2 asks you to develop "your position on what factors individuals need to consider when choosing to visit an aquarium or other sea-life attraction," so it would probably be best for you to focus on ethics, safety, education, entertainment, amusement, and economics.

With your list of ideas as a guide, you can now read the sources with focus. As you read, mark any sources that either directly or implicitly address one or more of the ideas you've identified, noting the idea in the margin. Or you can mark them in the charts you created in the previous lesson. On exam day, you can draw your own chart on scrap paper or in your prompt booklet, or you can annotate the sources in the margins near the text or images related to your focus ideas.

For example, review Source A from the aquariums prompt on the next page.

Jacobs, Bob. "The neural cruelty of captivity: Keeping large mammals in zoos and aquariums damages their brains." The Conversation, 24 Sept. 2020, theconversation.com/the-neural-cruelty-of-captivity-keeping-large-mammals-in-zoos-and-aquariums-damages-their-brains-142240.

The following is excerpted from an article written by a professor of neuroscience.

Many animals try to cope with captivity by adopting abnormal behaviors. Some develop "stereotypies," which are repetitive, purposeless habits such as constantly bobbing their heads, swaying incessantly or chewing on the bars of their cages. Others, especially big cats, pace their enclosures. Elephants rub or break their tusks.

Changing brain structure

Neuroscientific research indicates that living in an impoverished, stressful captive environment physically damages the brain. These changes have been documented in many, including rodents, rabbits, cats and humans.

Although researchers have directly studied some animal brains, most of what we know comes from observing animal behavior, analyzing stress hormone levels in the blood and applying knowledge gained from a half-century of neuroscience research. Laboratory research also suggests that mammals in a zoo or aquarium have compromised brain function.

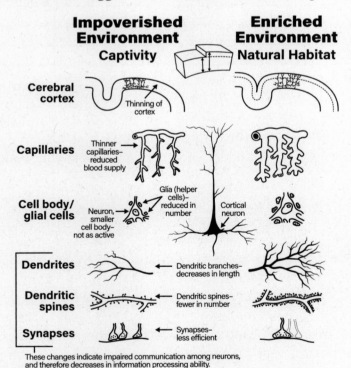

This illustration shows differences in the brain's cerebral cortex in animals held in impoverished (captive) and enriched (natural) environments. Impoverishment results in thinning of the cortex, a decreased blood supply, less support for neurons and decreased connectivity among neurons.
Arnold B. Scheibel, CC BY-ND

As you explore the text and images of the source, you should be able to see that this source relates directly to ethics, captivity, and safety. The word *captivity* is actually used in the source, and the behavioral findings based on studies suggest that keeping animals enclosed in an impoverished environment is damaging and therefore unsafe for their health and ultimately unethical.

To practice reading sources for ideas, begin by organizing the ways in which your sources explore certain ideas by marking the relationships in a chart or table like the ones below. Once you see that a source relates to a certain idea, you can put an **X** in the corresponding source box. The following charts are based on the sources for the aquariums prompt.

Synthesis Task 1 Ideas and Sources Organizer						
Ideas	**Source A**	**Source B**	**Source C**	**Source D**	**Source E**	**Source F**
Diversity of Marine Life		X		X		
Ethics	X	X	X		X	X
Captivity	X	X			X	X
Conservation		X	X	X	X	
Education		X	X	X	X	
Entertainment			X			

Synthesis Task 2 Ideas and Sources Organizer						
Ideas	**Source A**	**Source B**	**Source C**	**Source D**	**Source E**	**Source F**
Ethics	X	X	X			X
Safety	X	X		X	X	
Education		X	X	X	X	
Entertainment			X			
Amusement			X			
Economics			X	X	X	

A chart of ideas and sources makes writing body paragraphs significantly easier when you are ready to write. The benefit of a chart like this is that if you notice one source explores more ideas than others—like Sources B and C in the charts above—you'll know it's definitely one of the three sources you should cite when you write your essay. If you notice that multiple sources explore the same ideas, you can confidently use these sources in your body paragraphs. (See Lesson SYN.9.)

KEY POINT: Focusing on ideas while you read sources will make reading the sources significantly more meaningful. Doing so will also help you organize your sources for later, when you write your essay.

PRACTICE

Identify major ideas in the electric vehicles prompt on pages 13–14. You may want to consider using your work from Lesson SYN.3 of this writing guide. Then make corresponding "Ideas and Sources" organizers based on the two task types. (See next page.)

Synthesis Task 1 Ideas and Sources Organizer

Ideas	Source A	Source B	Source C	Source D	Source E	Source F

Synthesis Task 2 Ideas and Sources Organizer

Ideas	Source A	Source B	Source C	Source D	Source E	Source F

WRITE

Consider the information in your ideas and sources charts from the Practice activity. Then, for each source of the electric vehicles prompt on pages 14–21, write one brief sentence summarizing how that source could be used to answer the prompt. You should answer for both tasks when doing this. Consider creating an organizer like the one below to record your answers.

Synthesis Source Response Organizer

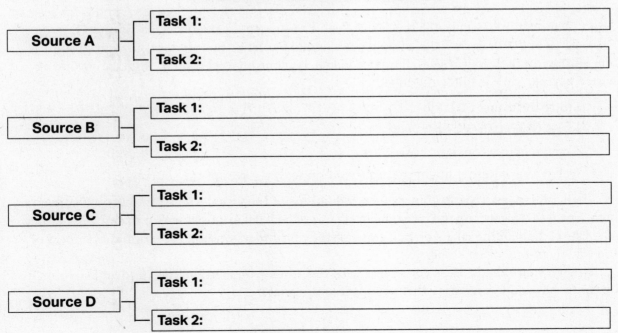

Source A — Task 1: / Task 2:

Source B — Task 1: / Task 2:

Source C — Task 1: / Task 2:

Source D — Task 1: / Task 2:

| Source E | Task 1: |
| | Task 2: |

| Source F | Task 1: |
| | Task 2: |

Watch this video (tinyurl.com/2n8k8958) in which Beth Hall provides very useful quick tips for annotating synthesis sources. Reflect on any strategies that you may want to adopt and combine with techniques you've learned and practiced above.

What's the Point? In one sentence, explain how this lesson can help you on the AP English Language and Composition exam.

_____

_____

_____

TEAM UP

You can also "read" visual sources for ideas, but you might need practice in translating the image or numbers of the visual sources into language expressing ideas. With your teacher's permission, meet in small groups to practice that translation now.

The prompt on sea-life attractions has three visuals, one each in Sources A and C (pages 3 and 6) and Source F (page 9). The electric vehicles prompt has two visuals, Sources D and F (pages 18 and 20). Each visual should be assigned to one or two students in your group (depending on the group's size). For your visual, become an expert on it. If you are working with a partner, do the following together.

- Study the visual carefully.
- Identify what ideas it conveys.
- Explain *how* it conveys those ideas.
- Determine where it fits in the conversation with the rest of the sources.

Then take turns sharing your expert evaluations of the visuals. As a group, try to come up with a process for getting the most meaning out of a visual as possible. For example, you may suggest reading all the labels or captions carefully or understanding the emotional impact of the visual, among other steps.

Finally, share the process you create with the other groups in the class and adjust yours in light of what you learn from other groups if appropriate.

LESSON SYN.7 From a General Claim to a Complex Thesis

Eyes on the Exam

Exam readers will be looking for your thesis statement. A complex thesis will help you produce a stronger essay.

LEARN

After you've read your prompt and your sources, you're ready to begin writing your essay. You should start this process by producing your thesis statement. Your **thesis statement** is the sentence that you will use to guide the rest of your essay. Thesis statements are usually placed at the end of a full introductory paragraph, but on exam day, you have the option of using your thesis as your *whole introductory paragraph*. That's right—one sentence can function as a full paragraph. By using your thesis as your first paragraph, you can save a significant amount of time that you can then use to focus on producing your body paragraphs.

To write your thesis statement, you first need an **overarching claim** about your position in response to the prompt. An overarching claim states your position on the topic from the prompt, while a thesis provides more complexity for that claim and also suggests some of the reasoning that justifies your claim. The overarching claim is a statement of your position; the thesis statement expresses how you intend to write about your position and develop your line of reasoning.

For example, to generate an overarching claim for Task 1 of the aquariums prompt on page 1, you would articulate your general position about the role such establishments play in education and wildlife conservation. So if you think that aquariums are beneficial in education and conservation, you could make the claim "Aquariums play a beneficial role in education and conservation."

Or to generate an overarching claim for Task 2 of the aquariums prompt, you would articulate your general position about what individuals need to consider when visiting an aquarium or other sea-life attraction. An overarching claim in response to this task might be "Individuals should consider how unethically animals are treated and the manipulative business practices of the establishments."

These overarching claims respond to the prompt, and each would earn the thesis point on exam day based on the scoring rubric. However, you should try to make these overarching claims more complex, since thought that is more complex is also more sophisticated. The easiest way to generate a **complex thesis** is to write your thesis in the form of a complex sentence. A **complex sentence** is a sentence that includes two clauses linked by a subordinating conjunction. **Subordinating conjunctions** show an inequality of ideas, adding layers of complexity to a sentence. Below is a list of common subordinating conjunctions:

Common Subordinating Conjunctions		
after	even though	until
although	if	when
as	since	whereas
as if	though	which
because	unless	while
before		

While the inclusion of any of the preceding words can make a sentence complex, the best words to use to turn your overarching claims into complex thesis statements are *because* and *since*. Including *because* or *since* in your thesis allows you to clearly delineate the reasoning for your argument. In other words, it allows you to begin projecting a clear line of reasoning, which is very important on exam day.

Below are examples that show how overarching claims can become complex thesis statements based on each task for the aquariums prompt on page 1.

Overarching Claim for Task 1: Aquariums play a major role in education and conservation.

Complex Thesis for Task 1: Aquariums play a beneficial role in education and conservation **since** they provide new opportunities for patrons to interact with marine life they may have never seen, and these establishments protect endangered species.

Overarching Claim for Task 2: Individuals should consider how unethically animals are treated and the manipulative business practices of the establishments.

Complex Thesis for Task 2: Individuals should consider how unethically animals are treated and the manipulative business practices of marine-life-based establishments **because** aquariums damage the lives of the animals they claim to serve and therefore should not be supported.

Each of these thesis statements now clearly outlines where the essay will go and clearly conveys the writer's position about aquariums.

The thesis statement for Task 1 posits that the essay will explore the ways in which new opportunities for patrons are beneficial for education and/or conservation and will then explore how protecting endangered species is beneficial for education and/or conservation.

The thesis statement for Task 2 posits that the essay will explore the lack of ethics in the ways animals are treated at aquariums and how their lives are damaged. Then the essay will go on to explore the ways in which the business practices of these establishments are harmful. Throughout the argument, the essay will also explain how the animals' poor treatment and the establishments' push for profits should encourage individuals not to support such organizations.

Both sample thesis statements have clear arguments. The thesis for Task 1 views aquariums favorably, while the one for Task 2 is considerably more critical. Nonetheless, both present a complex argument that the writer can support with evidence throughout the rest of the essay.

KEY POINT: Transforming your overarching claim into a **complex thesis statement** will help guide you in developing a stronger essay as you continue through the writing process. Create a complex sentence using *since* or *because* or another subordinating conjunction to help you achieve a complex thesis statement.

PRACTICE

After reading the electric vehicles prompt on pages 13–14, on separate paper, write overarching claims in response to both Task 1 and Task 2. The tasks are reproduced on the next page for easy reference. Make sure to keep these overarching claims general.

1. **Task 1** Write an essay that synthesizes material from at least three of the sources and develops your position on the extent to which electric vehicles should be embraced as the future of consumer transportation.

   Overarching claim:

2. **Task 2** Write an essay that synthesizes material from at least three of the sources and develops your position on what factors an individual should consider when buying an electric vehicle.

   Overarching claim:

WRITE

Now that you've created overarching claims for the electric vehicles prompt, transform them into complex thesis statements that will guide the rest of your essay. As you write these first drafts, make sure to include *because* or *since* as your subordinating conjunction. After you write your thesis, in one or two sentences describe how you would use it as the basis for structuring your essay. You may consider using any of the following templates. Write your first draft thesis statements on separate paper.

3. **Task 1**

   [Claim about synthesis topic] [**choose one:** *because/since*] [list two to three reasons that justify your claim].

   [Claim(s) about synthesis topic] [**choose one:** *because/since*] [identify a single unifying reason].

4. **Task 2**

   [Entity that needs to consider factors based on the prompt] should consider [factor 1] and [factor 2] [**choose one:** *because/since*] [insert unifying argument why the factors are important to consider].

   When discussing [topic of synthesis prompt], [factor 1] and [factor 2] are important to consider [**choose one:** *because/since*] [insert unifying reason why the factors are important to consider].

Watch this video (tinyurl.com/5n7cy7x2) in which Marco Learning CEO John Moscatiello gives his own tips for writing synthesis thesis statements. Then revise your complex thesis statements based on his suggestions.

What's the Point? In one sentence, explain how this lesson can help you on the AP English Language and Composition exam.

_____

_____

_____

LESSON SYN.8 Composing a Thesis with Opposing or Concessionary Views

Eyes on the Exam

One way to earn the sophistication point for synthesis is by "articulating implications or limitations of an argument by situating it within a broader context." Writing thesis statements that include opposing or concessionary views can help project the implications or limitations of your argument. *Concessionary* means "related to a concession." A concession is an admission that at least some part of a position different from yours has value.

LEARN

A thesis statement can be complex even if it doesn't consider any opposing viewpoints. However, addressing opposing viewpoints in your thesis can help make your thesis and your argument more sophisticated.

The easiest way to revise an already complex thesis statement to **address opposing viewpoints** (alternative perspectives) is by including one of the following words or phrases in it: *though, although, even though,* or *while*. When you include one of these words or phrases, you need to accurately summarize the opposing viewpoint. When you include an opposing viewpoint, you must *always* accurately summarize it. Oversimplifying an opposing viewpoint damages your argument rather than helps it.

It is often easiest to start a thesis statement with the opposing viewpoint(s). Even if you place the concession at the end of your thesis, your position will automatically be projected as the stronger one since the opposing view is preceded by a subordinating conjunction and is therefore part of the dependent clause.

Below are some examples of thesis statements that include opposing viewpoints. These thesis statements are based on the aquariums prompt on page 1.

Complex Thesis for Task 1: Aquariums play a beneficial role in education and conservation **since** they provide new opportunities for patrons to interact with marine life they may have never seen, and these establishments protect endangered species.

Opposing Viewpoint Thesis Task 1: Aquariums play a beneficial role in education and conservation **since** they provide new opportunities for patrons to interact with marine life they may have never seen, and these establishments protect endangered species, **even though** some individuals and organizations criticize the treatment of animals in these establishments.

Complex Thesis for Task 2: Individuals should consider how unethically animals are treated and the manipulative business practices of marine-life-based establishments **because** aquariums damage the lives of the animals they claim to serve and therefore should not be supported.

Opposing Viewpoint Thesis Task 2: Although some people and organizations seem to praise the efforts of aquariums and other sea-life establishments, individuals should consider how unethically animals are treated and the manipulative business practices of marine-life-based establishments **because** aquariums damage the lives of the animals they claim to serve and therefore should not be supported.

You may think that these thesis statements are long, and you're not wrong. But these thesis statements are also complex, punctuated correctly, and projecting lines of reasoning, so you can be sure that they are sophisticated.

> **KEY POINT:** Including an **opposing viewpoint in your thesis** can help you build a more sophisticated argument. Introducing the opposing view with one of the following subordinating conjunctions will keep that view in a weaker position than yours: *though, although, even though,* or *while.*

PRACTICE

Based on your positions and thesis statements for Task 1 and Task 2 of the electric vehicles prompt on page 1, on separate paper summarize an opposing viewpoint that could be used to challenge your position. The tasks are reproduced below for easy reference.

1. **Task 1** Write an essay that synthesizes material from at least three of the sources and develops your position on the extent to which electric vehicles should be embraced as the future of consumer transportation.

   Possible opposing viewpoint:

2. **Task 2** Write an essay that synthesizes material from at least three of the sources and develops your position on what factors an individual should consider when buying an electric vehicle.

   Possible opposing viewpoint:

WRITE

Based on your consideration of opposing views in the Practice activity, transform your complex thesis statements for the electric vehicles prompt (pages 13–14) into ones that address opposing views. As you write these, precede the opposing view with *though, although, even though,* or *while* as your subordinating conjunction. Use any of the following templates:

3. **Task 1**

   [Subordinating conjunction] [reasonably summarized claim of opposing side], [your claim about the synthesis topic] [**choose one:** *because/since*] [list two to three reasons that justify the claim].

   [Subordinating conjunction] [reasonably summarized claim of opposing side], [your claim(s) about synthesis topic] [**choose one:** *because/since*] [identify a single unifying reason].

   [Your claim about the synthesis topic] [**choose one:** *because/since*] [list two to three reasons that justify the claim], [subordinating conjunction] [reasonably summarized claim of opposing side].

4. **Task 2**

   While some may think it's most important to consider [one to two factors the opposition would reasonably suggest], it's actually more imperative that [entity that needs to consider factors based on the prompt] should contemplate [factor 1] and [factor 2] [**choose one:** *because/since*] [insert unifying argument for why the factors are important to consider].

Watch this video (tinyurl.com/25zsbwwp) by AP English teacher Beth Hall in which she explains how to write thesis statements that address opposing views. Consider revising one of your complex thesis statements based on her recommendations.

What's the Point? In one sentence, explain how this lesson can help you on the AP English Language and Composition exam.

_____

_____

_____

TEAM UP

Work in small groups as your teacher directs to share your work from the Write section. The sentence frames provided in this lesson will serve you well in developing your synthesis essay. Help one another smoothly fill in the sentence frames that result in a thesis with a counterargument. Provide feedback on clarity, strength of the argument, and adherence to the sentence frame structure.

Share your thesis statements from the Write activity on page 43. Discuss the challenges and successes you and your group members encountered in using sentence frames. Also discuss how using these frames has affected your understanding and creation of thesis statements. After these discussions, revise your thesis statements based on feedback from your group.

You may also want to experiment with other sentence frames that can be used for certain counterargument purposes. In your group, try using a few of the following frames:

1. **Addressing Misconceptions**: Although it is a common misconception that [counterargument], in reality, [your argument] due to [reason 1], [reason 2], and [reason 3].

2. **Balancing Perspectives:** Despite the arguments that [counterargument], the evidence more strongly supports [your argument], especially when considering [reason 1], [reason 2], and [reason 3].

3. **Concession and Stronger Argument:** While [counterargument] is a point to consider, it pales in comparison to [your argument], which is supported by [reason 1], [reason 2], and [reason 3].

Once again, discuss the challenges and successes you and your group members encountered in using sentence frames.

SYNTHESIS Thesis Review (Row A)

Eyes on the Exam

Readers will score your thesis based on Row A in the Synthesis rubric.

LEARN

Carefully read each section of the Row A rubric and scoring guide.

- Note the [4.B] at the end of the second row. It refers to the skill in the Course and Exam Description on which the score will be based. Skill 4.B is "Write a thesis statement that requires proof or defense and that may preview the structure of the argument."
- The first row under "Row A: Thesis . . ." explains in general terms how a response can fail to receive the point (first column). The second column explains, also in general terms, what a response needs to do to earn the point.
- The row beneath that provides *general examples* of ways to miss or earn the point.
- The second to the last row (next page) provides *specific examples* of the items in the previous row.
- The final row provides additional clarifications for acceptable thesis statements.

Question 1: Synthesis	
Row A: Thesis (0-1 points), Scoring Criteria [4.B]	
0 points For any of the following: There is no defensible thesis. The intended thesis only restates the prompt. The intended thesis provides a summary of the issue with no apparent or coherent claim. There is a thesis, but it does not respond to the prompt.	**1 point** Responds to the prompt with a thesis that presents a defensible position
Decision Rules and Scoring Notes	
Responses that do not earn this point: Only restate the prompt. Do not take a position, or the position must be inferred or is vague. Equivocate or summarize other's arguments but not the student's (e.g., some people say it's good, some people say it's bad). State an obvious fact rather than making a claim that requires a defense.	**Responses that earn this point:** Respond to the prompt by developing a position on the extent to which sea-life attractions enhance education and conservation rather than restate or rephrase the prompt. Clearly take a position rather than just stating there are pros/cons.

Examples that do not earn this point:	Examples that earn this point:
Restate the prompt	**Present a defensible position that responds to the prompt.**
"There are factors that need to be considered when choosing to visit an aquarium or other sea-life attraction."	*"Sea-life attractions should be regarded as positive contributors in education and conservation efforts.*
Address the topic of the prompt, but do not take a position	*"When choosing to spend the day at an aquarium or other sea-life attraction, individuals must consider the personal fun and bonding that these institutions offer."*
"Aquariums and other sea-life attractions are popular places to visit because people like seeing marine life."	*"While conservation efforts have saved certain marine species from extinction and often extended their longevity, the poor, cramped quality of life animals have in many aquariums minimizes the educational and ecological impacts that sea-life attractions have, especially in comparison to organizations that do not keep creatures in captivity."*
"Some organizations set out to protect the creatures that provide the main attraction at sea-life institutions."	
Address the topic of the prompt but state an obvious fact as a claim	
"A wide variety of sea creatures populate many marine-life attractions and need to be well taken care of."	

Additional Notes:

The thesis may be more than one sentence, provided the sentences are in close proximity. The thesis may be anywhere within the response.

For a thesis to be defensible, the sources must include at least minimal evidence that *could* be used to support that thesis; however, the student need not cite that evidence to earn the thesis point.

The thesis *may* establish a line of reasoning that structures the essay, but it needn't do so to earn the thesis point.

A thesis that meets the criteria can be awarded the point whether or not the rest of the response successfully supports that line of reasoning.

PRACTICE

Complete the following activities and answer the questions about the Row A Thesis rubric and scoring guide.

1. Can you earn the thesis point if you have a thesis, but it is on a related subject instead?

2. Explain the best way to earn the thesis point if you present different perspectives in the thesis.

3. Should your thesis be at the beginning or end of your essay? Identify the part of the rubric that answers that question.

4. Does a thesis statement need to be defensible with information from the sources? Identify the part of the rubric that answers that question.

5. Does the line of reasoning need to support the thesis for the essay to earn the thesis point? Identify the part of the rubric that answers that question.

You Be the Reader

Read sample essay SYN.1.C in the Appendix on page 274. Decide whether that essay earns the thesis point. Explain your answer.

Check your knowledge of the synthesis rubric with these quizlet flash cards (tinyurl.com/45pu8hd).

Revise

Review the thesis statement you have developed in response to the prompt about electric vehicles (pages 13–14). If you think it does not earn the thesis point based on this rubric, revise as needed to correct that. Even if you believe it earns the thesis point, revise your thesis to make it the best it can be.

TEAM UP

Row A of the Synthesis rubric provides all the criteria exam readers will use when scoring your thesis. However, you might want to develop a collaborative thesis checklist to understand the key components of an effective thesis statement in a synthesis essay.

Working in small groups as your teacher directs, read the following thesis statements on the topic of marine-life attractions:

1. Marine-life attractions have some educational benefits because they teach people about marine animals, but they might not always be good for the animals' welfare, which is important for conservation.

2. While marine-life attractions offer educational value to the public, their role in conservation is limited due to the inherent challenges of replicating natural habitats and the negative impact on the physical and psychological well-being of captive marine creatures, ultimately hindering genuine conservation efforts.

3. Aquariums and marine parks can sometimes help with conservation and educate the public, but there are also cases where these attractions fail to provide accurate information or contribute significantly to conservation efforts.

4. Marine-life attractions, such as aquariums and ocean parks, play a crucial role in conservation and education by providing unique opportunities for direct wildlife interaction, fostering public awareness of marine ecosystems, and supporting critical research initiatives that contribute to the protection of marine species.

With your group members, determine which thesis statements are strong and which are weak. Discuss what makes the strong statements effective and the weak ones less so. Then brainstorm and discuss the essential elements of a good synthesis thesis statement. After brainstorming, create a draft checklist of criteria for an effective synthesis thesis statement. The checklist should be concise and clear, ideally with five to seven key points.

Share and compare your checklist with that of another group, and talk through similarities and differences. Revise your group's checklist based on that discussion and any additional insights.

With your teacher's direction, integrate the different groups' checklist into one class-wide checklist to evaluate and improve your thesis statements.

Evidence and Commentary

LESSON SYN.9 Finding Evidence That Supports and Complements Your Argument

Eyes on the Exam

Exam readers will want to see that you include evidence from at least three different sources. Some or all of this evidence can be used to support and complement, or add to, your argument.

LEARN

An argument is effective when it is well supported. The best way to support an argument is to find evidence that supports your reasoning. Once you have a complex thesis in response to a synthesis prompt, you can begin developing the evidence that supports the reasoning that led you to your claim. The synthesis task requires you to integrate the words, ideas, and arguments of the provided sources with your own to create a new cohesive argument, so you need to identify the sources that state ideas or information that will help support and complement your argument.

Supporting evidence shows why your reasoning is strong. **Complementary evidence** makes your argument more complete. Complementary evidence either enhances and improves your argument in a way that will make your reasoning stronger, or it makes evidence from another source more complete as both work in support of your argument.

When identifying evidence for your synthesis body paragraphs, **locate sources that agree with your position.** For example, if your thesis for the aquariums prompt (page 1) Task 1 is "Aquariums play a beneficial role in education and conservation **since** they provide new opportunities for patrons to interact with marine life they may have never seen, and these establishments protect endangered species," you would search your sources for those that explore the importance of human experiences in aquariums. You would also search your sources for those that explore increased awareness of endangered species. For the aquariums prompt, Sources B and D provide the best information to support your reasoning about these parts of the thesis.

If your thesis for Task 2 is "Individuals should consider how unethically animals are treated and the manipulative business practices of marine-based establishments **because** aquariums damage the lives of the animals they claim to serve and therefore should not be supported," you would look for sources that explore ways in which animals are treated unethically and that explore the economic and business practices of marine-life-based establishments. Sources A and C provide the best information to support this argument.

Once you have found supporting sources, **pick out the lines of text** that you will eventually incorporate into your essay. Underline or circle those parts. You might also mark the evidence in the sources with abbreviations—supporting evidence with **S** and complementary evidence with **C**. The quotes you use in your essay should be no longer than about 13–15 words, so it may be best to find only two or three lines of text as you search for supporting or complementary textual evidence. You will need to **cite the source** of your evidence in your essay (Source A, for example), so make sure to include your citations as you organize your evidence. If you decide to use a visual source as supporting evidence, describe the picture or summarize or paraphrase the data when you incorporate it in your essay.

Look at the examples of supporting or complementary evidence that correspond to each thesis type in the tables below.

Task 1 Aquariums play a beneficial role in education and conservation **since** they provide new opportunities for patrons to interact with marine life they may have never seen, and these establishments protect endangered species.

Synthesis Argument and Supporting Evidence Organizer		
Source	**Textual Evidence**	**Citation**
B	"The AZA has published objective standards for what it means to provide proper care for a tapir, a tiger or a Japanese spider crab." "Many zoos and aquariums house hundreds of animal species. Each species exists because it occupies a unique niche in the ecosystem, so the conditions that produce ideal welfare for one species may not be the same as those for a different species." "Captive animals typically outlive their wild counterparts. Zoos and aquariums are the figurative lifeboat for an increasing number of species that are extinct in the wild." "Zoo-based efforts to save endangered species will succeed only if understanding of the animals' lives is fully integrated with husbandry standards."	(Source B)/ (Renner)
D	"The 175 million people who visit zoos or aquariums annually form a unique ecosystem where humans, exotic wildlife, domestic animals and local wildlife interact with each other on a daily basis." "Zoos and aquariums play beneficial roles in global conservation efforts and environmental and biomedical teaching and research." "In addition, zoos and aquariums enhance public understanding of wildlife and the conservation of the places animals live."	(Source D)/ (Johnson-Walker)

Task 2 Individuals should consider how unethically animals are treated and the manipulative business practices of marine-life-based establishments **because** aquariums damage the lives of the animals they claim to serve and therefore should not be supported.

Synthesis Argument and Supporting Evidence Organizer		
Source	**Textual Evidence**	**Citation**
A	"Many animals try to cope with captivity by adopting abnormal behaviors. Some develop 'stereotypies,' which are repetitive, purposeless habits such as constantly bobbing their heads, swaying incessantly or chewing on the bars of their cages." "Neuroscientific research indicates that living in an impoverished, stressful captive environment physically damages the brain." *continued*	(Source A)/ (Jacobs)

Synthesis Argument and Supporting Evidence Organizer		
Source	**Textual Evidence**	**Citation**
	"Laboratory research also suggests that mammals in a zoo or aquarium have compromised brain function." The picture in the source compares how captive animals have diminished cellular walls and more constrained neuropathways (which lead to decreases in processing for the animals) when compared with wild animals in their natural habitats that do not typically experience such significant neurological damage.	
C	"With an average visit of 3 to 4 hours, families visiting zoos and aquariums are uniquely 'in the moment', offering a rare opportunity for brands to engage with kids and their parents at one of their most authentic and connected moments, free from the many distractions that often compete for their attention." "Consumers believe that brands have the power to make the world better and research shows that brand actions and partnerships influence their purchase decision. Nine out of ten people feel better about a brand if they focus on an environmental or social cause." "For parents, a visit to the zoo or aquarium offers a respite from the chaos of everyday life allowing them to see more clearly through the eyes of their children, often evoking feelings of nostalgia. Additional core themes like discovery, curiosity, health, and wellness validate this market as ideal locations to drive positive brand sentiment." The graph details that attendance at zoos and aquariums is greater than most other forms of entertainment, even when major sports leagues' numbers are combined.	**(Source C)/ ("Marketing to Families")**

KEY POINT: You need to find evidence in your sources that will **support** or **complement** your argument.

PRACTICE

Based on your responses to, and the sources for, the electric vehicles prompt on pages 13–14, make a chart like the one below to record which sources best support or complement your argument. Then explain how you think these sources will support or complement your argument.

1. **Task 1**

Synthesis Argument and Supporting Evidence Organizer		
Source	**Support / Complement**	**Explanation**
	This source will . . . **Support / Complement** . . . my argument that . . .	

2. **Task 2**

Synthesis Argument and Supporting Evidence Organizer		
Source	**Support / Complement**	**Explanation**
	This source will . . . **Support / Complement** . . . my argument that . . .	

WRITE

Based on your responses to, and the sources for, the electric vehicles prompt, make an organizer like the ones below that clearly identifies the textual evidence from each source that best supports and/or complements your argument. Your textual evidence should be no longer than a few lines. Be precise during this step.

Remember: If you use a visual source, you need to describe the information with specific details, especially if there are no words to directly quote.

3. **Task 1**

Synthesis Argument and Textual Evidence Organizer		
Source	**Textual Evidence**	**Citation**

4. **Task 2**

Synthesis Argument and Supporting Evidence Organizer		
Source	**Textual Evidence**	**Citation**

Watch this video (tinyurl.com/3uaejp99) produced by CNET and narrated by Antuan Goodwin. As the speaker makes his claims, identify what evidence he includes to support his claims, and then explain how the evidence functions as he creates his arguments. While doing this, ask yourself these questions: "Does this evidence directly support a claim the speaker makes?" "Does this evidence complement a claim the speaker makes?" "Does this evidence complement other evidence that the speaker has already offered?" Compare your answers with those of your classmates.

What's the Point? In one sentence, explain how this lesson can help you on the AP English Language and Composition exam.

_____

_____

_____

LESSON SYN.10 Finding Evidence That Challenges Your Position

Eyes on the Exam

Exam readers will expect you to include evidence from at least three different sources. Exam readers also look for a nuanced argument by exploring disagreements between sources.

LEARN

While you can write a strong argument by including evidence from sources that only *support* your reasoning, the best complex arguments engage with the voices and arguments of those who *disagree*. In fact, engaging with the opposition is considered a significant move in making an argument more sophisticated. On exam day, if you can engage well with any opposing view, you will have a chance of being awarded the sophistication point. Keep in mind, though, that you can still write a high-scoring, sophisticated essay on exam day *without* engaging with opposing voices.

There are **three ways you can engage with the opposition** when you are producing an argument: you can concede, refute, or rebut.

- When you **concede,** you admit the merits of part of the opposing view's argument. However, you are not waving the white flag of surrender. When conceding, after admitting that the other side may have some reasonable points, you explain why you still have the stronger argument.

- When you **refute** an argument, you consider what the opposition has to say and systematically take down the entire argument by exposing flaws in the opposition's evidence and/or reasoning.

- When you **rebut** an argument, you introduce new evidence or offer a new line of reasoning for consideration in relation to what the opposition has already provided. A rebuttal differs from a refutation in that a refutation works to logically tear down the line of reasoning the other side has offered, while a rebuttal presents new information and/or new ways of thinking to challenge the reasoning of the opposition.

As you look for evidence to include in your essay, consider *not only evidence that will support your view but also evidence you can challenge by conceding, refuting, or rebutting.*

Challenging evidence can (1) challenge the direct claims of your thesis statement or (2) challenge some of the supporting evidence you've selected from other sources. So when reviewing sources, consider what your thesis statement claims and look for sources that contest your claim. Also consider your supporting evidence and look for other sources to challenge it.

For example, if your thesis for the aquariums prompt (page 1) Task 1 is "Aquariums play a beneficial role in education and conservation **since** they provide new opportunities for patrons to interact with marine life they may have never seen, and these establishments protect endangered species," search your sources to see which ones challenge the idea that aquariums are beneficial for any of the reasons you've stated. In the case of the information provided, Source A fits this bill well.

If your thesis for Task 2 is "Individuals should consider how unethically animals are treated and the manipulative business practices of marine-based establishments **because** aquariums damage the lives of the animals they claim to serve and therefore should not be supported," then you need to find sources that project marine-life establishments in a significantly more positive light. Sources B and D clearly provide this viewpoint.

Once again, after you have found these sources, select the pertinent textual evidence you will eventually engage with and combat in some way. Keep in mind that the quotes you use in your essay should be no longer than about 13–15 words, so limit yourself to two or three lines of textual evidence that challenges your argument. Remember to cite your evidence appropriately, either as Source A, Source B, etc., or by using the description in parentheses. On exam day, you can mark opposing evidence with O.

Look at the lines of opposing evidence that are selected for each task type in the tables below.

Synthesis Argument Opposing Evidence Organizer		
Task 1	Aquariums play a beneficial role in education and conservation **since** they provide new opportunities for patrons to interact with marine life they may have never seen, and these establishments protect endangered species.	
Source	**Textual Evidence**	**Citation**
A	"Many animals try to cope with captivity by adopting abnormal behaviors. Some develop 'stereotypies,' which are repetitive, purposeless habits such as constantly bobbing their heads, swaying incessantly or chewing on the bars of their cages." "Neuroscientific research indicates that living in an impoverished, stressful captive environment physically damages the brain." "Laboratory research also suggests that mammals in a zoo or aquarium have compromised brain function." The picture in the source compares how captive animals have diminished cellular walls and more constrained neuropathways (which lead to decreases in processing for the animals) when compared with wild animals that do not typically experience such significant neurological damage when in their natural habitats.	(Source A)/(Jacobs)

Synthesis Argument Opposing Evidence Organizer		
Task 2	Individuals should consider how unethically animals are treated and the manipulative business practices of marine-life-based establishments **because** aquariums damage the lives of the animals they claim to serve and therefore should not be supported.	
Source	**Textual Evidence**	**Citation**
B	"Accreditation is a mechanism for maintaining and pioneering best practices. Being accredited by the Association of Zoos and Aquariums is the highest level of professional recognition for North American zoos and aquariums." *continued*	(Source B)/(Renner)

Source	Textual Evidence	Citation
	"A recent revision to accreditation standards in 2018, however, supersedes this model in favor of a new goal—that a zoo or aquarium demonstrate it has achieved animal welfare. Not only must animals be healthy, but they should also display behavior typical of their species. Climbers must climb, diggers must dig and runners must run." "Zoos and aquariums are the figurative lifeboat for an increasing number of species that are extinct in the wild." "Zoo-based efforts to save endangered species will succeed only if understanding of the animals' lives is fully integrated with husbandry standards."	
D	"Zoos and aquariums play beneficial roles in global conservation efforts and environmental and biomedical teaching and research." "In addition, zoos and aquariums enhance public understanding of wildlife and the conservation of the places animals live."	**(Source D)/(Johnson-Walker)**

KEY POINT: Find viewpoints and evidence that challenge your own. **Engaging with opposing viewpoints** has the potential to make your argument more sophisticated.

PRACTICE

Based on your responses to, and the sources for, the electric vehicles prompt (pages 13–21), make a chart like the one below for each task. Choose which sources could best oppose your thesis and/or supporting evidence. Then explain how these sources may possibly challenge your argument or evidence. You do not need to decide if you are going to concede, refute, or rebut any opposing sources yet. Rather, at this point, you are just organizing your thoughts so that you can engage with opposing arguments later.

1. **Task 1**

Synthesis Argument Opposing Evidence Organizer		
Write an essay that synthesizes material from at least three of the sources and develops your position on the extent to which electric vehicles should be embraced as the future of consumer transportation.		
Source	**My Position/My Evidence**	**Explanation**
	This source will challenge [**choose one:** *my position that . . . /my evidence claiming . . .*]	

2. **Task 2**

Synthesis Argument Opposing Evidence Organizer		
Write an essay that synthesizes material from at least three of the sources and develops your position on what factors an individual should consider when buying an electric vehicle.		
Source	**My Position/My Evidence**	**Explanation**
	This source will challenge [**choose one:** my position that . . ./my evidence claiming . . .]	

WRITE

Based on your responses to, and the sources for, the electric vehicles prompt (pages 13–21), make an organizer for each task that clearly identifies the direct textual evidence from each source that best opposes your argument or supporting evidence. **Remember:** If you use a visual as a source, you need to describe the information with specific details, especially if there are no words to directly quote.

3. **Task 1**

Synthesis Argument Opposing Textual Evidence Organizer		
Source	**Textual Evidence**	**Citation**

4. **Task 2**

Synthesis Argument Opposing Textual Evidence Organizer		
Source	**Textual Evidence**	**Citation**

Watch this video (tinyurl.com/5yrfy8yz) from Edutopia about hexagonal thinking. Write your thesis on a hexagon and use this as your middle foundational shape. Then record your supporting and/or complementary evidence from Lesson SYN.9 and your opposing evidence from Lesson SYN.10 on other hexagons. Then connect and rearrange your evidence hexagons around your central argument while you consider the multitude of ways that all of the sources and lines of text relate to one another and your argument.

What's the Point? In one sentence, explain how this lesson can help you on the AP English Language and Composition exam.

_____

_____

_____

TEAM UP

Work in small groups as your teacher directs to develop your hexagonal thinking about your thesis, supporting or complementary evidence, and opposing evidence. After preparing your hexagons (see above near the link), first try to arrange them on your own to find the closest and most interesting connections. Then review the work of your other group members and point out any connections you see that a group member might have missed.

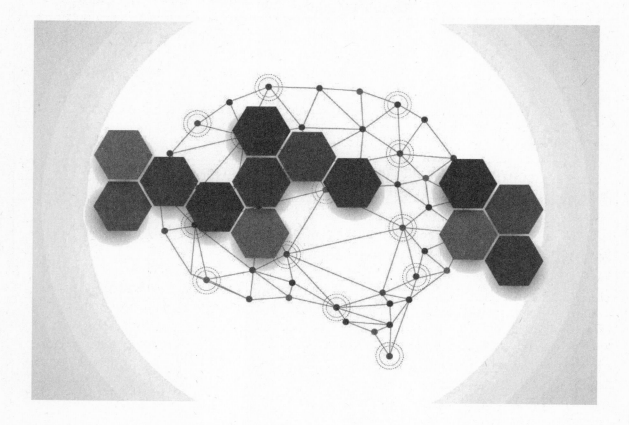

LESSON SYN.11 Writing Topic Sentences with Evidence and Argument in Mind

Eyes on the Exam

Exam readers look for your **line of reasoning**. Establishing strong topic sentences that relate to your thesis and project your evidence and commentary will help create that line of reasoning.

LEARN

Thesis statements drive entire essays. Topic sentences drive whole paragraphs. A topic sentence is usually the first sentence of each paragraph in the essay after the introductory paragraph. A strong topic sentence will make clear how to complete each body paragraph.

In fact, a good thesis statement will do most of the work to get you started on your body paragraphs. Take a close look at how the Task 1 thesis statement on the aquariums lays out the argument. The position being argued is underlined; the reasoning that justifies it is in italics.

Aquariums play a beneficial role in education and conservation **since** they *provide new opportunities for patrons to interact with marine life* they may have never seen, and these establishments *protect endangered species*.

Readers encountering this thesis statement would get a hint at the line of reasoning: you will show how aquariums provide new opportunities for learning, and you will then show how they protect endangered species. Expressing the two ideas of opportunities for learning and protecting endangered species as claims becomes the formula for your topic sentences.

In this example, the first topic sentence would logically make a claim about the diverse experiences of those who visit aquariums. The body of that paragraph would develop that idea with evidence that also relates to ideas in the thesis statement, specifically education and conservation. The second topic sentence would logically make a claim about how aquariums protect endangered species. Once again, the body of that paragraph would develop that idea with evidence that also relates to the more general idea of conservation.

Once you know the topics of your paragraphs, you are ready to go back to your evidence to see which sources would work best in each paragraph.

The chart below shows textual evidence from several sources you might use in your first body paragraph. The left-hand column contains direct quotes and their sources. The right-hand column provides a general summary of that evidence.

Textual Evidence	General Summary
(Source B)/(Renner) "The AZA has published objective standards for what it means to provide proper care for a tapir, a tiger or a Japanese spider crab."	Many people encounter diverse, meaningful, and even interactive displays of sea life each year.
(Source D)/(Johnson-Walker) "The 175 million people who visit zoos or aquariums annually form a unique ecosystem where humans, exotic wildlife, domestic animals and local wildlife interact with each other on a daily basis." "In addition, zoos and aquariums enhance public understanding of wildlife and the conservation of the places animals live."	

The general summary plays an important role in topic sentences. A strong topic sentence includes at least these two parts: a general summary of the evidence that will be specified later in the paragraph and an argument that in some way relates to your thesis statement.

Here is a **basic topic sentence template**:

[Insert a general summary of paragraph's evidence] + [your argument].

If you use that formula for a topic sentence for the first body paragraph on aquariums, the resulting topic sentence will be something like the following:

[Since many people annually encounter diverse, meaningful, and even interactive displays of sea life at aquariums,] + [those attractions play an important role in inspiring the public to preserve different ecosystems.]

Each part of this topic sentence clearly connects to the thesis statement, and it is appropriately complex. This sentence tells the reader you will provide specific details about the number of people that annually visit aquariums, specific details about the diversity in aquariums and experiences, and an explanation of how experiencing and interacting with the diverse aquatic life-forms can inspire patrons to promote conservation. You will use your sources to fill in the specifics.

For the aquariums prompt, as you saw above, you will need write at least one more body paragraph that considers endangered species and how aquariums are beneficial in supporting them. Below is textual evidence from multiple sources that you could consider putting in your second body paragraph as well as a general summary of the evidence,

Textual Evidence	General Summary
(Source B)/(Renner) "Captive animals typically outlive their wild counterparts. Zoos and aquariums are the figurative lifeboat for an increasing number of species that are extinct in the wild."	
(Source C)/("Marketing to Families") "In fact, zoos & aquariums are widely credited with saving several animal species from extinction."	Aquariums house many endangered species.
(Source D)/(Johnson-Walker) "Zoos and aquariums play beneficial roles in global conservation efforts and environmental and biomedical teaching and research."	

Using the formula for topic sentences repeated below, you might construct the following topic sentence:

[Insert a general summary of paragraph's evidence] + [your argument].

[Because aquariums house many endangered species,] [they serve a vital purpose in safeguarding against ecological disaster.]

If you were to outline an essay in response to the aquariums prompt by producing a complex thesis and topic sentences, all of which work to establish a line of reasoning, your work might look like this:

Task 1 Thesis: Aquariums play a beneficial role in education and conservation **since** they provide new opportunities for patrons to interact with marine life they may have never seen, and these establishments protect endangered species.

Topic Sentence 1: Since many people annually encounter diverse, meaningful, and even interactive displays of sea life at aquariums, those attractions play an important role in inspiring the public to preserve different ecosystems.

Topic Sentence 2: Because aquariums house many endangered species, they serve a vital purpose in safeguarding against ecological disaster.

KEY POINT: Strong **topic sentences guide body paragraphs** and make writing strong body paragraphs significantly easier.

PRACTICE

Based on your responses to the electric vehicles prompt (pages 13–14) and the sources provided, complete an organizer like the one below by collecting the evidence you intend to include in your body paragraphs. Then construct a general summary of the evidence you provided. Try to include evidence from multiple sources in each paragraph.

1. **Task 1 Topic Sentence/Evidence Organizer**

Textual Evidence	General Summary
Source	
Source	

2. **Task 2 Topic Sentence/Evidence Organizer**

Textual Evidence	General Summary
Source	
Source	

WRITE

Use your complex thesis statement from Lesson SYN.8 on the electric vehicles prompt and the general evidence summaries you just created to write topic sentences for at least two body paragraphs in your essay.

Watch this video (tinyurl.com/mup4fbzm) by AP English teacher Beth Hall in which she reviews writing topic sentences for synthesis. Then consider revising one of your topic sentences using the sentence frame she offers.

What's the Point? In one sentence, explain how this lesson can help you on the AP English Language and Composition exam.

_____

_____

_____

LESSON SYN.12 Writing Topic Sentences with Organization and Transitions in Mind

Eyes on the Exam

Exam readers will want to see that your synthesis essay has a line of reasoning. Organizing your topic sentences in a way that follows your thesis and adding transitional language to strong topic sentences will further establish the continuity and sophistication of your argument.

LEARN

In an essay, the **line of reasoning** is the logical sequence of claims that work together to defend the overarching thesis statement. You need to create a strong line of reasoning to score the highest number of points on exam day. One way is to generate topic sentences that generalize evidence and connect to ideas in your overarching argument. You can further establish your line of reasoning by properly ordering your topic sentences and by including purposeful transitional language in your topic sentences.

Review the following thesis statement in response to Task 2 of the aquariums prompt (page 1):

Individuals should consider how unethically animals are treated and the manipulative business practices of marine-based establishments **because** aquariums damage the lives of the animals they claim to serve and therefore should not be supported.

Now think about the following potential topic sentences for this essay (which are presented in no particular order):

A. Sea-life attractions offer partner companies chances to prey on the ignorance of families, particularly children, emphasizing their exploitative practices.

B. Sea-life establishments are unable to create and maintain environments that fully emulate many species' natural habitats, causing irreparable harm.

C. Quests for profits over actual conservation pervade entertainment-based aquatic institutions, highlighting the dubious motivations of those who oversee the industry.

These topic sentences are strong because they project the evidence that will be provided and tie those projections to an argument about how damaging aquariums and sea-life institutions are. However, based on the way the thesis is structured, the best order for these topic sentences would not be their current lineup. If you follow the thesis, the first topic sentence should be B, followed by C, followed by A. This order results in a much more organized paper because the thesis projects that the essay to follow will first discuss unethical treatment of animals and then discuss business practices, particularly manipulative ones.

Individuals should consider how unethically animals are treated (relates to sentence B) and the manipulative business practices of marine-based establishments (relates to sentences A and C) **because** aquariums damage the lives of the animals they claim to serve and therefore should not be supported.

Adding transitional language to your topic sentences further solidifies your line of reasoning by clearly and logically linking your ideas. Transitions give your ideas **coherence,** or logical flow, and allow you to seamlessly unify them as you build your argument.

Following is a chart of common transitional words and phrases that help create coherence.

Transitional Purpose	Transitional Language
Show importance	foundationally, above all, chiefly, most importantly, primarily, of critical importance, of less importance, less importantly
Connect (add) events or elements	additionally, and then, besides, equally important, further, furthermore, moreover, in addition to
Compare or contrast	whereas, but, yet, on the other hand, however, on the contrary, by comparison, conversely, although, in contrast, similarly
Indicate cause and effect	because, since, evidently, consequently, thus, therefore
Indicate exceptions or limitations	yet, still, however, in spite of, despite, sometimes
Emphasize	in fact, indeed, in any case, unquestionably, without a doubt, undeniably
Provide examples	for example, for instance, in this case, take the case of, to demonstrate, to illustrate

The chart above provides a few examples of the type of language writers should use to connect their ideas. Adding meaningful transitional phrases to emphasize importance, similarities, contrasts, and cause and effect makes an argument more cohesive and unified. A unified argument is a strong argument.

The template below provides a guide for constructing **topic sentences that include transitional language:**

[Transitional language] + [insert a general summary of your evidence] + [your argument].

Every topic sentence should include all of the above elements, although they do not always have to be in this order.

Review the thesis statement and topic sentences in response to Task 2 for the aquariums prompt again. This time, the essay outline is not only properly ordered, but the topic sentences also contain transitional language that further establishes the line of reasoning.

Task 2 Thesis: Individuals should consider how unethically animals are treated and the manipulative business practices of marine-based establishments **because** aquariums damage the lives of the animals they claim to serve and therefore should not be supported.

Topic Sentence 1: <u>**Most importantly**</u>, sea-life establishments are unable to create and maintain environments that fully emulate many species' natural habitats, causing irreparable harm to the wildlife.

Topic Sentence 2: <u>**In addition to**</u> the ecological inadequacies, quests for profits over actual conservation also pervade the industry, highlighting the dubious motivations of those who oversee entertainment-based aquatic institutions.

Topic Sentence 3: Sea-life attractions offer partner companies chances to prey on the ignorance of families, particularly children, <u>**further**</u> emphasizing their exploitative practices.

The transition can appear in different places, not always at the beginning. Reorder your language to avoid monotony by varying sentence structures as you project your argument.

PRACTICE

Using both Task 1 and Task 2 thesis statements (Lesson SYN.8) and topic sentences you created in response to the electric vehicles prompt (pages 13–14), complete the following tasks. You may wish to make a Synthesis Essay Organizer like the one below to record your responses. For each task, first copy your thesis statement. Then write your topic sentences (without transitional language) in the order that follows the line of reasoning projected in your thesis statement. Finally, explain why you have ordered your topic sentences the way you have, focusing on how doing so strengthens the relationships of ideas in your argument.

Your Thesis:	
Your first topic sentence:	Explain why this point is the one you are making first:
Your second topic sentence:	Explain why this point is the one you are making second:
Your third topic sentence:	Explain why this point is the one you are making third:

WRITE

Using your organized thesis statement and topic sentences in response to the electric vehicles prompt and the Practice activity above, revise your topic sentences by adding appropriate transitional language to build your argument and establish a strong line of reasoning. Complete this activity for both Task 1 and Task 2.

🖐 Watch this video (tinyurl.com/mtnrzw62) produced by Scribbr in which Jessica Liu models transitional language and its uses. Then consider revising one of your transitions in your topic sentences based on her recommendations.

What's the Point? In one sentence, explain how this lesson can help you on the AP English Language and Composition exam.

_____

_____

_____

LESSON SYN.13 Synthesizing Supporting and Complementary Sources

Eyes on the Exam

Exam readers will check to see that you include and cite at least three separate sources in your synthesis essay. Writing so your sources converse with one another will strengthen your essay and argument.

LEARN

The synthesis prompt requires you to cite at least three separate sources on your exam to score all four points in the Evidence and Commentary category. If you cite only two sources, the most you can get is one point. If you cite fewer than two sources, you will get *no* points in this category.

When including sources in your essays, you can choose to directly quote, paraphrase, or summarize. You can also mix all three; you just need to make sure that you cite your sources. A **direct quote** is exactly that: in your paper, you include actual word-for-word quotations from the sources enclosed in quotation marks. Direct quotes should typically be fewer than 13 words to avoid creating confusing sentences. When you **paraphrase,** you rewrite ideas from a source in your own words, but the length is usually about the same. For example, if you are paraphrasing two lines from the text, even though you put the information in your own words, it should still be about two lines. When you **summarize,** you condense the ideas from a source into a significantly shorter portion of text. When paraphrasing and summarizing, you should *not* use quotation marks to show you are referring to a source, but you must always cite your source.

The textual evidence chart below, based on the aquariums prompt (page 1), provides examples of a larger section of text directly quoted, paraphrased, and summarized.

(Source B)/(Renner)	Quote, Paraphrase, Summary
"Another major factor behind the AZA's new standard is its role in species conservation. Captive animals typically outlive their wild counterparts. Zoos and aquariums are the figurative lifeboat for an increasing number of species that are extinct in the wild. Simply keeping an animal alive is now no longer enough. Zoo-based efforts to save endangered species will succeed only if understanding of the animals' lives is fully integrated with husbandry standards."	**Direct Quote:** "Aquariums are the figurative lifeboat for an increasing number of species that are extinct in the wild" (Renner).
	Paraphrase: Aquariums are one of the only ways to keep some endangered species from going extinct (Renner).
	Summary: The AZA has new standards based on species conservation because they realize that zoos and aquariums need to keep animals from not only going extinct but also keep them healthy enough to be let back into the wild (Renner).

Citing sources indicates that you have taken information or ideas from the work of others. The most common method of citing a source is a called a parenthetical citation because the author information is put inside parentheses. However, if you mention the author's name in the sentence that contains the information from the source, you do not need to include a parenthetical citation. Further, on exam day you are permitted to cite any source you use as Source A, Source B, Source C, etc., rather than writing out the actual author information that is provided in the box at the beginning of the source. When writing for class and in college, you will need to cite your references more formally, but while you are working on a draft of a paper, this practice is acceptable.

When you write a synthesis essay, you can integrate your three separate sources in multiple places. The most common way to integrate different sources is as evidence in your body paragraphs, but you may want to consider integrating a short direct quotation from a source in your thesis. This tactic is useful on exam day because it will get one of your three sources in right at the beginning.

Here's how integrating sources would work if you were responding to the aquariums prompt:

Task 1 Thesis: Aquariums play a beneficial role in education and conservation **since** they provide new opportunities for patrons to interact with marine-life they may have never seen, and these establishments protect endangered species.

Task 1 Thesis with a Source: Aquariums play a beneficial role "in species conservation" (Source B) and education **since** they provide new opportunities for patrons to interact with marine-life they may have never seen, and these establishments protect endangered species.

Task 2 Thesis: Individuals should consider how unethically animals are treated and the manipulative business practices of marine-based establishments **because** aquariums damage the lives of the animals they claim to serve and therefore should not be supported.

Task 2 Thesis with a Source: Individuals should consider the animals' "impoverished, stressful captive environment[s]" (Source A) and the manipulative business practices of marine-based establishments **because** aquariums damage the lives of the animals they claim to serve and therefore should not be supported.

When you integrate direct quotations into your writing, remember these tips:

1. The textual evidence you include should flow seamlessly with your own words. You can know if you are creating this flow well because you won't be able to tell where your words end and the direct quotation begins. (Shorter pieces of textual evidence make this easier.)

2. You may never misquote a text to make it support a position contrary to what it originally says in the source. Doing so would be an unethical writing practice.

3. You are integrating sources to increase the credibility of your argument. If you put an author's name in the same sentence as your source information, make sure to present the author's credentials. Just naming someone doesn't add anything unless your reader knows why that person should be considered an authority.

4. Do not rely on words like *says*, *states*, and *claims* when you are referring to a source. Avoid using such phrases as *In the text it says* . . . or anything similar. Instead, as you introduce your quotations, consider using words like *argues, posits, theorizes, supports, confirms, refutes, challenges disproves, suggests, implies, presents, details, exposes,* or *qualifies.*

To initially integrate evidence in your body paragraphs, use your source material as examples to support the reasoning of your topic sentences. You might want to use the basic **templates for integrating evidence** on the next page.

1. For example, [**choose one:** *before/prior to/after/following*] [summarize the context before the textual evidence and then flow into the "fewer than 13 words you intend on quoting"] [citation in parentheses].

OR

2. For instance, [expert's or publication's name]—a [credentials that suggest authority in relation to the topic]—[**choose one:** *argues, presents, details, theorizes, exposes,* (anything but *says, states,* or *claims*)] [insert text followed by citation in parentheses].

Look at how the seamless integration of quotations would appear in a body paragraph in an essay responding to Task 2 of the aquariums prompt:

Topic Sentence 3

1. (*Template 1*) Sea-life attractions offer partner companies chances to prey on the ignorance of families, particularly children, **further emphasizing** their exploitative practices. For example, after revealing that young households annually attend zoos and aquariums more than major sporting events in their article, the Allionce Group encourages companies to capitalize on the "awe, wonder, and childhood joy" that the consumers experience in such a "trusted community," all for the sake of driving "positive brand sentiment" (Source C).

2. Sea-life attractions offer partner companies chances to prey on the ignorance of families, particularly children, **further emphasizing** their exploitative practices. (*Template 2*) For instance, the Allionce Group—a firm that focuses on marketing to young households—advises that companies heavily promote "positive brand sentiment" at aquariums while unsuspecting patrons are experiencing "awe, wonder, and childhood joy" (Source C).

In the above examples, notice the short length of the direct quotations and how they blend seamlessly with the writer's own language. They are only discernible because they are enclosed in quotation marks and followed by the source citation in parentheses.

When you integrate evidence in your supporting body paragraphs, try to provide at least two pieces per paragraph from two different sources when possible. If you can place *multiple sources in conversation with one another*, you will demonstrate a stronger knowledge of what synthesis entails. Consider how pairing complementary sources would look based on the first example from above:

Sea-life attractions offer partner companies chances to prey on the ignorance of families, particularly children, **further emphasizing** their exploitative practices. For example, after revealing that young families annually attend zoos and aquariums more than major sporting events—and contribute around "$16 billion to the economy" (Source D)—in their article, the Allionce Group promotes capitalizing on the "awe, wonder, and childhood joy" that the consumers experience in such a "trusted community," all for the sake of driving "positive brand sentiment" (Source C).

Notice how Source D provides a specific number to complement information mentioned in Source C. Both sources work together to support the reasoning of the topic sentence.

KEY POINT: Strengthen your argument by **quoting a least three sources** that support it.

PRACTICE

Part 1 Using the electric vehicles prompt (pages 13–14), find a short piece of textual evidence from a source that you can seamlessly integrate into your thesis.

Part 2 Using the electric vehicles prompt, find textual evidence from multiple sources that supports or complements other source information and arrange the direct quotes in an organizer like the one below. The first and third columns should represent different sources. Make one organizer for each body paragraph you intend to write.

Evidence Relationship Organizer

Source Text and Citation	Relationship	Source Text and Citation
	Circle One: Supports / Complements	

Part 3 Using the electric vehicles prompt, find larger portions of textual evidence (three to five lines) from at least three sources that will support and/or complement your argument. You may consider using work you've produced for previous lessons. Then make an organizer like the one below so you can practice selecting language you would like to directly quote, paraphrase, and summarize.

Evidence Quote, Paraphrase, and Summary Organizer

Source Text and Citation	Quote, Paraphrase, Summary
	Direct Quote:
	Paraphrase:
	Summary:

WRITE

Based on your previous responses (including those in previous lessons) to the electric vehicles prompt, integrate your supporting and complementing textual evidence into your thesis and body paragraphs. Remember to properly cite at least three different sources. Also remember to seamlessly integrate your quotations.

 Access this guide (tinyurl.com/8wa9fpw4) produced by Ursinus College's Center for Writing and Speaking for more in-depth methods and explanations of ways to integrate evidence in your essays. Consider revising your writing based on information found in the document.

What's the Point? In one sentence, explain how this lesson can help you on the AP English Language and Composition exam.

_____

_____

_____

TEAM UP

As your teacher directs, meet in small groups to share your work from the Write activity above on integrating evidence and quotations. Of course, not every word in every source is quote-worthy. Following are especially useful strategies for using exact quotes.

- Quote phrases or sentences that are particularly **significant, unique, or eloquent.** These might be statements that succinctly encapsulate an important idea or argument in a way that paraphrasing might not capture effectively.

- When a source provides **specific statistics, figures, or factual data** that are essential to your argument, quote these directly to ensure accuracy and credibility.

- Quote from **recognized authorities or experts** in the field relevant to your topic. These quotes can lend weight and legitimacy to your argument

- If a source offers a **definition or explanation** that is central to understanding the topic, consider quoting it directly, especially if the wording is precise or specialized.

- Quotes with particularly **persuasive or effective use of language, rhetorical devices, or stylistic elements** can be powerful in supporting your argument.

- If a source includes a statement that is **controversial, provocative, or captures a counterargument well,** quoting it can be effective for setting up a rebuttal or for discussing differing viewpoints.

Review one another's thesis and body paragraphs looking for quoted material and determining if it represents any of the above strategies. Provide feedback to the writer. Then revise your own work based on feedback and the strategies outlined above.

LESSON SYN.14 Synthesizing Opposing Sources

Eyes on the Exam

Exam readers will check to see that you include and cite at least three separate sources in your synthesis essay. Addressing opposing viewpoints in some way can help make your argument more sophisticated.

LEARN

As a writer, especially on exam day, you are not required to address an opposing point of view. You may want to, however, because addressing opposing views will make your argument more thoughtful, thorough, and nuanced, showing subtle differences of perspectives.

You can include an opposing viewpoint in your argument in several ways. You may

- Acknowledge that other arguments exist in relation to the topic.
- Concede that part of what the opposing viewpoint posits is actually true.
- Challenge the opposing argument by offering a rebuttal.
- Directly refute the opposing argument so that it no longer seems valid.

No matter your approach, addressing the opinions and arguments of others shows you have considered other positions and perspectives as you have generated your own argument. Addressing other views elevates your credibility and give your work an even-handedness lacking in arguments that refuse to consider opposing views.

You can begin synthesizing opposing viewpoints, or **counterarguments,** with your own argument as early as in your thesis statement. In Lesson SYN.8, you practiced writing counterargument thesis statements. In Lesson SYN.13, you saw how to quote a source when you write your thesis statement. Remember that a quote should seamlessly integrate with your own words and must accurately reflect the view of the source. Look at these examples based on thesis statements responding to Tasks 1 and 2 of the aquariums prompt (page 1).

Task 1 Opposing Viewpoint Thesis: Aquariums play a beneficial role in education and conservation **since** they provide new opportunities for patrons to interact with marine life they may have never seen, and these establishments protect endangered species, even though animals often exhibit suffering in captivity "by adopting abnormal behaviors" (Source A).

Task 2 Opposing Viewpoint Thesis: While some people and organizations seem to praise aquariums and other sea-life establishments for their "role in species conservation" (Source B), individuals should consider how unethically animals are treated and the manipulative business practices of marine-life-based establishments **because** aquariums damage the lives of the animals they claim to serve and therefore should not be supported.

Most of the time, you will integrate supporting sources as evidence for the claims in your topic sentences. But when you include opposing viewpoints in the body of your paragraphs, you may consider including the counterargument in your topic sentences as well, seamlessly, as in your thesis statement. When you include a counterargument in a topic sentence, though, you will most likely introduce it in a clause beginning with one of the following three words: *while*, *although*, or *though*. Using a **subordinating conjunction** like those listed in Lesson SYN.7 will make your claim appear stronger as the independent clause.

Here is a Task 2 example thesis and topic sentence for the first body paragraph responding to the aquariums prompt. Notice how the topic sentence begins by conceding a point but then shifts to focus on the argument at hand.

Task 2 Thesis: Individuals should consider how unethically animals are treated and the manipulative business practices of marine-based establishments **because** aquariums damage the lives of the animals they claim to serve and therefore should not be supported.

Topic Sentence 1: While it may be true that the "zoo and aquarium community" has been working to "embrace a higher standard of care" (Source B), sea-life establishments are unable to create and maintain environments that fully emulate many species' natural habitats, causing irreparable harm to the wildlife.

Including opposing views in your writing is not limited to brief quotes in your thesis statements and topic sentences. You can also integrate opposing sources in the evidence sections of your body paragraphs. When you include a counterargument in your evidence, establish a conversation between two separate sources that projects their contrasting viewpoints. Below you will find two templates you may wish to use when introducing counterarguments. You will also see each modeled with a thesis and topic sentences that respond to Task 1 of the aquariums prompt.

Templates for Integrating Opposing Evidence
1. [Summarize your argument or the context in the source before the textual evidence you'd like to quote and then flow into the] ["less than 13 words you intend to quote" (source citation)]; however, it must be admitted that [insert a point of concession in relation to the source's argument].
2. Although it may be [**choose one:** *argued, theorized, proposed, presented, accepted*] that ["insert source information that the paragraph will refute without mentioning source's name" (source citation)], [present your counterclaim, which may include evidence from another source].

Task 1 Thesis: Aquariums play a beneficial role in education and conservation **since** they provide new opportunities for patrons to interact with marine-life they may have never seen, and these establishments protect endangered species.

Template 1 Topic Sentence and Evidence: Since many people annually encounter diverse and meaningful displays of sea life at aquariums, those attractions play an important role in inspiring the public to preserve different ecosystems. For example, as over 195 million people (Source C) annually travel to and experience zoos and aquariums, adults and children can directly interact with institutions that "enhance public understanding of wildlife" (Source D). However, it must be admitted that all this family time in these institutions does offer significant "opportunit[ies] for brands to engage with kids" as they seek to "drive positive brand sentiment" (Source C).

Template 2 Topic Sentence and Evidence: Furthermore, because aquariums house many endangered species, they serve a vital role in safeguarding against ecological disasters. For instance, although research shows that animals in captivity develop "compromised brain function" (Source A), it is undeniable that "zoos and aquariums are the figurative lifeboat" for many "species that are extinct in the wild" (Source B).

You are not required to address opposing viewpoints. In fact, doing so just for the sake of it will probably weaken your argument. When they genuinely strengthen your argument, introduce opposing views seamlessly by following the models above. Take care to choose where, when, and why you introduce the positions and perspectives of others.

> **KEY POINT: Addressing counterarguments,** even if you think they are wrong, helps you generate a strong, sophisticated, and credible argument.

PRACTICE

Part 1 Using the electric vehicles prompt (pages 13–14), find a short piece of textual evidence from a source and then seamlessly integrate it into your thesis in the form of a counterargument.

Part 2 Using the electric vehicles prompt, find textual evidence that counters other source information and arrange the direct quotations in an organizer like the one below to set the sources in conversation. Make at least one organizer.

Evidence Relationship Organizer

Source Text and Citation	Relationship	Source Text and Citation
	Challenges	

WRITE

Based on your previous responses (including those in previous lessons) to the electric vehicles prompt, address counterarguments by including one or more in your thesis statement, topic sentences, or evidence sections of your body paragraphs. You do not need to address counterarguments in all three areas but try to do so in at least one. Remember to seamlessly integrate your quotations.

 Review this resource (tinyurl.com/y7m4uw29) from Cleveland State University, which further explores counterarguments. Based on information here, generate a list of additional ways you can include counterarguments in your essays and explain why you would consider doing so.

What's the Point? In one sentence, explain how this lesson can help you on the AP English Language and Composition exam.

_____

_____

_____

LESSON SYN.15 Providing Commentary for Supporting and Complementary Sources

Eyes on the Exam

Exam readers will look for well-developed commentary that explains how your examples relate to your thesis statement and works to establish a strong line of reasoning.

LEARN

The most important skill for you to demonstrate on your exam is the ability to produce accurate commentary. **Commentary** is the part of each paragraph that explains how your evidence supports the argument(s) you are making throughout your essay.

Often students can produce claims and evidence but have some trouble with commentary because the relationship between the thesis or topic sentence and the evidence may seem so obvious. Think of how many times you've told someone, "You know what I mean, right?" Or think about how many times you've written, "Obviously . . . ." However, the truth is that the relationship between your evidence and your argument is *not* obvious, so you need to explain it.

Consider this familiar example:

Claim: High schools should start later in the morning.

Evidence: Research shows that teen brains do not typically switch into gear until 8:00 am or later.

You might assume that the relationship between that claim and evidence is obvious. But a step is missing. How exactly does the biological evidence support the reasoning about the start of school? Commentary provides that missing link.

Commentary: Since teen brains are not working at their full potential before 8:00 am, they would not be as receptive to learning and as capable of performing cognitive tasks as they would be after 8:00.

An effective way to develop commentary skills is to use language in your commentary that is logical and based on cause-and-effect relationships. Following is a list of words that may help as you write your commentary.

Helpful Cause-and-Effect Words for Commentary	
because	therefore
consequently	due to
since	as
furthermore	so that
thus	

If you do not use the above words throughout your commentary, your argument is probably not as clear as you think it may be.

When you write commentary, explain the assumptions you are making as you relate your evidence to your argument. Articulating your assumptions shows your reader your thought processes and how your knowledge and experiences and the information in your sources influence the judgments you make as you construct your argument. If you ever get stuck writing your commentary, try including some language that helps you articulate your assumptions. Following is a list of words and phrases that can help you do so:

Helpful Words for Commentary That Explains Assumptions	
typically	most individuals
often	many individuals
most often	most people
generally	assuming that

Since commentary is a logical explanation of how your evidence supports your thinking about your claim(s), be sure your logic is strong. Commentary that suffers from **weak logic** doesn't actually explain the evidence in relation to the claim. You can avoid weak logic by using qualifiers. **Qualifiers** are words that make your claims less absolute, more limited. For example, rather than argue that captivity is *always* damaging, qualify or limit your claim by asserting it is *usually* damaging. Qualifying strengthens your argument—if you are challenged by an exception to it, you are prepared to respond. However, if you are absolutely sure of something, write about it absolutely. But most arguments are not entirely black and white, and you need to account for shades of gray. Recognizing these shades of gray is a mark of sophistication.

Helpful Words for Qualifying Claims		
usually	unlikely	commonly
probably	frequently	sometimes
possibly	rarely	rarely
in most cases	seldom	infrequently
most likely		

Below is part of a sample essay in response to Task 2 of the aquariums prompt (page 1). You will see a thesis, three topic sentences, and one complete body paragraph. The cause-and-effect language is bold and underlined; assumption clarifying language is bold and italicized; and qualifying language is in simply bold type so you can see how each contributes to detailed commentary.

Task 2 Thesis: Individuals should consider how unethically animals are treated and the manipulative business practices of marine-based establishments because aquariums damage the lives of the animals they claim to serve and therefore should not be supported.

Topic Sentence 1: Most importantly, sea-life establishments are unable to create and maintain environments that fully emulate many species' natural habitats, causing irreparable harm to the wildlife.

Topic Sentence 2: In addition to the ecological inadequacies, quests for profits over actual conservation also pervade the industry, highlighting the dubious motivations of those who oversee entertainment-based aquatic institutions.

Topic Sentence 3 (and Body Paragraph 3): Sea-life attractions offer partner companies chances to prey on the ignorance of families, particularly children, further emphasizing their exploitative nature. For example, after revealing that young families annually attend zoos and aquariums more often than major sporting events—and contribute around "$16 billion to the economy" (Source D)—in their article, the Allionce Marketing Group promotes capitalizing on the "awe, wonder, and childhood joy" that consumers experience in such a "trusted community," all for the sake of driving "positive brand sentiment" (Source C). Businesses leveraging these cherished times and feelings confirm how **potentially** exploitative the aquarium industry can be **because** sea-life attractions **typically** promote their establishments as family-friendly educational experiences, yet they are secretly recruiting brand loyalists that will allow both the institutions and partner companies to profit. **Consequently** *since most casual visitors* are oblivious to the financial schemes of the institutional overseers, they unknowingly subject themselves and those in their care to marketing propaganda under the guise of building memories and becoming well-rounded, considerate citizens. **Therefore**, while trying to better their communities, patrons are actually subjecting themselves to a **possible** future of financial servitude **because** these sea-life attractions and businesses **seemingly** seek to build their wealth on the backs of both their captive animals and their captive audiences. **As** the mighty dollar is **considerably more important** than anything else that these organizations claim to stand for, individuals should **probably** reconsider how they would like to invest in their own futures and choose to explore their free local forests and parks instead.

This paragraph is on topic and supports the argument because the very first sentence of commentary begins connecting the evidence to the topic sentence claim that "aquariums exploit others." The explanation that follows includes language that prompts commentary, and the final sentence connects the exploitative argument to the overarching thesis that "aquariums should not be supported." A strong line of reasoning runs throughout the paragraph. Now imagine that the first two body paragraphs were written in the same way and you will realize that this essay would be cohesive and coherent.

> **KEY POINT:** When you provide commentary, **explain how your evidence supports the reasoning that justifies the claims** in both your topic sentences and thesis statement. Develop commentary by articulating assumptions and using **cause-and-effect language.**

PRACTICE

Review your previous responses to the electric vehicles prompt (pages 13–14). For each supporting body paragraph, create an organizer like the ones below to help you conceptualize how your evidence relates to your topic sentence claim and the overarching arguments in your thesis statement.

Evidence Commentary Organizers

1. **Task 1 Body Paragraph #**

Summarize Evidence	Explain How This Evidence Relates to Your Topic Sentence Claim	Explain How This Evidence Relates to Your Thesis Statement Claim

2. **Task 2 Body Paragraph #**

Summarize Evidence	Explain How This Evidence Relates to Your Topic Sentence Claim	Explain How This Evidence Relates to Your Thesis Statement Claim

WRITE

Using your previous responses to the electric vehicles prompt, produce the commentary for all of the supporting body paragraphs for your essay. If you intend to have a body paragraph that addresses a counterargument, you do not have to write it now. Counterarguments will be addressed in the next lesson.

Watch this video (tinyurl.com/rcknw4s5) by AP English teacher Timm Freitas in which he models how to produce commentary in synthesis essays. Then, watch this video (tinyurl.com/5n6ajfv4) by AP English teacher Beth Hall. Consider the models and the points that each video makes and consider revising your work to more accurately convey the commentary in your supporting body paragraphs.

Access this handout (tinyurl.com/5dx9c5e9) about qualifiers produced by University of North Carolina at Chapel Hill. It lists common qualifiers and then goes on to compare absolute language and qualified language and explain strategies for using qualifiers. After reading this, revise your body paragraphs, changing some absolute language to qualified language.

What's the Point? In one sentence, explain how this lesson can help you on the AP English Language and Composition exam.

_____

_____

_____

LESSON SYN.16 Providing Commentary When Conceding and Refuting

Eyes on the Exam

Exam readers will want to see that you can identify opposing viewpoints and engage with them in a civil manner.

LEARN

When you write commentary for paragraphs that address counterarguments, you will use most of the same strategies you practiced in the previous lesson: include cause-and-effect language, explain your assumptions, and carefully choose qualifiers to avoid flawed reasoning.

However, as you write counterargument paragraphs, make sure your commentary reflects how you intend to address the opposing view. Do you intend to concede a point? Do you intend to rebut an argument? Do you intend to fully refute a point? Do you plan to mix these practices? How you answer these questions will determine your reason for including a counterargument in the first place.

Often, if you concede a point, you accept part of the opposing argument. But don't use all your commentary explaining the truth of the opposing view. Instead, after conceding the partial truth, explain the limitations of the opposing view. When you rebut, offer new evidence or new reasoning to challenge an opposing position.

Look at the sample body paragraph below. It contains the expected traits of commentary, but it also includes a combined concession and rebuttal. This rebuttal is achieved by providing a new way of thinking about the truth that is conceded. Essentially, this paragraph works to turn a concession into a positive supporting point for the argument in the thesis: aquariums are beneficial. The underlined phrases show how the writer engages with a different opposing viewpoint.

Task 1 Thesis: Aquariums play a beneficial role in education and conservation **since** they provide new opportunities for patrons to interact with marine-life they may have never seen, and these establishments protect endangered species.

Body Paragraph 1: Since many people annually encounter diverse and meaningful displays of sea life at aquariums, those attractions play an important role in inspiring the public to preserve different ecosystems. For example, as over 195 million people (Source C) annually travel to and experience zoos and aquariums, adults and children can directly interact with institutions that "enhance public understanding of wildlife" (Source D). However, **it must be admitted that** all of this family time in these institutions does offer significant "opportunit[ies] for companies to engage with kids" as various enterprises seek to "drive positive brand sentiment" (Source C). **Some may suggest that,** because aquariums often expose their customer base to different marketing materials, they should be avoided and labeled as exploitative profiteers. **Yet, since** most people would be unaware of these institutions if they didn't advertise, **it doesn't make sense** to demonize them for engaging in the same type of marketing, which in this case actually helps provide greater funding for these wildlife reserves. **In fact,** if people end up developing brand loyalties to the companies that provide financial support for these attractions, they not only benefit from their existence but may also learn the civic importance of carefully considering the type of companies they financially support. Furthermore, caring for the many varieties of wildlife that aquariums house is expensive, and these institutions need ways to fund themselves while lowering costs for their paying visitors. Acquiring funds through sponsorships is beneficial since it allows sea-life attractions to open their doors to more patrons so visitors can learn more about doing their part in maintaining and caring for balanced ecosystems.

You may concede a point by including words and phrases like the following.

Helpful Words for Conceding
most people will admit
admittedly
it must be admitted that

When you rebut a point, always establish a contrast between the opposing argument and the new information or reasoning you plan to introduce. If you forget to establish that contrast, you often end up only arguing in favor of the opposing viewpoint. On exam day, that omission will weaken your line of reasoning and significantly lower your score. To help you make the shift from the concession to the new information or reasoning you introduce, include words and phrases like the following.

Helpful Words for Shifting from Concession to Your Argument	
however	while it is true that
nevertheless	yet
more importantly	in fact
though this may be true	the truth is

Refutations are different from concessions and rebuttals and require a different strategy. Refutations directly challenge opposing viewpoints and their argumentative structure. They dismantle the opposing viewpoint's reasoning, rendering it not just weak but entirely invalid.

Look at the example thesis and body paragraph of a response to Task 2 of the aquariums prompt. Notice an initial concession. However, as the paragraph progresses, the argument moves to dismantle the opposing argument by criticizing the evidence offered to support it. The underlined phrases delineate the points at which the opposing viewpoint is refuted.

Task 2 Thesis: Although some people and organizations seem to praise the efforts of aquariums and other sea-life establishments, individuals should consider how unethically animals are treated and the manipulative business practices of marine-life-based establishments **because** aquariums damage the lives of the animals they claim to serve and therefore should not be supported.

Body Paragraph 1: <u>While it is true that</u> the "zoo and aquarium community" has been working to "embrace a higher standard of care" (Source B) for their animals, sea-life establishments are unable to create and maintain environments that fully emulate many species' natural habitats, causing irreparable harm to the wildlife. For example, many animals—including aquatic mammals—are often found "try[ing] to cope with captivity by adopting abnormal behaviors" (Source A). The reason these creatures exhibit such "repetitive, purposeless habits" is that they are "living in [...] impoverished, stressful captive environment[s]" which eventually compromise their "brain function" (Source A). <u>While it can be argued that</u> zoos and aquariums are beginning to change their practices to "optimize the welfare of animals under their care" (Source B), this <u>**doesn't mean that**</u> these establishments are not detrimental to captive animals in their current states. <u>**In fact,**</u> behavioral evidence suggests otherwise. Furthermore, only about "250 out of approximately

2,800" animal-based organizations that are licensed by the USDA are "[Association of Zoos and Aquariums] accredited" (Source B). **Therefore, even if** standards of care are changing, such changes have taken place in only a small number of accredited establishments, **thus minimizing** the positive effects that such changes might eventually have. Also, these care adjustments apply only to federally licensed facilities, leaving the majority of captive animals in exhibits that are neurologically damaging. Consequently, damaged animals with unnatural habits can never be released back into the wild, so the end goal of ecological conservation is essentially invalidated.

You might consider choosing from the following sentence templates when constructing your refutations.

Sentence Templates for Refutations
• Arguing that . . . doesn't mean that . . . .
• The argument that . . . doesn't seem to make sense when . . . .
• Despite these claims, the fact that . . . .
• It's not entirely true that . . . since . . . .
• When considering all of the evidence, it becomes clear that . . . .
• This argument is wrong because . . . .

KEY POINT: Practice using helpful **words and strategies to address opposing viewpoints** so you can add nuance and complexity to your argument.

PRACTICE

Read the electric vehicles prompt and sources (pages 13–14). Then fill in an organizer like the one below as you consider counterarguments to address in your essay.

Opposing Viewpoint	Cited Evidence That Supports the Opposing Viewpoint	Any Concession You May Be Willing to Make About the Opposing Position	What is Wrong with the Opposing Viewpoint's Position	Cited Evidence That Supports Your Position

WRITE

Using your previous responses (including those in previous lessons) to the electric vehicles prompt, produce a paragraph that addresses at least one counterargument.

Watch this video (tinyurl.com/mrxd3m4d) by AP English teacher Brian Tolentino. Then engage in the counterargument activity he presents.

Watch Timm Freitas explain how to avoid pseudo-commentary using the aquariums prompt at the companion website (tinyurl.com/2mrx3r99) for this book. There you will find other videos by the authors as well as all the links included in the lessons in this book.

What's the Point? In one sentence, explain how this lesson can help you on the AP English Language and Composition exam.

_____

_____

_____

TEAM UP

At this point in the synthesis-essay writing process, you have a nearly complete draft. This would be a good time to work in peer review groups, as your teacher directs. Each student should bring their work from the Write activity above. Before you begin, review the guidelines for peer review on page 11. Then add the following guidelines to focus on this review.

Focused Guidelines for Peer Review	
Set Clear Objectives	Clearly define the goals of the peer review. For this review, focus on thesis statements, topic sentences, and use of evidence.
Review Criteria	Provide a clear set of criteria that outlines what aspects of the writing should be evaluated. For this review, use Row B of the synthesis rubric (see next page). This ensures that the feedback is aligned with the writing assignment requirements.
Use "I" Statements	Frame your feedback in terms of your own reactions or understanding (e.g., "I found this part confusing . . ." or "I really liked how you . . ."). This can make the feedback feel less personal and more about the writing.
Reflect After Review	Reflect on the feedback you received and how you plan to use it to improve your work. This reflection can deepen your learning and make the peer review process more meaningful.

Begin by exchanging papers within your group. Each student should read one peer's writing, focusing on the objectives and review criteria. Then follow these steps.

- The first writer reads his or her paper to the group.
- The peer who read this paper offers feedback based on the objectives and review criteria.
- Others in the group add their feedback, using "I" statements.
- The writer replies to feedback, asking questions for clarification as needed and explaining what, if anything, will be revised based on the group's comments.

After all essays have been discussed, conclude the activity with a brief whole-class discussion. Share general insights or common themes you noticed during the peer reviews.

SYNTHESIS Evidence and Commentary Review (Row B)

Eyes on the Exam

Readers will score your evidence and commentary based on the criteria in Row B in the Synthesis rubric.

LEARN

Carefully read each section of the Row B rubric and scoring guide.

- The first 5-column row, arranged from 0 points on the left to 4 points on the right, explains in general terms what criteria need to be met to achieve each score. Note that there are criteria for both evidence and commentary.

- The second 5-column row describes characteristics of essays earning each point. In both of those rows, key words have been printed in bold type to help you see the similarities and differences between the rankings.

- The final row provides additional clarifications for acceptable evidence and commentary.

Row B: Evidence AND Commentary (0-4 points), Scoring Criteria [2.A, 4.A, 6.A, 6.B, 6.C]				
0 points	**1 point**	**2 points**	**3 points**	**4 points**
Simply **restates** thesis (if present), **repeats** provided information, or references **fewer than two of the provided sources.**	EVIDENCE: Provides evidence from or references **at least two** of the provided sources. AND COMMENTARY: Summarizes the evidence but **does not explain how the evidence supports the student's** argument.	EVIDENCE: Provides evidence from or references **at least three** of the provided sources. AND COMMENTARY: Explains how **some of the evidence** relates to the student's argument, but **no line of reasoning** is established, or the **line of reasoning is faulty.**	EVIDENCE: Provides **specific** evidence from **at least three** of the provided sources to **support all claims in a line of reasoning.** AND COMMENTARY: Explains how **some** of the evidence **supports a line of reasoning.**	EVIDENCE: Provides **specific** evidence from **at least three** of the provided sources to **support all claims in a line of reasoning.** AND COMMENTARY: **Consistently explains** how the evidence supports **a line of reasoning.**

Decision Rules and Scoring Notes

Typical responses that earn 0 points:	Typical responses that earn 1 point:	Typical responses that earn 2 points:	Typical responses that earn 3 points:	Typical responses that earn 4 points:
Are **incoherent** or **do not address the prompt.** May **be just opinion** with **no textual references** or references that are **irrelevant.**	Tend to focus on **summary or description of sources** rather than specific details.	Consist of a **mix of specific evidence and broad generalities.** May contain some **simplistic, inaccurate, or repetitive explanations** that don't strengthen the argument. May make one point well, but either **do not make multiple supporting claims** or do **not adequately support** more than one claim. Do not explain the connections or progression between the student's claims, so **a line of reasoning is not clearly established.**	**Uniformly offer evidence** to support claims. Focus on the importance of **specific words and details from the sources** to build an argument. Organize an argument **as a line of reasoning composed of multiple supporting claims.** Commentary **may fail to integrate some evidence or fail to support a key claim.**	**Uniformly offer evidence** to support claims. Focus on the importance of **specific words and details from the sources** to build an argument. Organize and support an argument as a **line of reasoning composed of multiple supporting claims**, each with **adequate evidence that is clearly explained.**

Additional Notes:

Writing that suffers from grammatical and/or mechanical errors that interfere with communication cannot earn the fourth point in this row.

Following are the skills from the Course and Exam Description that are assessed in Row B.

2.A Write introductions and conclusions appropriate to the purpose and context of the rhetorical situation.

4.A Develop a paragraph that includes a claim and evidence supporting the claim.

6.A Develop a line of reasoning and commentary that explains it throughout an argument.

6.B Use transitional elements to guide the reader through the line of reasoning of an argument.

6.C Use appropriate methods of development to advance an argument.

PRACTICE

Complete the following activities and answer the questions about the Row B Evidence and Commentary rubric and scoring guide.

1. In your own words, explain three ways in which an essay scoring a 2 is different from an essay earning a 3.

2. What is the highest score you can earn in Row B if your essay lacks a line of reasoning?

3. Describe the difference in evidence in an essay scoring a 2 and an essay earning a 3 in Row B.

4. What would you say is the biggest difference between an essay earning a 3 in Row B and an essay earning a 4? Explain your answer.

5. What is the highest score you can get if you do not make multiple supporting claims?

6. Can you have grammatical mistakes that don't interfere with communication and still earn 4 points if you meet all the other criteria?

You Be the Reader

Read sample essay SYN.1.A in the Appendix on page 271. Decide what score that essay earns in the Row B evidence and commentary category. Explain your answer.

Review the sample essay on this site (tinyurl.com/2cwabaj2) and the scores and comments they received from exam readers. Pay special attention to the Row B score.

_____

_____

_____

Revise

Review the evidence and commentary you have developed in response to Prompt B about electric vehicles. If you think it does not earn a 4 based on this rubric, revise as needed to raise your score. Even if you believe it earns 4 points as it is, revise your essay body to make it the best it can be.

LESSON SYN.17 Conclusions That Situate the Argument in a Broader Context

Eyes on the Exam

Exam readers will look for patterns of sophistication in your writing. One of the ways you can build sophistication is by producing a strong conclusion that articulates the implications of your argument by situating it within a broader context.

LEARN

You may believe that a conclusion paragraph simply summarizes the essay that precedes it; however, this is a limited view of what an essay's final paragraph can accomplish. If you produce a strong, meaningful conclusion, it will add to the sophistication of your argument, especially if you use it to elaborate on the intellectual discoveries you've made while writing your paper.

Conclusions are about *ideas*, not summaries. To write a strong conclusion, write it in a way that emulates or imitates the learning process. The learning process typically follows three stages: knowledge, understanding/application, and wisdom. So when writing a conclusion paragraph for your synthesis essay, begin by presenting an overarching statement of what you think your readers should know about the topic and the ideas that relate to it. Then express how the information you originally presented can be understood and applied to life in general. And finally, finish by producing a statement that provides wisdom for your reader.

Here are some steps and models that you can follow to help you generate your examples. The example conclusion will be in response to Task 1 of the aquariums prompt on page 1.

Step 1: List four to seven **ideas** that your essay explores and that relate to your topic. (You may use some of the same ideas you located in the prompt and your readings in Lesson SYN.3 if they are also explored in your essay.)
Ideas: education, conservation, diversity of life, ethics, entertainment, economics

Step 2: Write a **knowledge** statement that relates multiple ideas from Step 1 to the topic of your synthesis essay. You can write a general statement, or you can attempt to add some personal style by producing a pertinent metaphor.
Example Sentence 1: Visiting the aquarium has the incredible potential to inspire wonder and awe for the diverse life that exists below the surface of the ocean.
Stylized Example Sentence 1: Aquariums enlighten and inspire adults and children alike to explore the depth and importance of ecological diversity that lives beneath the surface of the ocean.

Step 3: Discuss how the knowledge statement from Step 2 can be applied to the lives of most, if not all, individuals. This statement will convey an **understanding** of how knowledge you explored in the previous sentence relates to the world at large. Here are a few tips to consider when writing this section of your conclusion:

- Use universal terms such as *individuals, people, a person* (but never the word *you*).
- Consider starting this sentence with the phrase *In a world where . . . .* This phrase works as a bridge from your understanding to your real-world/universal application.

Example: In a world where considering the environment is often sacrificed for the pursuit of private profits and shallow entertainment thrills, individuals and businesses alike must begin to recognize that they can partner to foster awareness of something significantly more valuable: conserving the natural world.

Step 4: Leave your readers with a piece of **wisdom** related to the topic of your essay. This wisdom should stem from the knowledge and understanding you have provided for them, and it should leave the audience feeling emotional (either positively or negatively, your choice). You may use this sentence to imply a call to action. As you produce this sentence, pick a source and try to synthesize a short, pertinent, direct quote that has not already been included in your essay. Doing so will showcase your synthesis skills one last time.

Example: Doing everything possible to provide "humans [and] exotic wildlife" the opportunity to "interact with each other on a daily basis" may just be the only way to ensure the survival of many species "before disaster strikes" (Source D).

Here is what the conclusion paragraph in response to Task 1 of the aquariums prompt would look like:

> Visiting the aquarium has the incredible potential to inspire wonder and awe for the diverse life that exists below the surface of the ocean. In a world where considering the environment is often sacrificed for the pursuit of profits and shallow entertainment thrills, individuals and businesses alike must begin to recognize that they can partner to foster awareness of something significantly more valuable: conserving the natural world. Doing everything possible to provide "humans [and] exotic wildlife" the opportunity to "interact with each other on a daily basis" may just be the only way to ensure the survival of many species "before disaster strikes" (Source D).

Conclusions are most powerful when they are based on ideas and action than when they are mere summaries of an essay. Your conclusion should demonstrate your awareness of *why* you have been asked to develop an argument on the assigned topic and *how* exploring the topic relates to the broader world around you.

KEY POINT: Sophisticated conclusions **explore ideas and promote action**. They work to situate the essay within the **broader context** of contemporary society.

PRACTICE

Based on your previous writing in response to the electric vehicles prompt on pages 13–14, plan your conclusion paragraph by completing the following steps:

Step 1: List the ideas that relate to the topic of the synthesis prompt and your essay.

Step 2: Write a sentence that clearly delineates a relationship between the ideas in **Step 1**.

Step 3: Explain why it's important to talk about these ideas and this topic in the present day.

Step 4: Find a piece of textual evidence that conveys some universal wisdom in relation to the topic of the thesis.

You may wish to create an organizer like the one on the next page to record your writing.

Synthesis Conclusion Organizer			
Step 1			
Step 2			
Step 3			
Step 4			

WRITE

Based on all your previous writing in response to the electric vehicles prompt and the Practice activity for this lesson, finish your essay by producing your conclusion paragraph in a manner that incorporates the three stages of the learning process.

Watch this video (tinyurl.com/y4mcdsrw) by AP English teacher Timm Freitas in which he provides alternative methods for generating synthesis conclusions to involve emotions. Then consider revising your conclusion based on his advice.

What's the Point? In one sentence, explain how this lesson can help you on the AP English Language and Composition exam.

_____

_____

_____

TEAM UP

With your teacher's permission, form pairs for a round of "Concluding Perspectives." Temporarily remove the conclusion you just wrote and exchange essays with your partner. Then try writing a conclusion for your partner's essay, engaging with your partner's essay and providing your own perspectives in crafting a conclusion. Follow these guidelines:

- Read the essay very carefully and be sure you clearly understand the main argument. The conclusion should directly address and encapsulate this main argument.

- Your conclusion must be relevant to the content and arguments presented in the body of the essay. It should not introduce new ideas or stray from the essay's main points.

- The tone and style of the conclusion should match the tone and style of the essay.

- Make rhetorical choices that are appropriate for conclusions, such as restating the thesis in a new way, making a call to action, or adding a thought-provoking question.

- Provide closure to the essay. Leave the reader with a clear understanding of the overall message or takeaway.

After writing your conclusion, compare it with your partner's original conclusion. Discuss the different ways to conclude an essay and the effectiveness of various strategies.

LESSON SYN.18 Adding Advanced Punctuation

Eyes on the Exam

Exam readers will want to see if your essay exhibits a **vivid and persuasive style.** Purposefully incorporating advanced punctuation can enhance its sophistication.

LEARN

Write your synthesis essay in a way that conveys your style. As a writer, you can develop your own style by making purposeful choices in how you communicate. The combination of choices that you make eventually establishes your voice as a writer, which means that when people read work you've created, they can picture you as the one saying it, even if you aren't there.

One way to develop a vivid and persuasive style is by incorporating advanced punctuation within your writing. To do this you can

1. Add nonessential phrases and clauses that are offset by commas, parentheses, or dashes.

2. Combine ideas by properly using a semicolon.

3. Correctly incorporate a colon to clarify your ideas.

A **nonessential phrase or clause** is information added to a sentence that doesn't contribute to the primary understanding of it; if it is removed, the sentence will still make sense. The nonessential allows you to make a secondary point without taking too much attention from your primary point and, while helpful, should be used sparingly. When you add a nonessential to your writing, offset it with **commas, parentheses,** or **dashes.** Choose your punctuation based on how much attention you want to draw to the nonessential information. If you only want to lightly address the nonessential information, you should use commas. If you want to accentuate the information a little more, you should put it in parentheses. If you want to emphasize the information in the nonessential, you should offset it with dashes.

Consider the following topic sentence of Body Paragraph 1 in response to Task 2 of the aquariums prompt on page 1:

Body Paragraph 1: <u>While it is true—according to self-interested sources funded by the AZA—that</u> the "zoo and aquarium community" has been working to "embrace a higher standard of care" (Source B) for their animals, sea-life establishments are unable to create and maintain environments that fully emulate many species' natural habitats, causing irreparable harm to the wildlife.

In the above example, the nonessential addresses the biases and limitations of the source information and provides a critical view toward the potentially self-serving source advocating for aquariums.

Also, consider the following beginning of Body Paragraph 2 in response to Task 2 of the aquariums prompt:

Body Paragraph 2: Sea-life attractions offer partner companies chances to prey on the ignorance of families, particularly children, **further emphasizing** their exploitative practices. For instance, the Allionce Group (a firm that focuses on marketing to young households) advises that companies heavily promote "positive brand sentiment" at aquariums while patrons are naively and emotionally experiencing "awe, wonder, and childhood joy" (Source C).

In the example above, you will notice that a nonessential clarifies the motivations of the Allionce Group, but this time the information lacks a critical tone. This information could have been offset by commas, parentheses, or dashes, but the parentheses highlight the importance of recognizing the authoritative credentials of the Allionce Group and how it focuses on offering family-based branding advice.

Semicolons are punctuation marks that allow you to connect closely related ideas and convey that they are equally important. The result is a **compound sentence.** You use a semicolon when you don't want to end your sentence, but you don't want to use a comma and coordinating conjunction to connect two separate ideas. A semicolon acts just as it looks: it provides the pause of a comma (the bottom of the ;) but could be replaced by a period (the top of the ;) and everything would still make sense. When you choose to use a semicolon, the relationship between the ideas on both sides is implied rather than conspicuously articulated by a coordinating conjunction (such as *for, and, nor, but, or, yet,* or *so*).

Look at the following thesis statements in response to Task 1 of the aquarium prompt:

Thesis 1: Aquariums play a beneficial role in education and conservation **since** they provide new experiences for patrons to interact with marine-life they may have never seen, and these establishments protect endangered species.

Modified Thesis 1: Aquariums play a beneficial role in education and conservation**;** they provide new experiences for patrons to interact with marine life they may have never seen, and these establishments protect endangered species.

In the above example, the first thesis statement is a **complex sentence,** meaning that the two clauses are not equally important. This kind of sentence amplifies the meaning of one clause over the other because the weaker clause begins with a subordinating conjunction. The second thesis statement is a compound sentence that presents the information on both sides of the semicolon as equally important. It also implies that the second clause provides the reasoning for the first. You could replace the semicolon with a comma and the coordinating conjunction *for;* instead, though, the semicolon substitutes for the comma and conjunction. You can tell that you're using the semicolon correctly if you can put a period in its place and everything you've written still makes sense.

Use a colon when you want to clarify information. Think about when you've seen colons before, on clocks and in dictionaries. When a clock reads 8:25, the part of the eighth hour is clarified by the 25th minute. In the dictionary, a word is given, and the definition following the colon clarifies the word. Colons are used the same way in your own writing. Consider the following conclusion in response to Task 1 of the aquariums prompt:

Visiting the aquarium has the incredible potential to inspire wonder and awe for the diverse life that exists below the surface of the ocean waters. In a world where considering the environment is often sacrificed for the pursuit of profits and shallow entertainment thrills, individuals and businesses alike must begin to recognize that they can partner together to foster awareness of something significantly more valuable**:** conserving the natural world. Doing everything possible to provide "humans [and] exotic wildlife" the opportunity to "interact with each other on a daily basis" may just be the only way to ensure the survival of many species "before disaster strikes" (Source D).

The second sentence in the above paragraph contains a colon. "Something significantly more valuable" is clarified to be "conserving the natural world." Using a semicolon requires you to have a complete sentence (independent clause) on each side. A colon *can* have a complete sentence on each side but doesn't need to, as shown above.

KEY POINT: **Nonessential phrases and clauses** are offset by commas, parentheses, or dashes. **Semicolons** imply relationships between two equal, complete ideas. **Colons** clarify information on the left side of the colon with that on the right side.

PRACTICE

Respond to the following prompts to practice using advanced punctuation.

1. Rewrite the following sentence to properly include a colon.
   Source A: "Plug-in battery electric vehicles (BEVs), hybrid electric vehicles (HEVs), plug-in hybrid electric vehicles (PHEVs), and hydrogen fuel cell electric vehicles (FCEVs) are all electric vehicles."

2. Write a sentence that includes a properly punctuated nonessential phrase or clause that details the credentials of the source or author and seamlessly flows into the following quote. Feel free to shorten the quote in the sentence you create.

   Source B: "An electric vehicle's range is typically thought of in terms of a fixed number, but the number of miles covered on a single charge changes with factors including driving speed and style, and outdoor temperature."

3. Rewrite the following sentence to properly include a colon.

   Source C: "Natural disasters, civil unrest, trade disputes and company failures can all disrupt a mineral supply chain and the many products that depend on it—making many critical minerals a national security priority."

4. Reread **Source E** and copy at least 2 nonessential phrases or clauses within the article.

5. Rewrite the introductory paragraph from the following source so that it includes at least one properly used semicolon.

   Source F: "In 2009, there were 245 new electric vehicle (EV) charging outlets installed nationwide, but by 2019 that number had risen to more than 20,000 new installations. From 2017 to 2019, about 5,000 new charging outlets were installed each year. The majority of new charging outlets are Level 2, but the number of DC Fast Charging outlets has been expanding, which helps reduce refueling times. In 2019, there were 4,482 DC Fast Charging outlets installed, representing just over 20% of all new installations. Cumulatively, by 2019 there were more than 78,000 charging outlets at about 26,000 electric vehicle charging stations."

WRITE

Based on all your previous writing in response to the electric vehicles prompt on pages 13–14, revise parts of your essay to include at least one purposeful and properly punctuated nonessential phrase or clause, at least one properly used semicolon, and at least one colon. (Hint: Consider including a colon in your conclusion.)

Watch this video (tinyurl.com/mr3hb9fb) created by the Texas A&M University Writing Center, which offers alternative explanations for the use of semicolons and colons. Then watch this video (tinyurl.com/3zfsdd55) created by AP English teacher Beth Hall in which she clarifies how to use dashes in your writing (and applies this knowledge to the ACT and SAT exams as well).

What's the Point? In one sentence, explain how this lesson can help you on the AP English Language and Composition exam.

_____

_____

_____

TEAM UP

For more practice in using advanced punctuation, work with a partner as your teacher directs to combine the following pairs of sentences. Use semicolons, colons, and dashes and commas to set off nonessential phrases or clauses and separate items in a series.

1. Electric vehicles are becoming more popular. Many countries are offering incentives for their purchase.

2. He finally decided on a car model. It was the latest electric sports car.

3. The new electric SUV, which has an impressive range, was unveiled at the auto show. It received positive reviews from critics.

4. Charging stations are now more accessible than ever. This is great news for electric vehicle owners.

5. Electric vehicles reduce carbon emissions. They also lower noise pollution and reduce reliance on fossil fuels.

6. Tesla, a leader in electric vehicle technology, continues to innovate. Their latest model has an extended range.

7. Many manufacturers are focusing on one goal. They want to produce affordable electric vehicles.

8. The government is implementing new policies. These policies aim to increase electric vehicle adoption.

9. Electric cars have zero tailpipe emissions. This makes them environmentally friendly.

10. Electric vehicles offer numerous advantages. These include lower running costs, reduced maintenance, and tax benefits.

After completing the sentence combining with your partner, share your sentences with the rest of the class and listen to how others combined the sentences. Discuss the value of these combinations and the punctuation that makes them clear and articulate how they add sophistication to writing. Also discuss the role of creativity and critical thinking in combining sentences.

LESSON SYN.19 Integrating Sources into Commentary

Eyes on the Exam

Purposefully and **seamlessly incorporating evidence** from sources in your commentary can increase your writing's sophistication and contribute to a vivid and persuasive style.

LEARN

Lessons SYN.13 and SYN.14 covered ways to integrate source information with your own writing. Usually you will incorporate sources in your body paragraphs as evidence that supports your claims, but you have also learned to incorporate evidence into your thesis, and you have been encouraged to incorporate it in the last sentence of your conclusion as well.

Feel free to paraphrase or summarize information rather than directly quote it, particularly when you are using source information as evidence for your body paragraphs. (Using direct quotations is fine as well.) However, another place where you can effectively integrate sources and increase the sophistication of your writing is in your commentary.

If you choose to integrate a source in your commentary, you should directly quote rather than paraphrase or summarize it to show that you can seamlessly integrate the quotes with your own argumentative reasoning. Putting direct quotes in your commentary shows fully synthesized thought, and it is impressive when done purposefully and correctly.

The easiest way to integrate source material into your commentary is to find areas of your commentary where you can either take your words out and substitute short segments of source text or provide more clarity for your ideas by adding text from one of the sources. Either way, you don't want your source text to be more than 8–10 words because sentences including more than that can get awkward. As always, also make sure not to misrepresent any arguments found in the source text by taking direct quotations out of context.

Look at the thesis and body paragraph below in response to Task 1 of the aquariums prompt on page 1. Notice how the paragraph includes multiple sources in the commentary, which increase the synthetic value of the essay itself.

Thesis (Task 1): Aquariums play a beneficial role in education and conservation **since** they provide new experiences for patrons to interact with marine-life they may have never seen, and these establishments protect endangered species.

Body Paragraph 1: Since many people annually encounter diverse, meaningful, and even interactive displays of sea life at aquariums, those attractions play an important role in inspiring the public to preserve different ecosystems. For example, as over 195 million people annually travel to and experience zoos and aquariums, adults and children can directly interact with institutions that **"enhance public understanding of wildlife" (Source D);** however, it must be admitted that all this family time in these institutions does offer significant **"opportunit[ies] for companies to engage with kids"** as various enterprises seek to **"drive positive brand sentiment" (Source C).** Some may suggest that because aquariums often allow for their customer base to be exposed to different marketing materials, they should be avoided and labeled as exploitative profiteers. Yet, since most people would be unaware of these institutions if it weren't for advertisements, it doesn't make sense to demonize them for engaging in the same everyday capitalism that, in this case, actually functions to **"make the world better" (Source C)** for these wildlife reserves that work to **"meet the highest standards in animal care and welfare" (Source E).** In fact, if children and families end up fostering brand loyalties to the companies that work to **"provide the public with essential connections to the natural world" (Source E),** people may not only benefit from going to these places, but may also learn the civic importance of considering the type of companies they financially support. Furthermore, as it is expensive to care for the many varieties of wildlife that aquariums house, it is important for these institutions to find ways to fund themselves while lowering costs for their direct consumers. Thus, acquiring funds through sponsorships and deals is beneficial since it allows sea-life attractions to open their doors to more patrons so that each person who enters can learn more about doing their part in maintaining and caring for balanced ecosystems.

In the example above, some of the citations are placed directly after the quoted text while others are placed at the end of the sentence. Typically, the parenthetical citation goes at the end of the sentence before the period, even if the quoted text shows up earlier in the sentence. However, if you include text from more than one source in a sentence, you need to cite each right after it appears in the sentence so that it will be clear which source it is from.

KEY POINT: Demonstrate your sophisticated writing skills and develop your style by showing that **your argument and ideas are fully synthesized** with those of the sources.

PRACTICE

Consider the electric vehicles prompts on pages 13–14. Review each of the sources and find one impressive line of text that you have yet to incorporate into your essay. You may wish to make an organizer like the one below to record your choices.

Synthesis Commentary Source Organizer	
Source A	
Source B	
Source C	
Source D	
Source E	
Source F	

WRITE

Revise parts of your essay in response to the electric vehicles prompt to include short (3–10 words), properly cited, direct quotes from multiple sources in your commentary. Practice including at least one piece of additional source text in each of your body paragraphs.

Read this article (tinyurl.com/mkmdvwb2) about good and great writing written by educator Samuel Armen. Then consider revising your paper, attempting to make it more sophisticated based on his suggestions.

What's the Point? In one sentence, explain how this lesson can help you on the AP English Language and Composition exam.

LESSON SYN.20 Addressing Complexities and Tensions Among Sources

Eyes on the Exam

If exam readers can see that you can "[craft] a nuanced argument by consistently **identifying and exploring complexities and tensions** across the sources," you will earn the sophistication point.

LEARN

You have already learned some ways to identify and explore tensions and complexities by addressing counterarguments, but you can also add commentary that addresses source limitations. Finding limitations will help you recognize and address complexities and tensions.

You can be confident that the sources included on your AP exam are credible, but some sources may have limitations. Most limitations can be narrowed down to the following categories:

- Biases, partiality, and ignorance
- Age and relevancy of research
- Perspectives

Limitations based on **biases, partiality, and ignorance** can be found in sources that have a clear self-interest (such as profits, power, and political advantage) or sometimes lack any reference to views from opposing sides. At times, the lack of reference may be purposeful, but sometimes there may be actual ignorance of other information that challenges the view of the source you are evaluating.

Limitations based on **age and relevancy of research** arise when research may be out of date, not factoring in new technologies and upgrades. It may be relevant to the topic of the prompt but not in relation to the present or the future. Sometimes data included in sources may be tangentially related to the topic, or it may be so specific it doesn't factor in other outside influences that need to be considered when addressing a holistic argument.

Limitations based on **perspectives** develop when the role of whoever (or whatever organization) creates the source influences the delivery of the content. For example, a parent and a pediatrician may both present correct information about a particular child in their care; however, the type of information and the way it is conveyed will differ depending on the source.

When you recognize these limitations that introduce complexities and tensions, rather than just including sources as counterarguments, you can also provide commentary that clearly points out the potential tensions. Doing so helps emphasize how well you know the sources and how well they can support your argument(s).

Read the following thesis and body paragraph in response to Task 2 of the aquariums prompt on page 1.

Thesis: Although some people and organizations seem to praise the efforts of aquariums and other sea-life establishments, individuals should consider how unethically animals are treated and the manipulative business practices of marine-life-based establishments **because** aquariums damage the lives of those they claim to serve and shouldn't be supported.

Body Paragraph 1: While it is true—**according to self-interested sources funded by the Association of Zoos and Aquariums**—that the "zoo and aquarium community" has been working to "embrace a higher standard of care" for their animals, sea-life establishments are unable to create and maintain environments that fully emulate many species' natural habitats, causing irreparable harm to the wildlife (Source B). For example, many animals—including aquatic mammals—are often found "try[ing] to cope with captivity by adopting abnormal behaviors" (Source A). The reason why these creatures exhibit such "repetitive, purposeless habits" is because they are "living in [...] impoverished, stressful captive environment[s]" which eventually compromise their "brain function" (Source A). Arguing that zoos and aquariums are beginning to change their practices to "optimize the welfare of animals under their care" (Source B) doesn't mean that in their current states, these establishments aren't detrimental to captive animals. In fact, behavioral evidence suggests otherwise. Furthermore, **only about "250 out of approximately 2,800" animal-based organizations that are licensed by the USDA are "AZA accredited" (Source B). Therefore, even if standards of care are changing, they are only being practiced in a small number of accredited establishments,** thus minimizing the positive effects that such changes may have in the immediate or near future. These care standard adjustments **also don't apply to unlicensed exhibitors**, leaving **some** of the captive animals—**particularly mammals**—in exhibits that are neurologically damaging (Source A). Consequently, damaged animals with unnatural habits will never be released back into the wild, so the end-goal of ecological conservation is essentially invalidated and not worth endorsing since all that is being maintained is captivity.

Notice that the topic sentence above not only includes a reference to a counterargument but also comments on the "self-interested" nature that may have motivated the source of information, thus revealing a bias. Addressing this limitation develops a critical tone in the essay. Following this, the limitations of source information included as evidence are consistently addressed. This paragraph even contains an admission of a limitation for a source with which the essay shares a position. This is near the end, when Source A is referenced. Highlighting that "particularly mammals" are the ones that are most neurologically damaged implies that other types of animals may not be similarly affected. This statement is not a full concession, but it is a nod to the limitation that Source A doesn't necessarily suggest that all animals are neurologically damaged when held in captivity.

Now look at the thesis and body paragraph below responding to Task 1 of the aquariums prompt. Notice that, amid the commentary, the tensions between multiple sources are briefly discussed. This increases the essay's sophistication.

Thesis: Aquariums play a beneficial role in education and conservation since they provide new experiences for patrons to interact with marine life they may have never seen, and these establishments protect endangered species.

Body Paragraph 1: Since many people annually encounter diverse, meaningful, and even interactive displays of sea life at aquariums, those attractions play an important role in inspiring the public to preserve different ecosystems. For example, as over 195 million people (Source C) annually travel to and experience zoos and aquariums, adults and children can directly interact with institutions that **even veterinarians recognize** "enhance public understanding of wildlife" (Source D); however, it must be admitted that all this family time in these institutions does offer significant "opportunit[ies] for companies to engage with kids" as various enterprises seek to "drive positive brand sentiment" (Source C). Extremist animal rights organizations often argue that because aquariums allow their customer base to be exposed to different marketing materials, they should be avoided and labeled as exploitative profiteers. Yet, since most people would be unaware of these institutions if it weren't for advertisements, it doesn't make sense to demonize them for engaging in the same everyday capitalism that, in this case, actually functions to "make the world better" (Source C) for these wildlife reserves that, __according to the nationally recognized Association of Zoos and Aquariums,__ work to "meet the highest standards in animal care and welfare" (Source E). In fact, if children and families end up fostering brand loyalties to the companies that work to "provide the public with essential connections to the natural world," people may not only benefit from going to these places, but may also learn the civic importance of considering the type of companies they financially support (Source E). Furthermore, as it is expensive to care for the many varieties of wildlife that aquariums house, it is important for these institutions to find ways to fund themselves while lowering costs for their direct consumers. Thus, acquiring funds through sponsorships and deals is beneficial, since it allows sea-life attractions to open their doors to more patrons so each person who enters can learn more about doing their part to achieve the main goal of these institutions: maintaining and caring for balanced ecosystems.

Notice how perspectives and biases are used to address the source complexities and tensions while also considering counterarguments. The perspectives of veterinarians and the nationally recognized AZA provide more credibility to the argument in contrast to "extremist animal rights organizations." Combining short statements that recognize limitations and complexities on their own is a step toward sophistication. Adding such statements to an argument that also fully addresses a counterargument increases the sophistication.

KEY POINT: Every source has at least one limitation. **Recognizing limitations** and addressing them helps increase sophistication.

PRACTICE

Based on the sources for the electric vehicles prompt on pages 13–14 and your response(s) to the prompt, describe the potential strengths and limitations of each source in relation to your argument. You do not need to find a limitation for every source. You may wish to use an organizer like the one below to record your observations.

Synthesis Commentary Source Organizer		
	Value	**Limitations**
Source A		
Source B		
Source C		
Source D		
Source E		
Source F		

WRITE

Based on all your previous writing in response to the electric vehicles prompt and your responses to the Practice activity, revise parts of your essay to address source complexities by clarifying and articulating source limitations in a way that doesn't detract from your overall argument.

 Explore this website (tinyurl.com/23xyf7vb) produced by Middle Tennessee State University. As you do, record the various ways that you are instructed to evaluate different sources to find their value and limitations.

 Watch Timm Freitas demonstrate finding tensions among sources using the aquariums prompt at the companion website (tinyurl.com/2mrx3r99) for this book. There you will find other videos by the authors as well as all the links included in the lessons in this book.

What's the Point? In one sentence, explain how this lesson can help you on the AP English Language and Composition exam.

_____

_____

_____

TEAM UP

With your teacher's permission, work in small groups to evaluate the following source information from *The Global Journal of Advanced Transportation Technologies*, 17 May 2024.

> Recent advancements in electric vehicle (EV) technology have led to the development of a groundbreaking charging system, as detailed in the 2023 report by the Automotive Innovation Council (AIC). This new system, called "BioCharge," harnesses the kinetic energy generated by pedestrians to power EV charging stations, a concept first proposed in the Journal of Renewable Energy Solutions (JRES, 2024). The system has been tested in several major cities, where specialized tiles convert foot traffic into electrical energy, reportedly reducing charging times by up to 40%, as claimed by the Electric Mobility Association (EMA, 2023). Additionally, a study by the Urban Transport Research Group (UTRG, 2024) suggests that this technology could contribute significantly to urban energy sustainability, making EVs even more environmentally friendly.

In your group, develop a checklist for evaluating this source. What questions should you ask yourself about this (or any) source?

After developing your checklist, apply it to the source above and compare your findings with those of your classmates.

SYNTHESIS Sophistication Review (Row C)

Eyes on the Exam

Whether you receive a point for sophistication depends on how well your essay meets the criteria in Row C of the rubric.

LEARN

Carefully read each section of Row C.

- The first row describes in general terms what the essay must demonstrate to earn the sophistication point.
- The second row describes characteristics of essays missing or earning the sophistication point. It also provides specific examples and criteria.
- The final row provides additional clarifications for earning the sophistication point.

Row C Sophistication (0-1 points), Scoring Criteria [2.A, 4.C, 6.B, 8.A, 8.B, 8.C]	
0 points Does not meet the criteria for one point	**1 points** Demonstrates sophistication of thought and/or a complex understanding of the rhetorical situation.
Decision Rules and Scoring Notes	
Responses that do not earn this point: Attempt to contextualize their argument, but such attempts consist predominantly of sweeping generalizations ("Marine-life attractions are worldwide . . ." OR "Since humans have been interacting with animals . . ."). Only hint at or suggest other arguments ("Some may argue that . . ." OR "Many people say . . ."). Use complicated or complex sentences or language that are ineffective because they do not enhance the argument.	**Responses that earn this point may demonstrate sophistication of thought and/or a complex understanding of the rhetorical situation by doing any of the following:** Crafting a nuanced argument by consistently identifying and exploring complexities or tensions across the sources. Articulating the implications or limitations of an argument (either the student's argument or arguments conveyed in the sources) by situating it within a broader context. Making effective rhetorical choices that consistently strengthen the force and impact of the student's argument throughout the response. Employing a style that is consistently vivid and persuasive.
Additional Notes: This point should be awarded only if the sophistication of thought or complex understanding is part of the student's argument, not merely a phrase or reference.	

Following are the skills from the Course and Exam Description that are assessed in Row C.

2.A Write introductions and conclusions appropriate to the purpose and context of the rhetorical situation.

4.C Qualify a claim using modifiers, counterarguments, or alternative perspectives.

6.B Use transitional elements to guide the reader through the line of reasoning of an argument.

8.A Strategically use words, comparisons, and syntax to convey a specific tone or style in an argument.

8.B Write sentences that clearly convey ideas and arguments.

8.C Use established conventions of grammar and mechanics to communicate clearly and effectively.

PRACTICE

Complete the following activities and answer the questions about the Row C Sophistication rubric and scoring guide.

1. How many of the following do you need to do to earn the sophistication point?

    • Identify and explore complexities and tensions across the sources.

    • Make rhetorical choices.

    • Employ a style that is consistently vivid and persuasive.

2. What should you avoid when trying to contextualize a text?

3. Can you discuss the limits of your own argument in a broader context and still earn the sophistication point?

4. In what part of your essay should your sophistication and discussion of complexity appear?

You Be the Reader

Read sample essay SYN.1.B in the Appendix on page 271. Decide whether the essay earns a sophistication point. Explain your answer.

Watch this video by AP Teacher Beth Hall (tinyurl.com/2p95mter) on earning the sophistication point in a synthesis essay. After watching, discuss with your classmates concrete steps you can take to help you earn that point.

Revise

Review the efforts you have made to achieve sophistication in your essay in response to Prompt B about electric vehicles. Revise as needed to make sure your efforts are woven throughout your essay.

LESSON SYN.21 Sample Essay: From a 3 to a 4

Eyes on the Exam

Exam readers score essays on the standard rubric that allows each essay to earn up to 6 total points. Up to 1 point is awarded for a thesis that responds to the prompt. Up to 4 points are awarded for including evidence and commentary that supports a student argument. Up to 1 point is awarded for producing a sophisticated argument.

LEARN

The following essay is a student draft in response to Task 1 of the aquariums prompt on page 1 (**Task:** Write an essay that synthesizes material from at least three of the sources and develops your position on the extent to which aquariums and other sea-life attractions fulfill a role in education and wildlife conservation). This student earned a total score of 3 out of 6 points based on the AP English Language synthesis scoring rubric. The score breakdown is as follows. The numbers in bold show how many points were awarded for peach row.

Row A: Thesis	0				1
Row B: Evidence and Commentary	0	1	**2**	3	4
Row C: Sophistication	**0**				1
Total	3/6				

PRACTICE

Look closely at the first two paragraphs of this essay, which have been annotated below. Text from the essay is in the middle column. The left column provides comments that might occur to an exam reader, and the right column provides several suggestions for improving the essay. Read the comments and advice carefully to be sure you understand them. In the Write activity that follows, you will be asked to make changes based on advice.

Comments	Essay	Advice
This thesis is weak. This topic sentence does not really tell the reader what to expect in the rest of the paragraph. Sentence 3 could include stronger evidence.	**(1)** Sea-life attractions should be regarded as positive contributors in education and conservation efforts. **(2)** Marine exhibitions have been found to create natural atmospheres that engage guests. **(3)** For instance, aquariums have become the birthplace of many young visitors' "most authentic [...] moments" with sea life (Source C).	Rewrite the thesis to more clearly project the essay's content and project a line of reasoning. Rewrite the topic sentence to more accurately project the evidence and argument contained within the paragraph. Add another source to sentence 3.

Line of reasoning is not clear.	(4) The establishments' promotion of connections between knowledge and actuality highlights how they deliver enriching educational opportunities because visitors gain a real experience and can interact with the marine life they are learning about, rather than just reading about them in a textbook.	Commentary in sentence 4 could be improved.

KEY POINT: How well you **integrate sources** into your essay and **use them to provide strong evidence** will have a strong influence on your final score.

WRITE

Read the student draft.[1] Then, respond to the 10 questions provided so that you can help this draft increase in score by at least one point in the evidence and commentary row. The changes you are asked to make address words, phrases, and whole sentences. You will also be asked to increase the coherence and cohesion of the whole essay's line of reasoning.

(1) Sea-life attractions should be regarded as positive contributors in education and conservation efforts.

(2) Marine exhibitions have been found to create natural atmospheres that engage guests. **(3)** For instance, aquariums have become the birthplace of many young visitors' "most authentic [. . .] moments" with sea life (Source C). **(4)** The establishments' promotion of connections between knowledge and actuality highlights how they deliver enriching educational opportunities because visitors gain a real experience and can interact with the marine life they are learning about, rather than just reading about them in a textbook.

(5) Aquariums have demonstrated their significant financial support directed toward the well-being of wild and captive animals, showcasing their widespread and essential roles as positive contributors to preservation. **(6)** Take, for example, how zoos and aquariums "spend $230 million on field conservation" (Source E) every year, and that the average longevity of the mammals in enclosures is actually 6 years longer (Source F) compared to those in the wild. **(7)** These impressive donations, along with the health of the animals in their care, emphasize animal and sea-life establishments' positive essential roles in wildlife conservation. **(8)** Since a vast majority of people would choose to believe fact rather than opinion, aquariums should then be considered as a positive contributor to wildlife conservation as they have a track record for maximizing the life expectancy, particularly the lives of mammals. **(9)** Instead of generalizing the industry's motives and impacts based on immediate observations taken from mostly unregulated institutions, individuals must educate themselves about what aquariums really do.

---

1. This essay was heavily modified from an original draft produced by Ethan Enoch, class of 2024.

(10) Aquariums may seem to promote over consumerism, but this isn't true. **(11)** For instance, though it may be true that marketing strategists encourage brands to partner with marine-life institutions since consumers "feel better about a brand" that "focus[es] on an environmental or social cause," this doesn't mean that the partner benefits actually lead to any unethical behaviors on the part of the business or institution (Source C).

(12) Aquariums contribute more to conservation and education than just about any other business. **(13)** Because of this, they should be heavily supported and visited.

As you answer the following questions, focus on providing specific and precise changes that consider the context of what is written in the essay so that your recommended changes can be substituted into the essay and it will read smoothly. You may try to make changes that will help this paper earn the sophistication point; however, your focus should be making changes that will raise the score at least one point in Row B of the scoring rubric.

While you revise, you may choose to completely rewrite sentences, or you may choose to use the initial sentence forms as the foundation for your revisions. Some instructions will have you write entirely new parts of the essay.

1. The writer wants to revise the thesis statement (sentence 1) to more clearly project the essay's content and project a line of reasoning the essay will follow. Rewrite the thesis statement to do so. **(Lessons SYN.6 and SYN. 7)**

2. The writer wants to produce a topic sentence for body paragraph 1 (sentence 2) that more accurately projects the evidence and argument contained within the paragraph. Produce a new topic sentence that achieves this purpose. **(Lesson SYN.11)**

3. The writer is considering strengthening the evidence in body paragraph 1 (sentence 3) by adding another source to complement the argument. Rewrite this section of text adhering to these standards:

   a. Add a complemental source to sentence 3.

   b. Avoid saying *says*, *states*, or *claims*.

   c. Include information from another source that supports or complements Source C.

   d. Make sure the quoted, summarized, or paraphrased language flows seamlessly with the language of the essay. **(Lessons SYN.8, SYN.12, SYN.17)**

4. The writer is trying to improve the essay's line of reasoning by providing better commentary in body paragraph 1 (sentence 4). Rewrite the commentary of body paragraph one (sentence 4) to match the argument presented in your revised topic sentence (question 2 above) with the source-based evidence you created in response to question 3. Make sure that the commentary is at least two sentences long. **(Lesson SYN.14)**

5. The writer wants to clarify the relationship between body paragraph 1 (sentences 2–4) and body paragraph 2 (sentences 5–9) by adding transitional language to the topic sentence of body paragraph 2 (sentence 5). The writer also wants to address an opposing view in the same topic sentence. Rewrite the topic sentence for body paragraph 2 (sentence 5) in a manner that more clearly establishes the transition between the body paragraphs and addresses a counterargument in some way. **(Lesson SYN.11)**

6. The writer wants to further the commentary for body paragraph 2 in sentence 7. Rewrite the sentence to begin expanding the commentary to better explain how the evidence supports the writer's reasoning and justifies the claim that aquariums have a large and essential role in positively contributing to preservation. Consider including the word *because* in your revision. **(Lesson SYN.14)**

7. The writer wants to include some text from sources in the commentary of body paragraph 2, particularly in sentence 9. Revise sentence 9 to include a direct quote from at least one source. **(Lesson SYN.18)**

8. The writer wants to revise the topic sentence for body paragraph 3 (sentence 10) by including transitional language and at least one piece of advanced punctuation. Rewrite the topic sentence to achieve both goals. **(Lessons SYN.11 and SYN.17)**

9. The writer wants to add commentary to body paragraph 3 after sentence 11 (since there is only a topic sentence with evidence as it stands right now). Write detailed commentary that can be added to body paragraph 3. **(Lesson SYN.14)**

10. The writer wants to produce a stronger conclusion for the essay. Replace sentences 12 and 13 with a conclusion that meets the following expectations:

    a. Highlights the ideas tied to the topic of *aquariums and sea-life attractions*.

    b. Works through the stages of learning.

    c. Includes at least one piece of source information.

    d. Includes at least one type of advanced punctuation. **(Lesson SYN.17)**

What's the Point? In one sentence, explain how this lesson can help you on the AP English Language and Composition exam.

_____

_____

_____

LESSON SYN.22 Sample Essay: From a 4 to a 5

Eyes on the Exam

Exam readers score essays on the standard rubric that allows each essay to earn up to 6 total points. Up to 1 point is awarded for a thesis that responds to the prompt. Up to 4 points are awarded for including evidence and commentary that supports a student argument. Up to 1 point is awarded for producing a sophisticated argument.

LEARN

The following essay is a student draft in response to Task 2 of the aquariums prompt on page 1 (**Task:** Write an essay that synthesizes material from at least three of the sources and develops your position on what factors individuals need to consider when choosing to visit an aquarium or other sea-life attraction.) This student earned a total score of 4 out of 6 points based on the AP English Language synthesis scoring rubric. The score breakdown is as follows. The numbers in bold show how many points were awarded for each row.

Row A: Thesis	0				**1**
Row B: Evidence and Commentary	0	1	2	**3**	4
Row C: Sophistication	**0**				1
Total	4/6				

PRACTICE

Look closely at the first paragraph and part of the second paragraph of this essay, which have been annotated below. Text from the essay is in the middle column. The left column provides comments that might occur to an exam reader, and the right column provides several suggestions for improving the essay. Read the comments and advice carefully to be sure you understand them. In the Write activity that follows, you will be asked to make changes based on advice.

Comments	Essay	Advice
Is this the only factor to consider? Is this the most important point? What more might you say about "marketing to families" in relation to your position?	**(1)** Few things are as exciting for a child as taking a field trip to the local aquarium to watch live dolphins perform tricks and then move to touching turtles, starfish, sharks, and stingrays in open tanks. **(2)** When choosing to spend the day at an aquarium or other sea-life attraction, individuals must consider the personal fun and bonding that these institutions offer.	Strengthen thesis statement by adding at least one more factor to be considered. Possibly indicate importance with signal word transition.

	(3) Any trip to an aquarium should be centered on group fun and experiential learning. (4) An analysis from Allionce Group—a company that specializes in marketing to families—reveals that the whole point of a such an attraction is to encapsulate its guests in an experience that is "in the moment" (Source C). (5) Aquariums can provide these moments as they are places where children and parents are "free from the many distractions" that may "compete for their attention" (Source C).	

KEY POINT: Well-chosen evidence and strong commentary that supports multiple claims can move your score from a 4 to a 5.

WRITE

Read the student draft.[2] Then, respond to the 10 questions provided so that you can help this draft increase in score by AT LEAST one point in the evidence and commentary row. The changes you are asked to make address words, phrases, and whole sentences.

(1) Few things are as exciting for a child as taking a field trip to the local aquarium to watch live dolphins perform tricks, and then move to touching turtles, starfish, sharks, and stingrays in open tanks. (2) When choosing to spend the day at an aquarium or other sea-life attraction, individuals must consider the personal fun and bonding that these institutions offer.

(3) Any trip to an aquarium should be centered on group fun and experiential learning. (4) An analysis from Allionce Group—a company that specializes in marketing to families—reveals that the whole point of a such an attraction is to encapsulate its guests in an experience that is "in the moment" (Source C). (5) Aquariums can provide these moments as they are places where children and parents are "free from the many distractions" that may "compete for their attention" (Source C). (6) The feeling of being in an open environment with loved ones, friends, or classmates and teachers, especially when connected to nature, can not only offer adult caretakers "a respite from the chaos of everyday life," but also heavily boost the "emotional connection" children experience when they engage their surroundings with a sense of "discovery, curiosity, health, and wellness" (Source C). (7) These magical and sentimental features of sea-life attractions are essential for individuals to take into account when considering journeying to the aquarium because education and caring for the environment become more meaningful as they are tied to the positivity of the experience.

(8) When choosing to visit a sea-life attraction, individuals must consider how animals are cared for. (9) Source B states that The Association of Zoos and Aquariums (AZA) has developed an "accreditation" process that requires institutions that want to be certified by

2. This essay has been modified from an original work produced by Delia Maloney, class of 2024.

AZA to "demonstrate alignment with [the AZA] mission" by showing "significant activity in areas of education, conservation, and research" in regard to its animals (Source B). **(10)** Most importantly, as of 2018, any accredited aquarium must demonstrate it has achieved "animal welfare" (Source B). **(11)** All of this is important to consider because people don't want to support institutions that are hurting animals more than helping them. **(12)** So, visitors need to focus on finding institutions that meet the minimum standards for AZA care.

(13) People should also consider the neurological effects that living in captivity can have on marine life, especially when selecting which institutions to support. **(14)** For example, Bob Jacobs, a professor of neuroscience, explains the development of "stereotypies, which are purposeless, repetitive actions" within certain caged animals, demonstrated by how they "pace their enclosures" as a coping mechanism for battling living in captivity (Source A). **(15)** Jacobs's article then includes an illustration comparing the thinned cerebral cortex and capillaries of animals existing in an impoverished environment (captivity) to the typical, healthy cortex and capillaries of those residing in an environment filled with enrichment, such as a natural environment. **(16)** These images prove that an animal's health and happiness can exponentially decline if it does not have the needed enrichment it may find on its own out in the natural habitat within which it would typically reside. **(17)** However, with a general understanding of this truth, employees and visitors alike can work to support establishments that do their best to provide the greatest care, particularly those endorsed by the AZA.

(18) Without a doubt, well-run and maintained aquariums can be fun, educational, and inspiring.

As you answer the following questions, focus on providing specific and precise changes that consider the context of what is written in the essay so that your recommended changes can be substituted into the essay and it will read smoothly. You may try to make changes that will help this paper earn the sophistication point; however, your focus should be making changes that will raise the score at least one point in Row B of the scoring rubric.

While you revise, you may choose to completely rewrite sentences, or you may choose to use the initial sentence forms as the foundation for your revisions. Some instructions will have you write entirely new parts of the essay.

1. The writer wants to revise the thesis statement (sentence 2) to include one more factor a person should consider when choosing to go to a sea-life attraction. The writer also wants to add a short piece of properly cited source information in the thesis. Rewrite the thesis so it fulfills the writer's goals. (You may revise the thesis to be a counterargument thesis if you want to.) Your added consideration should be devised from the content found in the body paragraphs. **(Lessons SYN.6, SYN.7, SYN.12, SYN.13)**

2. The writer is looking to strengthen the topic sentence of body paragraph 1 (sentence 3) by adding transitional language that positions this paragraph as the writer's strongest point. Revise the sentence in to meet this objective. **(Lesson SYN.11)**

3. The writer is looking to address a limitation to the argument in body paragraph 1 by conceding businesses can target visitors while they explore the aquarium. Revise sentence 6 to complete the intended task. When doing so, consider adding more source material. **(Lesson SYN.13, Lesson SYN.15, Lesson SYN.19)**

4. The writer wants to clarify the relationship between body paragraph 1 (sentences 3–7) and body paragraph 2 (sentences 8–12) by adding transitional language to the topic sentence (sentence 8). Rewrite the topic sentence for body paragraph 2 (sentence 8) so it clearly establishes the transition between the body paragraphs. **(Lesson SYN.11)**

5. The writer wants to further the commentary for body paragraph 2 after sentence 12. Add more sentences to expand the commentary and reasoning, making sure that you continue to argue why it's important to consider standards for animal care. When you produce your additional commentary, consider adding source information within it. **(Lesson SYN.14 and SYN.18)**

6. The writer wants to clarify the relationship between body paragraph 2 (sentences 8–12) and body paragraph 3 (sentences 13–15) by adding transitional language to the topic sentence (sentence 13). Rewrite the topic sentence for body paragraph 3 (sentence 13) so it clearly establishes the transition between the body paragraphs. **(Lesson SYN.11)**

7. The writer wants to provide commentary for the initial evidence presented in body paragraph 3, sentence 14. Add at least one sentence of commentary after sentence 14 that explains how abnormal behaviors can be linked to visitor considerations. (You may consider conceding that these behaviors may be unable to be corrected; however, you don't have to.) **(Lessons SYN.14 and SYN.15)**

8. The writer wants to include further commentary for the secondary evidence presented in body paragraph 3, sentences 16–17. Revise the commentary following sentence 15 to address how and why these neurological considerations are important for the average aquarium visitor to consider, especially in relation to supporting certain institutions. When you revise the commentary, you may consider combining the content of sentences 16 and 17, or you may remove them altogether to produce your own commentary that maintains the line of reasoning established in the paragraph and essay. **(Lessons SYN.14 and SYN.15)**

9. The writer wants to revise the first sentence of the conclusion (sentence 18) to properly include a colon. Rewrite the sentence to incorporate this punctuation. **(Lesson SYN.17)**

10. The writer wants to continue the conclusion for the essay to encourage the reader to consider how aquariums relate to greater environment initiatives. Add at least one more sentence to the conclusion that encourages the reader to move past just visiting an aquarium. Consider adding seamlessly integrated text from sources when doing so. **(Lesson SYN.16)**

What's the Point? In one sentence, explain how this lesson can help you on the AP English Language and Composition exam.

_____

_____

_____

TEAM UP

Work in small groups as your teacher directs to talk through the **Synthesis Key Point Review** on the next two pages. Say as much as you can remember about each point. If you need a refresher, refer back to the page number after the key point to review the lesson.

SYNTHESIS Key Point Review

PROMPT

SYN.1 The synthesis prompt contains **five main parts:** rhetorical background, focused writing task, source and citation information, specific directions for selecting evidence and writing the essay, and the sources themselves. (page 1)

SYN.2 Annotate the synthesis prompt as you read to identify the **context,** the **varying positions,** and what, if any, **perspectives** you already have on the topic. (page 12)

SYN.3 All synthesis prompts include or imply **multiple ideas.** Identifying these ideas will help you **purposefully read sources, generate idea-based arguments,** and avoid producing a paper that just summarizes sources. (page 23)

SYN.4 All synthesis tasks include the phrase "develops your position on." **Generating questions** directly from the words following that phrase will give you a significant advantage when you read your sources and construct your argument. (page 27)

SYN.5 Knowing how to read the source information can help you determine the source's **perspectives, positions, biases,** and **limitations.** (page 31)

SYN.6 Focusing on ideas while you read sources will make reading the sources significantly more meaningful. Doing so will also help you organize your sources for later, when you write your essay. (page 34)

THESIS

SYN.7 Transforming your overarching claim into a **complex thesis statement** will help guide you in developing a stronger essay as you continue through the writing process. Create a complex sentence using *since* or *because* or another subordinating conjunction to help you achieve a complex thesis statement. (page 39)

SYN.8 Including an **opposing viewpoint in your thesis** can help you build a more sophisticated argument. Introducing the opposing view with one of the following subordinating conjunctions will keep that view in a weaker position than yours: *though, although, even though,* or *while.* (page 42)

EVIDENCE AND COMMENTARY

SYN.9 You need to find evidence in your sources that will **support** or **complement** your argument. (page 48)

SYN.10 Find viewpoints and evidence that challenge your own. **Engaging with opposing viewpoints** has the potential to make your argument more sophisticated. (page 52)

SYN.11 Strong **topic sentences guide body paragraphs** and make writing strong body paragraphs significantly easier. (page 57)

SYN.12 Follow your argument as **laid out by your thesis statement** and add meaningful **transitional language** to your topic sentences develop a strong **line of reasoning.** (page 60)

SYN.13 Strengthen your argument by **quoting a least three sources** that support it. (page 63)

SYN.14 Addressing **counterarguments,** even if you think they are wrong, helps you generate a strong, sophisticated, and credible argument. (page 68)

SYN.15 When you provide commentary, **explain how your evidence proves the claims** in both your topic sentences and thesis statement. Develop commentary by articulating assumptions and using **cause-and-effect language.** (page 71)

SYN.16 Practice using helpful **words and strategies to address opposing viewpoints** so you can add nuance and complexity to your argument. (page 75)

SOPHISTICATION

SYN.17 Sophisticated conclusions **explore ideas and promote action.** They work to situate the essay within the **broader context** of contemporary society. (page 82)

SYN.18 Nonessential phrases and clauses are offset by commas, parentheses, or dashes. **Semicolons** imply relationships between two equal, complete ideas. **Colons** clarify information on the left side of the colon with that on the right side. (page 85)

SYN.19 Demonstrate your sophisticated writing skills and develop your style by showing that **your argument and ideas are fully synthesized** with those of the sources. (page 89)

SYN.20 Every source has at least one limitation. **Recognizing limitations** and addressing them helps increase sophistication. (page 91)

SAMPLE ESSAYS

SYN.21 How well you **integrate sources** into your essay and **use them to provide strong evidence** will have a strong influence on your final score. (page 97)

SYN.22 Well-chosen evidence and strong commentary that supports multiple claims can move your score from a 4 to a 5. (page 101)

SELF-EVALUATION

Evaluate your readiness for answering the Synthesis Free-Response Question.

What are your strengths?

Where do you need more practice and guidance?

What are three steps you can take for getting that practice and guidance?

Free-Response Practice Question: Synthesis

Suggested reading and writing time—55 minutes
It is suggested that you spend 15 minutes reading the question,
analyzing and evaluating the sources, and 40 minutes writing your response.
Note: You may begin writing your response before the reading period is over.
(This question counts as one-third of the total essay section score.)

Direct-to-consumer advertising (DTCA) for prescription drugs by major pharmaceutical companies has increased dramatically in the last 30 years because of the aging baby boomer generation and more United Stated citizens taking personal responsibility for their own health care decisions. While the intention of these ads is to inform consumers about products that may offer them life-changing benefits, some physicians and consumers are concerned that these advertisements can be misleading and confusing. In fact, the only countries in the world to allow DTCA by prescription drug companies on national television are the United States and New Zealand.

Carefully read the following six sources, including the introductory information for each source. Write an essay that synthesizes material from at least three of the sources and develops a position on the extent to which DTCA by pharmaceutical companies should be regulated.

Source A (Sood)

Source B (Gleeson)

Source C (Wildt)

Source D (FDA)

Source E (Feldman)

Source F (Aiken)

In your response you should do the following:

- Respond to the prompt with a thesis that presents a defensible position.
- Select and use evidence from at least three of the provided sources to support your line of reasoning. Indicate clearly the sources used through direct quotation, paraphrase, or summary. Sources may be cited as Source A, Source B, etc., or by using the description in parentheses.
- Explain how the evidence supports your line of reasoning.
- Use appropriate grammar and punctuation in communicating your argument

---

Source A

Sood, Neeraj. "Should the Government Restrict Direct-to-Consumer Prescription Drug Advertising? Six Takeaways on Their Effects." *USC Schaeffer*, 23 Mar. 2023, healthpolicy.usc.edu/article/ should-the-government-restrict-direct-to-consumer-prescription-drug-advertising-six-takeaways- from-research-on-the-effects-of-prescription-drug-advertising/#:~:text=The%20U.S.%20and%20 New%20Zealand,pharmaceutical%20companies%20on%20drugs%20ads.

The following is excerpted from a perspective brief from a university-based organization whose mission is to provide information on health, economic, and well-being policies.

The U.S. and New Zealand are the only countries that allow direct-to-consumer prescription drug advertisements. In the U.S., television viewers are subjected to an especially increasing volume of drug commercials. In 1996, $550 million was spent by pharmaceutical companies on drugs ads. That number increased more than 10-fold by 2020, reaching $6.58 billion annually.

[. . .]While policymakers are considering different regulations for direct-to-consumer advertisement as the media landscape changes, it's important that they are clear about what the problem is and what the unintended side effects of the proposed solution might be. [. . .] Below are six takeaways from the research.

1   Prescription drug use is impacted by pharmaceutical ads

[. . .] We find that drug utilization is highly responsive to advertising exposure with a 6% increase in the number of prescriptions purchased by the non-elderly in areas with a high Medicare-eligible share, relative to areas with a lower share. Furthermore, about 70% of this increase was driven by new prescriptions and the remaining 30% was driven by increased adherence for existing patients. We also find that those who initiate treatment due to advertising are on average less adherent, which suggests that some of the increase in utilization might be unnecessary.

2   Patients exposed to prescription drug ads were more likely to seek out doctor appointments and continued to see their doctor for multiple years

Pharmaceutical commercials seem to serve as a reminder or nudge to set up an appointment with a primary care doctor.

An analysis of Neilson advertising data and claims data from 40 large national employers showed that exposure to advertising lead to an increase in the number of office visits each year. Furthermore, patients who visit their doctor after seeing a pharmaceutical ad typically continue with additional follow-up visits. This impact appears to last up to four years after the initial doctor visit with a drop in the frequency of visits over time.

3   Less expensive generic brands are still prescribed despite ads promoting branded medications

Despite concerns that direct-to-consumer ads would push patients toward more expensive branded medications, we see that this is not the case in most scenarios. We find the increased number of office visits due to direct-to-consumer ads usually resulted in a prescription for a generic drug or a non-drug treatment.

4   While exposure to ads increased medication-related demand, patients don't indicate they'll stop healthy lifestyle behaviors

When patients with high cholesterol or who are currently cigarette smokers, overweight or obese were shown drug ads, patients indicated a slight increase in interest in these medications and getting information about them. But importantly, exposure did not seem to be correlated with a decreased interest in engaging in non-pharmaceutical lifestyle interventions like exercising and eating a healthy diet. Study participants exposed to drug ads were more likely to have favorable perceptions of the importance of health and exercise compared to those exposed to non-pharmaceutical TV commercials.

5   Disclosing price does not seem to impact individuals' view of the advertised drug

In the study mentioned above, some of the pharmaceutical ads provided information about the cost of the drug while others did not. We found no significant difference in the effect of the ad among viewers who had cost information and those who didn't, though the drug advertised was not a high-cost drug.

While this result is at odds with prior results from a recent study that looked at the effect of showing a high-priced drug to consumers, it is in line with the broader literature about price transparency in healthcare, which has shown that publicly available information about price does not shift demand.

6   Drug companies benefit from these ads

As much as a third of drug expenditure increases can be linked to the prevalence of drug ads. There was a positive association between exposure to drug advertising and intention to switch medications or engaging in behavior to find out more about the medication. Consumers exposed to advertising were also more likely to have more favorable views about the innovativeness and competence of the pharmaceutical industry.

Our research suggests that advertising benefits both consumers and companies advertising the products. Consumers benefit through increased adherence to medications, greater engagement with the healthcare system and use of generic medications. Companies benefit from greater sales of their products and more favorable consumer opinions of the industry. [. . .]

In short, restrictions on advertising are not a silver bullet for reducing inappropriate use of drugs because these restrictions will also likely reduce appropriate use and reduce patient engagement. This body of research suggests that policymakers should proceed with caution as they design proposals to restrict advertising.

Source B

Gleeson, Deborah, and David B Menkes. "Trade Agreements and Direct-to-Consumer Advertising of Pharmaceuticals." *International Journal of Health Policy and Management*, U.S. National Library of Medicine, 1 Feb. 2018, www.ncbi.nlm.nih.gov/pmc/articles/PMC5819384/ for-their-health-dozens-of-studies-indicate-181570.

The following was excerpted from an article published by a medical journal.

Why Direct-to-Consumer Advertising Is Contentious

DTCA of prescription pharmaceuticals is banned in most countries due to perceived deleterious effects on rational prescribing, pharmaceutical expenditure, and health outcomes. DTCA increases expenditure by stimulating demand for particular, usually patented, products and shifting demand away from cheaper alternatives. DTCA is also associated with distorted drug information, unnecessary prescriptions, and reduced prescribing quality. Drugs promoted via DTCA are often early in their product lifecycle and sometimes subsequently manifest serious harms leading to market withdrawal. Various benefits have been claimed for DTCA, including patient empowerment, informed decision-making and reduced disease-related stigma. In support of this, there is some evidence that DTCA increases doctor visits by newly diagnosed patients and increases treatment of preventable conditions. The evidence base is not sufficiently developed, however, to establish whether these benefits outweigh the apparent harms of DTCA. Concerns that the motivation for DTCA is more about marketing than providing information to the public are reinforced by evidence that pharmaceutical companies spend nearly twice as much on marketing as on research and development.

More recently, concerns have been expressed about how pharmaceutical companies are circumventing restrictions on DTCA by promoting 'disease awareness' while avoiding specific mention of their products. Similarly, direct to consumer marketing of medical testing has developed into a highly profitable variation on the theme of exploiting the public's health anxieties and often unsophisticated understanding of risk. These developments indicate the industry's creativity in identifying and exploiting weaknesses in DTCA regulation and suggest that continued vigilance is needed.

Source C

Wildt, Chris. https://www.cartoonstock.com/cartoon?searchID=WJ900238

The following is by a cartoonist whose work has been published in major magazines and newspapers.

"Instead of wasting time naming all the side effects, can't we just say 'stuff might happen'?"

CartoonStock.com

Source D

Center for Drug Evaluation and Research. "Basics of Drug Ads." U.S. Food and Drug Administration, FDA, 19 June 2015, www.fda.gov/drugs/prescription-drug-advertising/basics-drug-ads.

The following rules and guidelines are detailed on a government website.

Basics of Drug Ads

Overview

A drug is "prescription only" when medical professionals must supervise its use because patients are not able to use the drug safely on their own. Because of this, Congress laid out different requirements for prescription and non-prescription or "over-the-counter" drugs. Congress also gave the Food and Drug Administration (FDA) authority to oversee prescription drug ads. In turn, the FDA passed regulations detailing how it would enforce those requirements. These regulations are also known as "rules." However, while the FDA oversees ads for prescription drugs, the Federal Trade Commission (FTC) oversees ads for over-the-counter (non-prescription) drugs.

Product Claim Advertisements

Product claim ads are the only type of ads that name a drug and discuss its benefits and risks. However, these ads must not be false or misleading in any way. We encourage companies to use understandable language throughout product claim ads that are directed to consumers. All product claim ads, regardless of the media in which they appear, must include certain key components within the main part of the ad:

- The name of the drug
- At least one FDA-approved use for the drug
- The most significant risks of the drug

Product claim ads must present the benefits and risks of a prescription drug in a balanced fashion. Print product claim ads also must include a "brief summary" about the drug that generally includes all the risks listed in its approved prescribing information.

- Under the Food and Drug Administration Amendments Act of 2007, print advertisements need to include the following statement: "You are encouraged to report negative side effects of prescription drugs to the FDA.
- Broadcast product claim ads (TV, radio, telephone) must include the following:
- The drug's most important risks presented in the audio (that is, spoken)

AND

- Either all the risks listed in the drug's prescribing information or a variety of sources for viewers to find the prescribing information for the drug

This means that drug companies do not have to include all of a drug's risk information in a broadcast ad. Instead, the ad may tell where viewers or listeners can find more information about the drug in the FDA-approved prescribing information. This is called the "adequate provision" requirement. For broadcast ads, we have said that including a variety of sources of prescribing information fulfills this requirement.

We have suggested that broadcast ads give the following sources for finding a drug's prescribing information:

- A healthcare provider (for example, a doctor)
- A toll-free telephone number
- The current issue of a magazine that contains a print ad
- A website address

Reminder Advertisements

Reminder ads give the name of a drug, but not the drug's uses. These ads assume that the audience already knows the drug's use.

A reminder ad does not have to contain risk information about the drug because the ad does not say what the drug does or how well it works. Unlike product claim ads, reminder ads cannot suggest, in either words or pictures, anything about the drug's benefits or risks. For example, a reminder ad for a drug that helps treat asthma should not include a drawing of a pair of lungs because this implies what the drug does.

Reminder ads are not allowed for certain prescription drugs with serious risks. Drugs with serious risks have a special warning, often called a "boxed warning," in the drug's FDA-approved prescribing information. Because of their seriousness, the risks must be included in all ads for these drugs.

Help-Seeking Advertisements

Help-seeking ads describe a disease or condition but do not recommend or suggest a specific drug treatment. Some examples of diseases or conditions discussed in help-seeking ads include allergies, asthma, erectile dysfunction, high cholesterol, and osteoporosis. The ads encourage people with these symptoms to talk to their doctor. Help-seeking ads may include a drug company's name and may also provide a telephone number to call for more information. When done properly, help-seeking ads are not considered to be drug ads. Therefore, we do not regulate true help-seeking ads, but the FTC does regulate them. If an ad recommends or suggests the use of a specific drug, however, it is considered a product claim ad that must comply with FDA rules.

[. . .]

Risk Disclosure Requirements for Different Types of Advertisements

Different advertisements require different amounts of benefit and risk information. Reminder ads do not have to include any risk information because they cannot include any claims or pictures about what a drug does or how it works. Reminder ads are only for drugs without certain specified serious risks. Print product claim ads may make statements about a drug's benefit(s). They must present the drug's most important risks in the main part of the ad. These ads generally must include every risk, but can present the less important risks in the detailed information known as the "brief summary."

Also, print product claim and reminder ads must include the following statement: "You are encouraged to report negative side effects of prescription drugs to the FDA. [. . .]"

Broadcast product claim ads may make statements about a drug's benefit(s). They must include the drug's most important risk information in a way that is clear, conspicuous, and neutral. In addition, they must include either every risk or provide enough sources for the audience to obtain the drug's prescribing information.

Source E

Feldman, Robin. "Perspective: The Problem with Direct-To-Consumer Pharmaceutical Advertising." The Washington Post, WP Company, 2 Mar. 2023, www.washingtonpost.com/made-by-history/2023/03/02/drug-advertising-consumers/.

The following is a perspective published on the website for a national newspaper.

If only medicines could do everything advertisers claim.

Consider an inspiring ad for an AIDS drug, featuring a former basketball star suggesting the drug can help most or all HIV patients. In reality, however, the drug was only effective for 37 percent of patients. A prescription medication for thicker eyelashes displayed a stunning fashion model on its website, while downplaying the risk that hair could grow outside the treatment area or that the person's eye color could be permanently darkened.

Although supporters of direct-to-consumer advertising contend that the practice provides an important educational resource to patients, research shows that advertising medicine to consumers prompts inappropriate prescriptions, increases adverse patient outcomes and boosts drug prices. The problem may loom even larger as direct-to-consumer telehealth companies and pharmacies move into the online space. A recent investigation found a new danger with quick, online access to medicine: 25 percent of the websites investigated were leaking sensitive patient information to advertising platforms.

From snake oil to opioids, advertising medicine directly to consumers has a long and sordid history in the United States. Well before modern images of talking stomachs or couples in separate bathtubs, drugmakers aggressively marketed cures for a whole host of illnesses, real and invented.

With vibrant names like Hamlin's Wizard Oil and Dr. Kilmer's Swamp Root, such "medicines" tended to keep their actual ingredients — often alcohol or opium — a closely guarded secret. Ultimately, the marketing prowess of the "patent medicine" industry was its own undoing, as public outrage led to increased regulation in the first half of the 20th century. But now, changes in the media landscape have allowed the practice of appealing directly to patients to take off once again — with potential to harm vulnerable communities as in the past. [. . .]

Drugmakers were not required to test the safety of their products, nor was the accuracy of their medical claims verified. These conditions enabled snake oil salesmen to thrive: Tablets made of cannabis and chloroform were advertised for "women's ailments," a mixture of opium and alcohol was marketed to treat rabies, tetanus and "nervous irritability," while strychnine poison was peddled as an aphrodisiac.

These solutions were not just deceptive. They were dangerous.

Public outrage about the fraudulence of "patent medicine" claims led, in part, to the 1906 Pure Food and Drugs Act. The law focused on labeling, and it marked the emergence of the Food and Drug Administration (FDA) as a consumer protection agency.

But the act's shortcomings were tragically exposed in the 1930s when dozens of children died after taking "Elixir Sulfanilamide," a sweetened cough syrup that contained alcohol. Following these tragedies, it was clear that more than labeling was needed. Thus, in 1938, Congress passed the Food, Drug and Cosmetics Act, which mandated safety testing for new drugs, pre-marketing approval by the FDA and beefed-up labeling requirements. [. . .]

The potential for abuse may increase as companies hone their ability to target specific groups of prospective patients, in particular elderly individuals who may be more susceptible to drug advertising. Indeed, the rise of online advertising enables much greater precision for advertisers to target marginalized or vulnerable communities. A predisposition or even a worry about certain medical conditions could be extrapolated from the patient's internet footprint (e.g., internet searching or order history), prompting a drugmaker to bombard the patient with online advertisements for a drug.

This surge of contemporary television and internet advertising has coincided with a notable drop-off in FDA enforcement, perhaps from the sheer volume of work as the agency has been asked to shoulder safety and efficacy issues for medical devices, tobacco products and dietary supplements. The FDA may simply be overwhelmed. Meanwhile, its sister agency, the FTC—which has extensive day-to-day experience regulating all manner of consumer advertising—has been sidelined in the case of advertising medicine, with its jurisdiction primarily restricted to over-the-counter drugs and "self-help" messages.

But these two agencies have the institutional capacity to work together. They have coordinated with other agencies in areas outside of prescription medication and could do so here. For example, the FDA cooperates with the U.S. Department of Agriculture to ensure food safety, and the FTC shares responsibility for merger oversight with the Department of Justice. Clearly, the FTC has the experience and regulatory structure to lead the effort, with an assist from the FDA. The FTC could gauge whether prescription drug advertisements are appropriate from a consumer communication perspective, while directing questions about safety and efficacy to the FDA for evaluation.

Other tweaks to the laws governing drug advertising to consumers could help as well. While banning the practice is worth consideration, it probably won't occur. But lawmakers could rescind the tax deduction that drug manufacturers currently receive for direct-to-consumer advertising expenditures. At a time when legislators scramble to find sources for funding initiatives, this tax benefit could provide an option. Furthermore, boosting regulatory resources through industry user fees could help support the necessary agency effort, irrespective of which agency is at the helm.

As was the case a century ago, more comprehensive oversight of pharmaceutical advertising is warranted. If the United States is going to lead the rest of the world in allowing advertising medicine directly to consumers, its regulatory system should keep pace.

Source F

Aiken, Kathryn J., *et al* "Consumers' Experience with and Attitudes toward Direct-to-Consumer Prescription Drug Promotion: A Nationally Representative Survey." Health Mark Q. 2021 Jan–Mar; 38(1): 1–11, https://www.ncbi.nlm.nih.gov/pmc/articles/PMC8815450/.

The chart below was published in an article about the impact of pharmaceutical marketing.

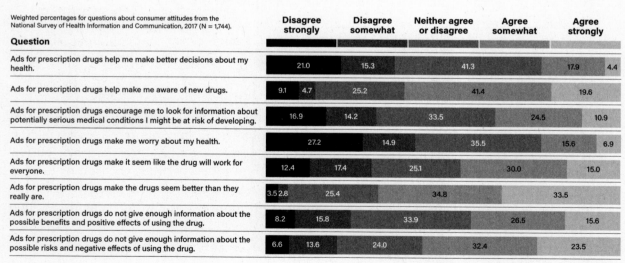

Weighted percentages for questions about consumer attitudes from the National Survey of Health Information and Communication, 2017 (N = 1,744).

Question	Disagree strongly	Disagree somewhat	Neither agree or disagree	Agree somewhat	Agree strongly
Ads for prescription drugs help me make better decisions about my health.	21.0	15.3	41.3	17.9	4.4
Ads for prescription drugs help make me aware of new drugs.	9.1	4.7	25.2	41.4	19.6
Ads for prescription drugs encourage me to look for information about potentially serious medical conditions I might be at risk of developing.	16.9	14.2	33.5	24.5	10.9
Ads for prescription drugs make me worry about my health.	27.2	14.9	35.5	15.6	6.9
Ads for prescription drugs make it seem like the drug will work for everyone.	12.4	17.4	25.1	30.0	15.0
Ads for prescription drugs make the drugs seem better than they really are.	3.5	2.8	25.4	34.8	33.5
Ads for prescription drugs do not give enough information about the possible benefits and positive effects of using the drug.	8.2	15.8	33.9	26.5	15.6
Ads for prescription drugs do not give enough information about the possible risks and negative effects of using the drug.	6.6	13.6	24.0	32.4	23.5

Note. These items were included in the 2002 FDA survey (Aikin et al., 2004).

Prompt

LESSON RA.1 The Rhetorical Analysis Prompt

Eyes on the Exam

Exam readers will evaluate your rhetorical analysis essays based on how effectively you **respond to the specific tasks** required in the prompt.

LEARN

The goal of the Rhetorical Analysis Free-Response Question is to demonstrate your understanding of the choices a writer or speaker makes in a given situation and to express that understanding in a well-developed essay.

Following is a rhetorical analysis prompt modeled on the one you will need to respond to in the free-response section of the exam.

The first paragraph of the prompt provides important **background** information. The final sentence of that paragraph also contains **important directions** explaining the task. The **task** (underlined below) contains key words, such as *read, analyze,* and *write*. It also provides a focus point, narrowing the subject. The final part of the task will always include one of the following phrases: *convey a message* (as in the prompt below), *develop an argument*, or *achieve a purpose*.

The second paragraph contains more **specific directions** for writing and lets you know what the exam readers will be expecting to see. The passage for analysis follows those bulleted directions. (The parts are labeled in the example below, but they are not labeled on the exam.)

[Background]

The Statue of Liberty was officially unveiled in New York on October 28, 1886, and quickly came to symbolize freedom and the American Dream. In preparation for its centennial (100-year) celebration, the statue underwent a two-year restoration from 1984–1986. On the evening of July 3, 1986, then U.S. President Ronald Reagan delivered remarks at the base of the statue that were broadcast across the nation. At the end of his remarks, he turned on the floodlights that illuminated the statue's golden torch. *[Task]* <u>After reading President Reagan's speech, write a well-developed essay in which you analyze how President Reagan makes rhetorical choices to convey his message about American values.</u>

[Specific directions]

In your response you should do the following:

- Respond to the prompt with a thesis that analyzes the writer's rhetorical choices.
- Select and use evidence to develop and support your line of reasoning.
- Explain the relationship between the evidence and your thesis.
- Demonstrate an understanding of the rhetorical situation.
- Use appropriate grammar and punctuation in communicating your argument.

[Passage for analysis]

[1] While we applaud those immigrants who stand out, whose contributions are easily discerned, we know that America's heroes are also those whose names are remembered by only a few. Many of them passed through this harbor, went by this lady, looked up at her torch, which we light tonight in their honor.

[2] They were the men and women who labored all their lives so that their children would be well fed, clothed, and educated, the families that went through great hardship yet kept their honor, their dignity, and their faith in God. They passed on to their children those values, values that define civilization and are the prerequisites of human progress. They worked in our factories, on ships and railroads, in stores, and on road construction crews. They were teachers, lumberjacks, seamstresses, and journalists. They came from every land.

[3] What was it that tied these profoundly different people together? What was it that made them not a gathering of individuals, but a nation? That bond that held them together, as it holds us together tonight, that bond that has stood every test and travail, is found deep in our national consciousness: an abiding love of liberty. For love of liberty, our forebears—colonists, few in number and with little to defend themselves—fought a war for independence with what was then the world's most powerful empire. For love of liberty, those who came before us tamed a vast wilderness and braved hardships which, at times, were beyond the limits of human endurance. For love of liberty, a bloody and heart-wrenching civil war was fought. And for love of liberty, Americans championed and still champion, even in times of peril, the cause of human freedom in far-off lands.

[4] "The God who gave us life," Thomas Jefferson once proclaimed, "gave us liberty at the same time." But like all of God's precious gifts, liberty must never be taken for granted. Tonight we thank God for the many blessings He has bestowed on our land; we affirm our faithfulness to His rule and to our own ideals; and we pledge to keep alive the dream that brought our forefathers and mothers to this brave new land.

[5] On this theme the poet Emma Lazarus, moved by this unique symbol of the love of liberty, wrote a very special dedication 100 years ago. The last few lines[1] are ones we know so well; set to the music of Irving Berlin, they take on tonight a special meaning.

{Here a chorus sings.}

[6] We are the keepers of the flame of liberty. We hold it high tonight for the world to see, a beacon of hope, a light unto the nations. And so with joy and celebration and with a prayer that this lamp shall never be extinguished, I ask that you all join me in this symbolic act of faith, this lighting of Miss Liberty's torch."

---

1 These are the final lines of the poem "The New Colossus" by Emma Lazarus, spoken by the "Mother of Exiles," the Statue of Liberty.

"Give me your tired, your poor,

Your huddled masses yearning to breathe free,

The wretched refuse of your teeming shore.

Send these, the homeless, tempest-tost to me,

I lift my lamp beside the golden door!"

PRACTICE

Complete the following activities.

Part 1 Answer the following questions using the information provided in the **background.**

1. What do you learn about the Statue of Liberty in the background information?

2. What do you learn about President Reagan?

3. In your own words, describe the **task** you are expected to complete.

4. How does the first paragraph narrow the subject?

Part 2 In your own words, describe what the first three bullet points in the **specific directions** ask you to do.

Part 3 Write a sentence that states the main idea of each of the paragraphs in Reagan's speech.

WRITE

Number your paper 1–4. Each number represents a paragraph in a rhetorical analysis essay. Next to each number, describe what that paragraph might contain. You don't have to include details related to this specific prompt. You can just describe the type of information that would be in each paragraph. For example, one thing you might say after #1 is, "This paragraph would contain the thesis statement." Use the information in the different parts of the prompt to help you complete this activity.

Watch this video (tinyurl.com/33ce9eu6) by AP teacher Timm Freitas about breaking down the AP rhetorical analysis prompt. After watching, you may want to revise what you have written for the description of your four paragraphs to add more information.

Watch Beth Hall explain the details of the rhetorical analysis task using the Reagan liberty speech prompt at the companion website (tinyurl.com/2mrx3r99) for this book. There you will find other videos by the authors as well as all the links included in the lessons in this book.

What's the Point? In one sentence, explain how this lesson can help you on the AP English Language and Composition exam.

_____

_____

_____

NOTE: The links included in these lessons have been coded to be ad free. Occasionally you may see a message saying that a video is not available. In that case, just refresh your browser and the video will load.

LESSON RA.2 Unpacking the Prompt: The Rhetorical Situation

Eyes on the Exam

Exam readers will be looking for how effectively you demonstrate an understanding of the prompt, including the rhetorical situation and the background information.

LEARN

Every communication takes place with a rhetorical situation. Writers make key decisions about what to say and how to say it based on their specific situation.

These are the elements in every rhetorical situation:

- **Exigence** (the **impetus** of or reason for the text)
- **Purpose** (the **goals** the writer or speaker wants to achieve)
- **Audience** (**receivers** of the message who often have a variety of needs, values, and beliefs)
- **Writer or speaker** (a **unique voice** with values and beliefs)
- **Context** (the **background**: time, place, and occasion)
- **Message** (the **substance and focus** of the writer's or speaker's main points)

You can picture the rhetorical situation this way.

The Rhetorical Situation

The elements of a rhetorical situation are usually easy to identify. The table on the next page shows the rhetorical situation of the speech by former President Reagan.

Rhetorical Situation of Reagan's 1986 Speech at the Statue of Liberty	
Exigence	The lighting of the Statue of Liberty's recently restored torch on July 3rd (likely in anticipation of July 4th and the centennial celebration)
Purpose	Use the rededication of the Statue of Liberty to address a wide audience of Americans.
Audience	Most likely Americans present at the ceremony and those listening or watching at home
Speaker	Ronald Reagan, who was president at the time
Context	The Statue of Liberty was unveiled in 1886. It was restored in 1984-1986.
Message	According to the prompt, the message of the speech pertains to American values.

Although the prompt contains all the information you need to complete the task, you also likely have some relevant additional knowledge to help you understand this passage. You might ask yourself the following questions related to the different elements of the rhetorical situation. Possible answers are provided in parentheses.

Speaker

1. What are the *needs, beliefs,* or *values* of the speaker? (Given his role as U.S. President, Reagan likely values the American Dream, freedom, hard work, history, and tradition.)

2. What, if any, relevant outside information do you know about the speaker? (Reagan was the 40th president (1981–1989); he was a Republican from California.)

Audience

3. What *needs, beliefs,* or *values* does the audience presumably share? (The audience likely shares many of the same values as the president.)

4. Will the audience likely be receptive, reluctant, or defensive upon hearing the speaker's message? Why? (The audience will likely be receptive to the message since it addresses shared beliefs and values.)

Context

5. What, if any, relevant *background information* do you know about the context—in this case, for example, the late 1800s, the Statue of Liberty, and/or Ellis Island? (The Statue of Liberty has a poem by Emma Lazarus on the pedestal. Those emigrating from Europe primarily entered the U.S. through Ellis Island. America was then known as the "melting pot," suggesting that immigrants aspired to assimilate into American culture.)

6. To what extent is the topic relevant today? (Immigration is still a relevant issue today, though the metaphor of the "melting pot" has been replaced with the metaphor of the "salad bowl" to embrace America's diverse population.)

Message

7. What are examples of the *focus* of the prompt (in this case, "American values")? ("American values" can include freedom, hard work, and diversity, among others.)

After you've read a prompt, label the components of the rhetorical situation, such as by adding **S** above the speaker's name (President Reagan) or **C** above the context (rededication of the Statue of Liberty). Or, you may decide to add notes about the rhetorical situation or any background information in the margin.

KEY POINT: Adding labels or notes can help you remember to connect the rhetorical choices to the rhetorical situation when you begin planning and writing.

PRACTICE

Read the following prompt based on a speech by former President Barack Obama. Note that this prompt uses the phrase *achieve his purpose* rather than *convey his message* as in the Reagan prompt. Label the components of the rhetorical situation: **S** for speaker, **A** for Audience, **C** for Context, **E** for Exigence, and **M** for Message. You will read excerpts from the speech in the next lesson.

On May 19, 2013, then president Barack Obama delivered a commencement speech to the graduating class of Morehouse College, an all-male, historically Black college in Atlanta, Georgia, established in 1867. Read the excerpt of the speech carefully and analyze how President Obama makes rhetorical choices to achieve his purpose of inspiring the graduates.

WRITE

Answer the following questions related to the different elements of the rhetorical situation to recall additional background information you already know about Obama.

Speaker

1. Given his role as U.S. President, what does Obama presumably *need, believe,* or *value*?
2. What, if any, relevant outside information do you know about Obama's presidency?

Audience

3. What *needs, beliefs,* or *values* does the audience presumably share?
4. Will the audience likely be receptive, reluctant, or defensive upon hearing Obama's message? Why?

Context

5. What, if any, relevant background information do you know about the time period of the founding of Morehouse?
6. To what extent is the topic of inspiring graduates relevant today?

Message

7. What are examples of the *focus* of the prompt? In other words, what other sources might provide inspiration for college graduates or young people in general?.

 Watch this video (tinyurl.com/y38mdwbd) from the Jamestown University Writing Center. It explains the rhetorical situation from the point of view of the writer instead of the reader and may help you understand rhetorical choices.

What's the Point? In one sentence, explain how this lesson can help you on the AP English Language and Composition exam.

_____

_____

_____

TEAM UP

Work in small groups as your teacher directs. Each group should collect a few text messages they have sent or received (ensuring privacy and appropriateness). These messages can be real or created for the purpose of this exercise. Then discuss the following:

- The intended audience of the message.
- The purpose of the message (inform, persuade, entertain, for example).
- The context in which the message was sent (time, location, relationship between sender and receiver).
- How the message might be interpreted differently if any of these elements were changed.

Each group should then present one of their text messages and their analysis to the class, explaining how the rhetorical situation influenced the content and style of the text message.

Remember that every communication, even a text message exchange, takes place within a rhetorical situation. In the exchanges to the left, the high school student communicates one way with her mother and another way with her friend Izzy even though the **message** is not that different. These exchanges show the strong influence the **audience** and **purpose** have on the choices a writer makes.

LESSON RA.3 Annotating the Passage

Eyes on the Exam

Given the time constraints of the exam, develop and use a system of **meaningful annotations** to help you quickly understand the passage.

LEARN

In the previous lesson, you annotated the prompt to identify the rhetorical situation and answer questions about your prior knowledge. After you have then read and understood the passage, annotating the passage itself is another useful strategy. "What/Why" annotations can be an efficient way to mark up the passage. The chart below shows some examples of what a speaker might do and why a speaker might do that. The items in the "What?" column are rhetorical choices. The "Why?" column explains their effect on the audience.

What?	Why?
Ask questions	Makes the listener think and feel connected
Make strong word choices	Appeals to the listener's emotions
Repeat words or sentence structures	Emphasizes the repeated idea
Use a serious tone	Elevates the importance of the idea
Tell personal anecdotes (brief stories)	Engages the listener's empathy
Use humor	Creates bond with audience through laughter
Quote authorities	Establishes trust with the listener

For example, you might answer the "what" and "why" questions about paragraph 2 of the Reagan speech as shown below. You can make a simple chart like the one shown, or you can write your "What?" notes in the left margin of the passage and your "Why?" notes in the right margin. You can also underline or circle words within the passage.

What?	Paragraph 2	Why?
Starts with questions Repeats "that bond" 4 repetitions of "love of liberty" 4 sentences in a row with the same structure	What was it that tied these profoundly different people together? What was it that made them not a gathering of individuals, but a nation? That bond that held them together, as it holds us together tonight, that bond that has stood every test and travail, is found deep in our national consciousness: an abiding love of liberty. For love of liberty, our forebears—colonists, few in number and with little to defend themselves—fought a war for independence with what was then the world's most powerful empire. For love of liberty, those who came before us tamed a vast wilderness and braved hardships which, at times, were beyond the limits of human endurance. For love of liberty, a bloody and heart-wrenching civil war was fought. And for love of liberty, Americans championed and still champion, even in times of peril, the cause of human freedom in far-off lands.	Questions get audience actively engaged Repetition emphasizes bond Repetition emphasizes love of liberty The repeated sentence structure creates rising drama

To streamline the process and conserve space, you may consider using abbreviations or bullet points.

Q's	What was it that tied these profoundly different people together? What was it that made them not a gathering of individuals, but a nation? <u>That bond</u> that held them together, as it holds us together tonight, <u>that bond</u> that has stood every test and travail, is found deep in our national consciousness: an abiding love of liberty. . . .	*Engages*
Reps "bond" and "love of lib."		*emphasizes*

> **KEY POINT: "What/Why" annotations** help you engage with the passage as you reread. These annotations will help you with future steps in the writing process.

PRACTICE

Using the "What/Why" annotations on paragraph 2 above as a model, add "What/Why" annotations for paragraphs 3–5 below. Find the annotation style that suits you best.

What?	Paragraph 3	Why?
	"The God who gave us life," Thomas Jefferson once proclaimed, "gave us liberty at the same time." But like all of God's precious gifts, liberty must never be taken for granted. Tonight we thank God for the many blessings He has bestowed on our land; we affirm our faithfulness to His rule and to our own ideals; and we pledge to keep alive the dream that brought our forefathers and mothers to this brave new land.	

Paragraph 4

On this theme the poet Emma Lazarus, moved by this unique symbol of the love of liberty, wrote a very special dedication 100 years ago. The last few lines are ones we know so well; set to the music of Irving Berlin, they take on tonight a special meaning.

Paragraph 5

We are the keepers of the flame of liberty. We hold it high tonight for the world to see, a beacon of hope, a light unto the nations. And so with joy and celebration and with a prayer that this lamp shall never be extinguished, I ask that you all join me in this symbolic act of faith, this lighting of Miss Liberty's torch.

WRITE

The prompt you analyzed in Lesson RA.2 refers to the following excerpts from Barack Obama's commencement speech at Morehouse College. (The paragraphs are numbered for easy reference.] Read the passage once through to understand the main message. Then annotate the passage with "what" and "why" notes showing what rhetorical choices Obama made and why he might have made them given the rhetorical situation. Underline or circle words with special impact. Two examples are done for you.

What?	Obama's Speech at Morehouse	Why?
Refers to Benjamin Mays and quotes him	[1] Benjamin Mays, who served as the president of Morehouse for almost 30 years, understood [the school's sense of pride] better than anybody. He said—and I quote—"It will not be sufficient for Morehouse College, for any college, for that matter, to produce clever graduates . . . but rather <u>honest</u> men, men who can be trusted in public and private life—men who are sensitive to the wrongs, the sufferings, and the injustices of society and who are willing to accept responsibility for correcting [those] ills."	*Establishes a sense of honor and integrity*
Gives historical context	[2] It was that mission—not just to educate men, but to <u>cultivate good men</u>, strong men, upright men—that brought community leaders together just two years after the end of the Civil War. They assembled a list of 37 men, free blacks and freed slaves, who would make up the first prospective class of what later became Morehouse College. Most of those first students had a desire to become teachers and preachers—to better themselves so they could help others do the same.	*History reminds listeners of long tradition*
	[3] A century and a half later, times have changed. But the "Morehouse Mystique" still endures. Some of you probably came here from communities where everybody looked like you. Others may have come here in search of a community. And I suspect that some of you probably felt a little bit of culture shock the first time you came together as a class in King's Chapel. All of a sudden, you weren't the only high school sports captain, you weren't the only student council president. You were suddenly in a group of <u>high achievers,</u> and that meant you were expected to do something more.	
	[4] That's the unique sense of purpose that this place has always infused—the conviction that this is a training ground not only for individual success, but for leadership that can change the world.	

[5] Dr. King was just 15 years old when he enrolled here at Morehouse. He was an unknown, undersized, unassuming young freshman who lived at home with his parents. And I think it's fair to say he wasn't the coolest kid on campus—for the suits he wore, his classmates called him "Tweed." But his education at Morehouse helped to forge the intellect, the discipline, the compassion, the soul force that would transform America. It was here that he was introduced to the writings of Gandhi and Thoreau, and the theory of civil disobedience. It was here that professors encouraged him to look past the world as it was and fight for the world as it should be. And it was here, at Morehouse, as Dr. King later wrote, where "I realized that nobody . . . was afraid."

[6] Not even of some bad weather. I added on that part. (Laughter.) I know it's wet out there. But Dr. Wilson told me you all had a choice and decided to do it out here anyway. (Applause.) That's a Morehouse Man talking. Now, think about it. For black men in the '40s and the '50s, the threat of violence, the constant humiliations, large and small, the uncertainty that you could support a family, the gnawing doubts born of the Jim Crow culture that told you every day that somehow you were inferior, the temptation to shrink from the world, to accept your place, to avoid risks, to be afraid— that temptation was necessarily strong.

[7] And yet, here, under the tutelage of men like Dr. Mays, young Martin learned to be unafraid. And he, in turn, taught others to be unafraid. And over time, he taught a nation to be unafraid. And over the last 50 years, thanks to the moral force of Dr. King and a Moses generation that overcame their fear and their cynicism and their despair, barriers have come tumbling down, and new doors of opportunity have swung open, and laws and hearts and minds have been changed to the point where someone who looks just like you can somehow come to serve as President of these United States of America. (Applause.)

[8] So the history we share should give you hope. The future we share should give you hope. You're graduating into an improving job market. You're living in a time when advances in technology and communication put the world at your fingertips. Your generation is uniquely poised for success unlike any generation of African Americans that came before it.

[9] But that doesn't mean we don't have work—because if we're honest with ourselves, we know that too few of our brothers have the opportunities that you've had here at Morehouse. In troubled neighborhoods all across this country—many of them heavily African American—too few of our citizens have role models to guide them. Communities just a couple miles from my house in Chicago, communities just a couple miles from here—they're places where jobs are still too scarce and wages are still too low; where schools are underfunded and violence is pervasive; where too many of our men spend their youth not behind a desk in a classroom, but hanging out on the streets or brooding behind a jail cell.

[10] My job, as President, is to advocate for policies that generate more opportunity for everybody—policies that strengthen the middle class and give more people the chance to climb their way into the middle class. Policies that create more good jobs and reduce poverty, and educate more children, and give more families the security of health care, and protect more of our children from the horrors of gun violence. That's my job. Those are matters of public policy, and it is important for all of us—black, white and brown—to advocate for an America where everybody has got a fair shot in life. Not just some. Not just a few. (Applause.)

[11] But along with collective responsibilities, we have individual responsibilities. There are some things, as black men, we can only do for ourselves. There are some things, as Morehouse Men, that you are obliged to do for those still left behind. As Morehouse Men, you now wield something even more powerful than the diploma you're about to collect—and that's the power of your example. So what I ask of you today is the same thing I ask of every graduating class I address: Use that power for something larger than yourself. Live up to President Mays's challenge. Be "sensitive to the wrongs, the sufferings, and the injustices of society." And be "willing to accept responsibility for correcting [those] ills."

Watch Obama deliver the entirety of <u>his speech to Morehouse graduates</u> (tinyurl.com/yc6w4s8b). (The portion of the speech presented here starts at 6:10 in the recording.) After watching, you may want to make additional annotations to the excerpts above.

What's the Point? In one or two sentences, explain how this lesson can help you on the AP Language and Composition exam.

_____

_____

_____

TEAM UP

Meet in small groups as your teacher directs. Compare your "What?" and "Why?" notes with those of your group members. Go through the passage paragraph by paragraph, sharing what you noted. As you go, discuss differences among the group's annotations, especially in the "Why?" column. Revise your annotations as you see fit after the discussion.

Next, plan a commencement speech that any one of your group members might deliver at a middle school graduation in your district. Outline the components of the rhetorical situation in the chart below. Given the other elements of the rhetorical situation, decide on what message you want to convey.

Rhetorical Situation of Middle School Commencement Speech	
Exigence	
Purpose	
Audience	
Speaker	
Context	
Message	

Keeping in mind the needs, beliefs, and values of the audience, plan out the basic outline of a speech you might deliver from the perspective of someone who has experienced high school and the changes that can take place between middle school and high school. Identify what you might address in the beginning, middle, and ending of the speech. Then discuss with your group what rhetorical choices (the "whats" you might make in each part of the speech) and the effect (the "whys") you hope each would have on the audience. Think of a few specific examples and write them down. For example, you might say, "In the first paragraph, I might tell a story from the day I was in their shoes at middle school graduation. I hope it will have the effect of establishing a connection with the graduates." Or, "In the second paragraph, I might ask students to reflect on what they learned from middle school. By asking questions, I might keep them listening and paying attention."

Share the plan for your speech and examples of rhetorical choices with the rest of the class when everyone has finished.

LESSON RA.4 Lines of Reasoning

Eyes on the Exam

Exam readers will look for your understanding of a text's line of reasoning as well as for your ability to establish a line of reasoning in your own writing.

LEARN

The **line of reasoning** is the logical sequence of ideas that work together to justify the overall message or claim of a speaker or writer. Dividing a passage into sections can help you follow the speaker's line of reasoning. Each section contributes a key idea to the text and helps justify the main idea. Shorter passages may have only two sections, but longer passages may have three or more sections. Sections in a text do not have to be equal in length.

Many exam-length passages can be divided into three main parts: beginning, middle, and end. To identify where one section ends and the next begins, look for shifts in topic or ideas, rhetorical choice, or tone. These shifts help identify the "movements" of the passage.

In the Reagan speech, for example, shifts might be noted at the following points in this abbreviated version. (You can read the entire speech on page 116.)

[1] While we applaud those immigrants who stand out, whose contributions are easily discerned, we know that America's heroes are also those whose names are remembered by only a few . . . .

[2] They were the men and women who labored all their lives . . . . They worked in our factories, on ships and railroads, in stores, and on road construction crews. They were teachers, lumberjacks, seamstresses, and journalists. They came from every land.

The key idea of paragraphs 1 and 2 is that immigrants remembered only by their families passed by here from all over the world and worked hard.

[3] What was it that tied these profoundly different people together? What was it that made them not a gathering of individuals, but a nation? . . . And for love of liberty, Americans championed and still champion, even in times of peril, the cause of human freedom in far-off lands.

A shift happens in paragraph 3 when Reagan asks questions, and the idea shifts from the arrival of people from different places to the bond that unites them—the love of liberty. He goes on to give historical examples of Americans championing liberty. The tone also becomes more serious and dramatic.

[4] "The God who gave us life," Thomas Jefferson once proclaimed, "gave us liberty at the same time." But like all of God's precious gifts, liberty must never be taken for granted. Tonight we thank God for the many blessings . . . and we pledge to keep alive the dream that brought our forefathers and mothers to this brave new land.

Another shift happens in paragraph 4. Reagan quotes a founding father and with the word "but" shifts to make the key point that liberty can't be taken for granted. Everyone needs to pledge to keep it alive.

[5] On this theme the poet Emma Lazarus, moved by this unique symbol of the love of liberty, wrote a very special dedication 100 years ago . . . [that] take[s] on tonight a special meaning.

[6] We are the keepers of the flame of liberty. . . . I ask that you all join me in this symbolic act of faith, this lighting of Miss Liberty's torch.

Paragraph 5 appeals to the values and emotions of the audience with the stirring words of the poem. Paragraph 6 then calls everyone to commit to keeping liberty safe.

Reagan's line of reasoning can be expressed as follows:

1. The United States was built by hard-working immigrants from many lands. (paragraphs 1 and 2)

2. Despite their many differences, these people were united by a love of liberty. Americans have continued to champion liberty throughout history. (paragraph 3)

3. From the nation's founding, people knew that liberty could not be taken for granted. Everyone has an obligation to keep it alive. (paragraph 4)

4. The poem on the Statue of Liberty movingly recognizes the symbolic power of the statue. Reagan asks everyone to be part of the lighting of the torch as the keepers of the flame. (paragraphs 5 and 6)

One way to section the speech into beginning, middle, and end is as follows:

• Beginning—paragraphs 1 and 2
• Middle—paragraphs 3 and 4
• End—paragraphs 5 and 6

Note that there are often several ways to divide a text. As long as you have an explanation for your divisions, do not worry if they are the "right" ones.

Use the divisions you created and the line of reasoning you identified to write claims about what happens in the beginning, middle, and end of the text. For the Reagan speech, those claims may appear as follows.

1. Reagan begins his speech by acknowledging the contributions of diverse immigrants to emphasize the crucial role they have played in American history.

2. Reagan continues by underscoring the value of liberty that has united America for generations but points out that it cannot be taken for granted.

3. Reagan concludes his speech at the torch-lighting ceremony by unifying the crowd to further reinforce the value of liberty in American society and the need to keep it alive.

KEY POINT: Determine the **line of reasoning** by dividing the text into different sections and identifying the key idea of each section. Use this analysis to write claims about what happens in the beginning, middle, and end of the text.

PRACTICE

Part 1 Divide Obama's speech at Morehouse College into sections based on shifts in topic or idea, rhetorical choices, or tone. Annotate the text on pages 124–126 to show its divisions. Add brief notes about the shifts you see.

Part 2 Based on the divisions you created, on separate paper describe Obama's line of reasoning in a numbered list like that on page 129.

Part 3 Mark the speech to show the beginning, middle, and end.

WRITE

Write a claim about what Obama does in each section. Use the provided sentence frames if needed.

1. Obama begins his speech by . . . to . . .
2. Obama continues by . . . because . . .
3. Obama concludes his commencement speech at Morehouse College by . . . to . . . .

While Reagan focused on newcomers to America, this 1923 speech by Ruth Muskrat Bronson to President Calvin Coolidge (tinyurl.com/mtw4bc3p) presents the perspective of Native Americans. Read it and identify its parts and line of reasoning.

Miss Ruth Muskrat, a Cherokee Indian, presents Mr. Coolidge with a copy of *The Red Man in the United States*, a survey of the present day American Indian, December 13, 1923.

Source: Library of Congress

What's the Point? In one or two sentences, explain how this lesson can help you on the AP Language and Composition exam.

_____

_____

_____

LESSON RA.5 Identifying Rhetorical Choices

Eyes on the Exam

The first bullet point in the directions of the rhetorical analysis prompt requires you to "respond to the prompt with a thesis that analyzes the writer's rhetorical choices." Knowledge of **rhetorical choices** will help you carry out this part of the directions.

LEARN

Rhetorical choices are the strategic decisions a speaker or writer makes when creating a message. They are the "what" you have been identifying in previous lessons. These choices go beyond the basic mechanics of language into the intentional use of devices, structures, and appeals to achieve an outcome or a specific effect on the audience. The "achieve an outcome or specific effect" is the "why" you have been noting.

Sometimes a writer may make a rhetorical choice to use a rhetorical device. A *rhetorical device* is something the speaker "uses." Therefore, when writing about devices, use nouns. Conversely, a *rhetorical choice* is something the speaker "does." Therefore, when writing about rhetorical choices, use verbs.

Review the table of common rhetorical devices and choices before proceeding to the practice section.

Rhetorical Devices or Appeals (Noun Form)	Rhetorical Choices (Verb Form)
Allusion	alludes to, implies, references
Anecdote	recalls a time when, recounts an experience when, reminisces on/about
Call to Action	calls, galvanizes, implores, rouses, rallies
Comparison (Allusion, Analogy, Metaphor, Simile)	compares X to Y, equates X to Y
Definition	clarifies the meaning of X, defines X, redefines X
Description/Imagery	describes, offers a detailed description of, provides a detailed account of, vividly describes
Diction	includes the term "...," incorporates the phrase "...," incorporates ____ language (such as formal or informal)
Examples/Exemplification	exemplifies, lists examples of, offers examples of, provides an example of
Juxtaposition	contrasts, juxtaposes

Rhetorical Devices or Appeals (Noun Form)	Rhetorical Choices (Verb Form)
Organization	organizes, structures, moves from . . . to, varies sentence structure
Pronoun Use	incorporates inclusive diction, includes divisive diction, directly addresses the audience
Repetition	echoes, repeats
Logos	appeals to logic, logically asserts
Ethos	bolsters his/her credibility, strengthens his/her credibility, testifies that
Pathos	elicits a sense of " . . . ," evokes a feeling of " . . . "

The directions in the prompt require you to not only identify but also to analyze the writer's rhetorical choices. Analyzing rhetorical choices involves examining how writers or speakers use language and communication strategies to persuade, inform, or engage their audience.

Review Reagan's speech at the Statue of Liberty. These are the rhetorical choices and devices you might identify when analyzing the speech.

Rhetorical Choices and Devices in Reagan's Speech	
Paragraphs 1–2	Lists, diction (word choice), repetition
Paragraphs 3–4	Question, repetition, historical examples, quoting
Paragraphs 5–6	Allusion (to the poem by Emma Lazarus), repetition, pronoun use/inclusive diction

KEY POINT: Review your knowledge of **rhetorical choices** and *devices* so you can efficiently analyze how and why a writer or speaker makes or uses them.

PRACTICE

Make a chart like the one below to identify the rhetorical choices and devices Obama uses in his speech to Morehouse graduates on pages 124–126.

Rhetorical Choices and Devices in Obama's Speech	
Paragraphs 1–4	
Paragraphs 5–7	
Paragraphs 8–11	

WRITE

Look over your list of devices and choices. Then determine one rhetorical choice or device from each section you believe you could write about best. Number your paper 1–3 and write a brief explanation of why you made each determination.

 Use these Quizlet flashcards (tinyurl.com/2p8u4fes) to help you review the variety of rhetorical choices and devices writers and speakers tend to choose. After working your way through the deck, review you list of choices and devices in Obama's speech and make any additions you might have noticed.

What's the Point? In one sentence, explain how this lesson can help you on the AP English Language and Composition exam.

_____

_____

_____

TEAM UP

Practice using rhetorical devices and identifying rhetorical choices by working together in small groups as your teacher directs to complete the following activity.

Your school is organizing a food drive and has released this information about it:

This fall, the Key Club is sponsoring a food drive to help our community food pantries and homeless shelters. Please bring nonperishable food items to school and place them in the receptacles at the south entrance by October 30th.

With your group, decide how to craft a message to be read during announcements that would encourage students to take part in this food drive. As a group, decide which of the choices or devices in the chart in this lesson you will use to shape your message, which should be about a paragraph long. For example, you might choose juxtaposition and begin your paragraph this way:

On any Saturday, you may sit down to lunch at your comfortable home and enjoy a freshly made grilled cheese sandwich and a bowl of tomato soup. On that same Saturday, a number of hungry community members may wait in line at the church whose turn it is to provide the week's soup kitchen. . . .

Collaborating with your group, write a complete paragraph based on the rhetorical strategy you chose. When every group has finished, one member from each group should read the paragraph to the whole class. The class should then determine which rhetorical strategy was used and discuss its effectiveness.

LESSON RA.6 From Claim to Thesis Statement

Eyes on the Exam

On the exam, you'll receive one point for writing a **defensible thesis**.

LEARN

A fact is a statement that can be proven true. A **claim** is an idea asserted to be true but open to disagreement.

> **Fact:** President Reagan gave a speech at the Statue of Liberty on July 3, 1986. (See page 116.)

> **Claim:** In his July 3, 1986 speech at the Statue of Liberty, Ronald Reagan subtly hinted at the need for environmental conservation and awareness.

Nobody can dispute the first statement. The second statement, however, asserts a claim that, in this case, almost *everybody* would dispute. Defending this claim with an argument using the textual evidence in the speech would be challenging, since environmental conservation and awareness are never even mentioned.

> **Defensible Claim:** In his July 3, 1986 speech at the Statue of Liberty, Ronald Reagan's main idea was national unity.

This claim is open to disagreement—not everyone may believe national unity was the *main* idea. However, the speech does include textual evidence that could support or defend an argument developed around this claim.

If you look at the part of the prompt reproduced below, though, you will see that the task and directions ask for more than a claim. They require you to develop a **thesis** analyzing Reagan's **rhetorical choices** to convey a message about American values.

After reading President Reagan's speech, write a well-developed essay in which you analyze how President Reagan makes rhetorical choices to convey his message about American values.

In your response you should do the following:

- Respond to the prompt with a **thesis that analyzes the writer's rhetorical choices.**
- Select and use evidence to develop and support your line of reasoning.
- Explain the relationship between the evidence and your thesis.
- Demonstrate an understanding of the rhetorical situation.
- Use appropriate grammar and punctuation in communicating your argument.

The thesis is the overarching claim of your essay. You can use the last part of the task statement in the prompt as the first step in formulating your thesis by turning it into a question. Your answer to that question becomes a starting point for your thesis.

Turning the task into a question: How does President Reagan make rhetorical choices to convey his message about American values?

Answer (and first step toward thesis statement): President Reagan makes a variety of rhetorical choices to convey his message about American values.

However, that preliminary thesis is actually a fact. No one can deny that Reagan makes rhetorical choices. To create a *defensible* thesis, you need to assert a more specific claim about which rhetorical choices he makes and why he makes them. Think about your "what" and "why" notes to fill in the necessary details. The underlined parts in the defensible thesis below provide those details.

Defensible thesis: In his July 3, 1986, speech at the Statue of Liberty, President Reagan lists diverse immigrants, repeats key words and ideas, and stirs patriotic emotions to convey the message that liberty is one of the most important values Americans share.

Your thesis is like a road map: it tells your reader what your argument is and suggests an order in which your argument will unfold. A thesis can be a single sentence or multiple consecutive sentences.

For rhetorical analysis, you will usually need to refer to two to three major rhetorical choices in your thesis. When listing the choices in your thesis, think about the order in which they appear in the text. A choice at the beginning of the passage should be listed in your thesis before a choice at the end of the passage.

The order of the choices in your thesis determines the order of the body paragraphs in your essay. The first choice in your thesis will be the main idea of your first body paragraph. The second choice will align with your second body paragraph. If you have a third choice, that choice will be the main idea of the third paragraph.

In addition to mentioning the rhetorical choices you intend to analyze in your essay, you should also include the specific message, argument, or purpose in your thesis. The example above accomplishes that through the clause "liberty is one of the most important values Americans share."

On exam day, your rhetorical analysis prompt will include one of the following phrases: **convey a message** (as the Reagan prompt does), **develop an argument,** or **achieve a purpose.** Underline or circle this phrase in the prompt to remind you of your task.

Some prompts will provide a brief explanation of the message, argument, or purpose. In the Reagan prompt, for example, you learn the message is about American values. In these cases, use the brief explanation only as a guide. As you construct your thesis, ask yourself questions about what *values* really means so you can be more specific about the speaker's message, argument, or purpose.

KEY POINT: Your prompt will include one of the following phrases: convey a message, develop an argument, or achieve a purpose. To truly answer the prompt, **your thesis should include the specific message, argument, or purpose**.

PRACTICE

1. The thesis statements below refer to Obama's commencement speech (pages 124–126) and are **not** defensible. Read the statements and write a sentence on separate paper explaining why these thesis statements are not defensible.
    A. President Obama makes several rhetorical choices in his speech.
    B. In his speech, President Obama talks about the Morehouse legacy.

2. The thesis statements below *are* defensible. Circle the specific rhetorical choices and underline the message.

A. In his speech at the 2013 commencement at Morehouse College, then President Barack Obama quotes Benjamin Mays and holds up the example of Dr. King to achieve his purpose of inspiring Morehouse graduates to live up to the important responsibilities they carry out into the world.

B. To highlight the individual responsibilities of "Morehouse Men," President Obama addresses the graduates with inclusive language, focuses on a well-known example, and issues a call to action.

WRITE

Using the provided sentence frame if needed, write a defensible thesis in response to the Morehouse prompt. Circle your rhetorical choices and underline the purpose.

Prompt: On May 19, 2013, then president Barack Obama delivered a commencement speech to the graduating class of Morehouse College, an all-male historically Black college in Atlanta, Georgia established in 1867. Read the excerpt of the speech carefully and analyze how president Obama makes rhetorical choices to achieve his purpose of inspiring the graduates.

Sentence Frame for Thesis

In his [TONE] speech at [EVENT], then President Barack Obama [CHOICE 1 and CHOICE 2] to achieve his purpose of inspiring . . . .

My thesis:

 Watch this video (tinyurl.com/2k6dd7sw) by AP Teacher Beth Hall on writing a defensible thesis and note how you can make a strong thesis when avoiding the word *use*. Revise your thesis to eliminate *use* if it is now in your thesis statement.

What's the Point? In one or two sentences, explain how this lesson can help you on the AP Language and Composition exam.

_____

_____

_____

LESSON RA.7 Crafting an Engaging Introduction

Eyes on the Exam

Although an introduction is not required on the AP English Language and Composition exam, developing one that includes your defensible thesis may provide an opportunity to add depth and sophistication.

LEARN

Think of an introduction as an inverted triangle. Your introduction should start broadly and become more specific. This type of introductory paragraph has three common components: hook, context, and thesis.

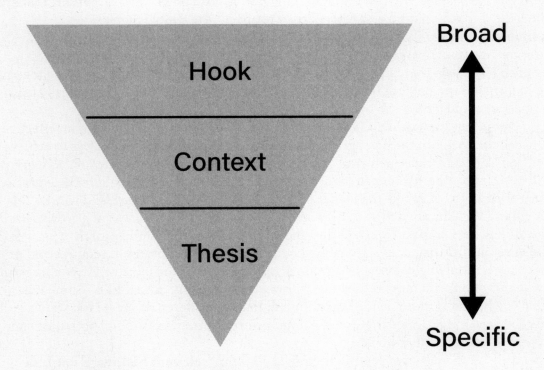

- A **hook** is an engaging opening, typically one to two sentences.
- The **context** is an explanation of the specific elements of the rhetorical situation of the passage.
- The **thesis** is the overarching claim of the essay that mentions the specific rhetorical choices you intend to analyze in your essay.

You may find it challenging to come up with a hook under time pressure. If so, focus on the context and the thesis. *You don't need a long introductory paragraph for a timed essay; spend most of your time developing your body paragraphs instead.*

In Lesson RA.6, you practiced writing a defensible thesis. But what about the other components of an introduction? How do you write an effective hook and provide adequate context? The chart on the next page provides examples of weak hooks and more effective hooks. Avoid the types of hooks identified in the first column. Below the chart are examples. They are sentences that would come before the thesis statement.

Less Effective Hooks	More Effective Hooks
• Rhetorical questions • Trite expressions (since the dawn of time or throughout history) • Quotes • First person statements (In this essay, I'm going to tell you about…)	• Meaningful fragments • Universal truths • Vivid description • False assumptions (that you will challenge) • Relevant historical context

A **meaningful fragment** is a short, powerful thought that is not a complete sentence. The meaningful fragment should be related to the topic or theme of the passage in some way. You'll likely need to provide another sentence after the meaningful fragment to smoothly clarify the connection to the passage. EXAMPLE: A melting pot. A salad bowl. These are terms that are sometimes used to express the great diversity of people in the United States.

A **universal truth** is a general statement that applies to a broad range of situations, including the one in the passage. The universal statement does not mention the specific speaker of the passage—that happens in the context. EXAMPLE: When people come together, uniting in purpose and pooling their resources, skills, and perspectives, they typically achieve more than they could alone.

If you enjoy creative writing, **vivid description** may be more your style for an effective hook. Just as the writer of the passage you are analyzing made rhetorical choices to achieve a purpose, you, too, can make rhetorical choices to craft an engaging introduction. To work well, the vivid description should be related to the topic of the passage and should include precise adjectives or adverbs to "hook" the reader. EXAMPLE: The night was dark and windy. The speaker's stand was illuminated with decorative, golden lights in the shape of a crown. Beyond that, the dark waters around Liberty Island showed no sign of the familiar torch.

A **false assumptions** hook is arguably the most challenging because it requires you to anticipate a commonly held false assumption about the topic of the passage. After addressing the false assumption, you must refute it, or show why it is wrong. EXAMPLE: Some may think that the nation is more divided than united, that our differences create too wide a gulf to bridge. However, the United States has a long history of strength through both unity and diversity, both in the spirit of liberty.

Depending on the passage, you might know additional **relevant historical context** about the speaker, audience, or time period. Additionally, you might find relevant details in the passage that could help you use a broader understanding of the historical context as an effective hook. EXAMPLE: In 1986, as President Reagan gave his remarks on the lighting of the Statue of Liberty, the United States and the Soviet Union were in a Cold War (1947–1991). The central conflict stemmed from the clash between two opposing ideologies: American capitalism and democracy versus Soviet communism. Both sides actively promoted their systems and competed for influence around the world. Reagan used the opportunity of rededicating the Statue of Liberty to remind the world of the liberty cherished by Americans.

See how the hook, context, and thesis work together in the paragraph below. The hook is in *italics*, the context is <u>underlined</u>, and the thesis is in **bold type.**

Sample Introductory Paragraph

Some may think that our nation is more divided than united, that our differences create too wide a gulf to bridge. However, the United States has a long history of strength through both unity and diversity, both in the spirit of liberty. <u>This was the theme President Ronald Reagan chose to emphasize in his speech on July 3, 1986, at the lighting of the torch of the newly restored Statue of Liberty.</u> **President Reagan lists diverse immigrants, repeats key words and ideas, and stirs patriotic emotions to convey the message that liberty is one of the most important values Americans share.**

> **KEY POINT: Introductory paragraphs** commonly contain three parts: **hook, context, and thesis.** For timed essays, a hook is optional. However, do include appropriate specifics about the rhetorical situation and a defensible thesis to avoid a jarringly abrupt introduction.

PRACTICE

The examples below are in response to the prompt about the speech by Obama at Morehouse College (pages 124–126). Read the examples of effective hooks below and determine which type of hook each is: a meaningful fragment, a universal truth, a vivid description, a false assumption, or relevant historical context. Some examples might contain more than one technique.

1. On January 9, 2009, for the first time in American history, an African American— Barack Obama—was inaugurated as President of the United States. Four years later, he was inaugurated for his second term. And just a few months after that, this barrier-breaking president visited Morehouse College, a historically all-Black male school, to present the commencement address.

2. Proud parents endured a soaking rain on May 19, 2013, tempered by warm humor from the speaker of the day, President Barack Obama.

3. Individual responsibilities. In 2013, Morehouse graduates heard an inspiring speech stressing the obligation graduates have to take on their individual responsibilities.

4. Everyone stands on the shoulders of those who have come before.

5. Some may think that when Black American men graduate from college, they turn their backs on the neighborhoods they grew up in or the problems that less privileged Black Americans may face. Try telling that to a "Morehouse Man," especially after the inspiring commencement address they heard from then-President Barack Obama in May of 2013.

WRITE

Select one of the five methods for crafting an engaging hook and create one that is different from the examples above. Write an introductory paragraph in response to the prompt about President Obama's speech at Morehouse (pages 124–126). Your paragraph should contain a hook, context, and thesis.

 Visit this site (tinyurl.com/yc4prh3a) to get another perspective on the introductory paragraph. It includes two videos—one on hooks and one on background. When you have finished reading and watching, revise your paragraph if appropriate.

What's the Point? In one sentence, explain how this lesson can help you on the AP English Language and Composition exam.

_____

_____

_____

TEAM UP

In small groups, take turns reading your introductory paragraphs aloud. After each reading, the group should provide constructive feedback, focusing specifically on the effectiveness of the hook and its connection to the overall argument of the rhetorical analysis. Feedback should consider how well the hook:

- Engages the reader
- Sets the tone
- Introduces the main focus of the analysis

After that discussion, collaboratively create a different type of hook for each paragraph from the "More Effective Hooks" column of the chart on page 138. Compare the effectiveness of the hooks.

Conclude the activity with a reflection on the various strategies for creating effective hooks and how these strategies can be applied to future writing tasks. Each member should share key takeaways and insights gained from the activity.

LESSON RA.8 Topic Sentences for Body Paragraphs

Eyes on the Exam

Constructing effective topic sentences will help you clarify your line of reasoning and move smoothly from one idea to the next in your rhetorical analysis essays.

LEARN

A topic sentence is usually the first sentence of a body paragraph. It is a claim that conveys the main idea of the paragraph. Since topic sentences also help writers move from one main idea to the next, effective topic sentences also clarify the line of reasoning of the essay. For a rhetorical analysis essay, a strong topic sentence will include the "what" (the choice) and the "why" (the reason the choice was used).

Your thesis is a road map to your line of reasoning, so it also provides direction for your topic sentences. Topic sentences tell the reader the main idea of each body paragraph.

Consider the following first-draft thesis statement in response to the Reagan prompt.

Thesis Statement: In his July 3, 1986, speech at the Statue of Liberty, President Reagan lists diverse immigrants, repeats key words and ideas, and stirs patriotic emotions to convey the message that liberty is one of the most important values Americans share.

The three **rhetorical choices** mentioned in that thesis are *listing examples, repeating key words and phrases*, and *appealing to emotions*. Each of the choices will become the focus of a body paragraph that begins with a strong topic sentence and then includes plentiful evidence from the speech. The order in which the choices are mentioned is the order in which the topic sentences and their paragraphs should appear. Typically, this order follows the order of the rhetorical choices in the text.

The topic sentences built into this thesis statement might be as follows:

Topic sentence for the first body paragraph: President Reagan offers examples of diverse workers and occupations to highlight both the immigrants' unique skills and their importance to the building of the nation. (This relates to listing examples.)

Topic sentence for the second body paragraph: President Reagan repeats "bond" and "love of liberty" to emphasize the ties that unify Americans despite their differences. (This relates to repeating key words and phrases.)

Topic sentence for the third body paragraph: As he concludes his speech, President Reagan stirs listeners with the moving ideals of liberty and each person's responsibility to keep it safe. (This relates to the appeal to emotions.)

Note that although the topic sentences connect back to each idea in the thesis, they do not use the same wording as the thesis. For example, if it simply picked up the wording from the thesis, the first sentence might begin: President Reagan lists diverse immigrants . . . . Varying the wording of your thesis statement as you compose your topic sentences will avoid repetitiveness and add interest to your essay.

The final topic sentence shows how topic sentences can serve as transitions from one part of your line of reasoning to another with the clause "As he concludes his speech." With that in mind, you can link the other topic sentences clearly by reworking them with similar phrases and clauses. The first topic sentence might start with "As he begins his speech . . . ." The second might start with "After acknowledging the diversity and importance of immigrants through well-chosen examples, Reagan then shifts to . . . ." Use your understanding of the beginning, middle, and end of the text (see Lesson RA.4) to help you write these transitional connections.

> **KEY POINT:** Look to your **thesis statement** for the **main ideas and order of your topic sentences.** Link them with **transitions** that show how your ideas are moving from the beginning of the speech to the end.

PRACTICE

Analyze your thesis statement to clearly identify the language that corresponds with each of your main ideas. Write it out and then underline the first main idea, circle or italicize the second main idea, and put the third main idea, if you have one, inside a box or in bold type, just so you can see the separate parts. You can also color code them with highlighting—green for idea one, yellow for idea two, and blue for idea three, for example.

WRITE

Write a topic sentence for each of your body paragraphs. You may use any of the provided sentence frames as needed, modifying them according to the specifics of your thesis. Underline or highlight the parts of each topic sentence that match the marking you did in your thesis.

Frames for Body Paragraphs
Body Paragraph 1
• [SPEAKER] begins by [insert first rhetorical choice] in order to [insert PURPOSE].
• [SPEAKER] begins by [insert first rhetorical choice], thus establishing his message that [insert MESSAGE].
• In order to [insert PURPOSE], [SPEAKER] begins his speech by [insert first rhetorical choice].
Body Paragraphs 2–3
• [SPEAKER] continues by [insert second rhetorical choice] to [insert PURPOSE].
• In order to further [insert PURPOSE], [SPEAKER] continues by [insert rhetorical choice].
• [SPEAKER] then shifts from [main idea of body paragraph 1] to [main idea of body paragraph 2].
• Having already established that [refer to the main idea of body paragraph 1], [SPEAKER] then [introduce the main idea of body paragraph 2].
• [SPEAKER] concludes his speech by [insert rhetorical choice] in order to [insert PURPOSE].

Watch AP teacher <u>Timm Freitas present topic sentence templates</u> (tinyurl.com/mwcebvd). After you watch, review your work and make any changes you think will improve your topic sentences.

What's the Point? In one or two sentences, explain how this lesson can help you on the AP Language and Composition exam.

_____

_____

_____

Eyes on the Exam

Readers will score your thesis based on Row A in the Rhetorical Analysis rubric.

LEARN

Carefully read each section of the Row A rubric and scoring guide. You will answer questions about this part of the rubric on the next page.

- Note the **[1.A, 4.B]** at the end of the second row. They refer to the skills in the Course and Exam Description on which the score will be based. Skill 1.A is "Identify and describe components of the rhetorical situation: the exigence, audience, writer, purpose, context, and message." Skill 4.B is "Write a thesis statement that requires proof or defense and that may preview the structure of the argument."

- The first row under "Row A: Thesis . . ." explains in general terms how a response can fail to receive the point (first column). The second column explains, also in general terms, what a response needs to do to earn the point.

- The row beneath that provides general examples of ways to miss or earn the point.

- The second to the last row provides specific examples of the items in the previous row.

- The final row provides additional clarifications for acceptable thesis statements.

QUESTION 2: Rhetorical Analysis	
Row A: Thesis (0-1 points), Scoring Criteria [1,A, 4.B]	
0 points	**1 point**
For any of the following:	Responds to the prompt with a defensible thesis that analyzes the writer's rhetorical choices.
• There is no defensible thesis. • The intended thesis only restates the prompt. • The intended thesis provides a summary of the issue with no apparent or coherent claim. • There is a thesis, but it does not respond to the prompt.	
Responses that do not earn this point:	**Responses that earn this point:**
Only restate the prompt. Fail to address the rhetorical choices the writer of the passage makes. Describe or repeat the passage rather than making a claim that requires a defense.	Respond to the prompt rather than restate or rephrase the prompt and clearly articulate a defensible thesis about the rhetorical choices Reagan makes to convey his message.

Examples that do not earn this point:	Examples that earn this point:
Restate the prompt	**Present a defensible thesis that analyzes the writer's rhetorical choices**
"Reagan gave a speech when the Statue of Liberty's torch was rededicated in 1986."	*"With inclusive language and emphasizing the ties that bind Americans, Reagan used the rededication of the Statue of Liberty as an opportunity to highlight the fundamental American values of diversity and liberty."*
"Reagan spoke about American values."	
Make a claim, but do not address the writer's rhetorical choices	
"Reagan makes the point that we all share a love of liberty."	
Repeat provided information from the passage	
"In paragraph 2, Reagan relates information about the many immigrants who arrived."	

Additional Notes:

The thesis may be more than one sentence, provided the sentences are in close proximity.

The thesis may be anywhere within the response.

For a thesis to be defensible, the passage must include at least minimal evidence that could be used to support that thesis; however, the student need not cite that evidence to earn the thesis point.

The thesis may establish a line of reasoning that structures the essay, but it needn't do so to earn the thesis point.

A thesis that meets the criteria can be awarded the point whether or not the rest of the response successfully supports that line of reasoning.

PRACTICE

Complete the following activities and answer the questions about the Row A Thesis rubric and scoring guide.

1. In your own words, explain three problems that could keep you from earning the thesis point.

2. Explain whether summarizing the prompt is a useful strategy. Identify the part of the rubric that addresses that.

3. Does a thesis statement need to present a line of reasoning? Identify the part of the rubric that answers that question.

4. Does a thesis statement need to contain evidence? Identify the part of the rubric that answers that question.

5. Will you miss the point if your thesis statement is not in the first paragraph? Identify the part of the rubric that answers that question.

You Be the Reader

Read sample essay RA.2.B in the Appendix on page 277. Decide whether that essay earns the thesis point. Explain your answer.

Watch AP teacher Beth Hall talk through Row A of the Rhetorical Analysis rubric (tinyurl.com/mr2rf9fr) beginning at 1:24 and continuing until 6:15.

Revise

Review the thesis statement you have developed in response to Obama's Morehouse speech. If you think it does not earn the thesis point based on this rubric and Beth Hall's explanations, revise as needed to correct that, Even if you believe it earns the thesis point, revise your thesis to make it the best it can be.

TEAM UP

Exam readers, often hundreds at a time seated at tables in a convention hall, approach their scoring with collaboration. They receive training; they agree on how to apply the rubric; and they read for eight hours a day—all responses to the same essay question—for seven days. When they are uncertain how to score an essay, they may talk to someone at their table, and if they can't resolve a question that way, they ask a "table leader" or "question leader" who has extensive experience in scoring essays. The philosophy of AP exam readers is that they are looking for ways to *award* points, not ways to withhold them.

In that spirit of collaboration, and as your teacher directs, work in small groups to read sample essay RA.2.A in the Appendix on page 276. Go over Row A of the rubric part by part to make sure everyone understands it. Then discuss the sample essay to see if you can agree on whether it earns the thesis point. Report your decision to the whole class when everyone is done, and, if there are disagreements, argue your respective positions on why it should or shouldn't receive the thesis point until you can reach agreement.

You may also want to share with your group the thesis statement you have developed in response to Obama's Morehouse speech for feedback from your co-readers.

Evidence and Commentary

LESSON RA.9 Selecting Evidence

Eyes on the Exam

Use **specific and sufficient evidence** to support each of the claims in your line of reasoning.

LEARN

Each of your topic sentences asserts a claim in support of your thesis. Your body paragraphs need to "prove" each claim with evidence from the text. Evidence can be a short, direct quote or a paraphrase. The key is to reference specific portions of the passage.

Consider this claim about the beginning of Reagan's speech at the Statue of Liberty Torch-Lighting Ceremony that might be the first topic sentence of an essay: "President Reagan begins by listing many examples of hardworking Americans to highlight the diversity and determination of immigrants and their strength in numbers." The underlined portions in the following paragraphs of the speech all serve as textual evidence to support the reasoning of the topic and, as a result, justify its claim.

> [. . .]
>
> They were the <u>men and women who labored all their lives</u> so that their children would be well fed, clothed, and educated, the <u>families that went through great hardship</u> yet <u>kept their honor, their dignity, and their faith in God</u>. They passed on to their children those values, values that define civilization and are the prerequisites of human progress. They worked <u>in our factories</u>, <u>on ships and railroads, in stores</u>, and <u>on road construction crews</u>. They were <u>teachers</u>, <u>lumberjacks</u>, <u>seamstresses</u>, and <u>journalists</u>. They came from every land.

Here is a second possible topic sentence: "As Reagan continues, the fundamental principles of 'bond' and 'liberty' echo through effective repetition to emphasize the main theme of his speech." The underlined portions below show textual evidence you might use to support the reasoning of the topic and, as a result, justify its claim.

> What was it that tied these profoundly different people together? What was it that made them not a gathering of individuals, but a nation? That <u>bond</u> that held them together, as it <u>holds us together</u> tonight, that <u>bond</u> that has stood every test and travail, is found deep in our national consciousness: an abiding <u>love of liberty</u>. <u>For love of liberty</u>, our forebears—colonists, few in number and with little to defend themselves—fought a war for independence with what was then the world's most powerful empire. <u>For love of liberty</u>, those who came before us tamed a vast wilderness and braved hardships which, at times, were beyond the limits of human endurance. <u>For love of liberty</u>, a bloody and heart-wrenching civil war was fought. And <u>for love of liberty</u>, Americans championed and still champion, even in times of peril, the cause of human freedom in far-off lands.

Notice that these underlined sections are not complete sentences. Finding evidence in only parts of sentences is useful because one way to present your evidence is to embed quotes into your own sentences. Shorter quotes work best for that.

Example of quoted evidence: Reagan honored the immigrants' contributions by noting they "labored all their lives so that their children would be well fed, clothed, and educated."

You can also paraphrase evidence from your source, expressing the same idea in your own words.

Example of paraphrased evidence: Reagan honored the immigrants' contributions by noting *their lifelong hard work on behalf of their children's comfort and education.*

KEY POINT: Choose **specific, clear evidence** from your text to support your reasoning and justify the claim each topic sentence asserts about rhetorical choices the speaker or writer makes. When selecting direct quotes as evidence, look for short quotes (roughly 3–12 words).

PRACTICE

Select at least two pieces of evidence that could be used with each of the claims below from Obama's Morehouse speech (reproduced on the next two pages for easy reference). Your evidence can be a short, direct quote from the passage or a paraphrase. You may wish to make a chart like the one below to record your answers.

1. President Obama begins his commencement address by referencing Morehouse College's history to engage the audience and create a context for his message.

2. Obama continues by shifting his focus from the college's history to one of its most noteworthy graduates, Dr. Martin Luther King Jr., to convey the message that he, too, was once a young man uncertain of his future.

3. Obama concludes his speech by calling on the graduates to lead by example.

Claims	Evidence
1.	
2.	
3.	

WRITE

Using the topic sentences you developed in Lesson RA.8, select supporting evidence from the Morehouse speech, reproduced on the next two pages for easy reference.

Make a chart like the one below to record your evidence. Add more rows or leave one blank as necessary for your topic sentences.

Topic Sentences	Evidence (include location, such as para. 3)
1.	
2.	
3.	

[1] Benjamin Mays, who served as the president of Morehouse for almost 30 years, understood [the school's sense of pride] better than anybody. He said—and I quote—"It will not be sufficient for Morehouse College, for any college, for that matter, to produce clever graduates . . . but rather honest men, men who can be trusted in public and private life—men who are sensitive to the wrongs, the sufferings, and the injustices of society and who are willing to accept responsibility for correcting [those] ills."

[2] It was that mission—not just to educate men, but to cultivate good men, strong men, upright men—that brought community leaders together just two years after the end of the Civil War. They assembled a list of 37 men, free blacks and freed slaves, who would make up the first prospective class of what later became Morehouse College. Most of those first students had a desire to become teachers and preachers—to better themselves so they could help others do the same.

[3] A century and a half later, times have changed. But the "Morehouse Mystique" still endures. Some of you probably came here from communities where everybody looked like you. Others may have come here in search of a community. And I suspect that some of you probably felt a little bit of culture shock the first time you came together as a class in King's Chapel. All of a sudden, you weren't the only high school sports captain, you weren't the only student council president. You were suddenly in a group of high achievers, and that meant you were expected to do something more.

[4] That's the unique sense of purpose that this place has always infused—the conviction that this is a training ground not only for individual success, but for leadership that can change the world.

[5] Dr. King was just 15 years old when he enrolled here at Morehouse. He was an unknown, undersized, unassuming young freshman who lived at home with his parents. And I think it's fair to say he wasn't the coolest kid on campus—for the suits he wore, his classmates called him "Tweed." But his education at Morehouse helped to forge the intellect, the discipline, the compassion, the soul force that would transform America. It was here that he was introduced to the writings of Gandhi and Thoreau, and the theory of civil disobedience. It was here that professors encouraged him to look past the world as it was and fight for the world as it should be. And it was here, at Morehouse, as Dr. King later wrote, where "I realized that nobody . . . was afraid."

[6] Not even of some bad weather. I added on that part. (Laughter.) I know it's wet out there. But Dr. Wilson told me you all had a choice and decided to do it out here anyway. (Applause.) That's a Morehouse Man talking. Now, think about it. For black men in the '40s and the '50s, the threat of violence, the constant humiliations, large and small, the uncertainty that you could support a family, the gnawing doubts born of the Jim Crow culture that told you every day that somehow you were inferior, the temptation to shrink from the world, to accept your place, to avoid risks, to be afraid—that temptation was necessarily strong.

[7] And yet, here, under the tutelage of men like Dr. Mays, young Martin learned to be unafraid. And he, in turn, taught others to be unafraid. And over time, he taught a nation to be unafraid. And over the last 50 years, thanks to the moral force of Dr. King and a Moses generation that overcame their fear and their cynicism and their despair, barriers have come tumbling down, and new doors of opportunity have swung open, and laws and hearts and minds have been changed to the point where someone who looks just like you can somehow come to serve as President of these United States of America. (Applause.)

[8] So the history we share should give you hope. The future we share should give you hope. You're graduating into an improving job market. You're living in a time when advances in technology and communication put the world at your fingertips. Your generation is uniquely poised for success unlike any generation of African Americans that came before it.

[9] But that doesn't mean we don't have work—because if we're honest with ourselves, we know that too few of our brothers have the opportunities that you've had here at Morehouse. In troubled neighborhoods all across this country—many of them heavily African American— too few of our citizens have role models to guide them. Communities just a couple miles from my house in Chicago, communities just a couple miles from here—they're places where jobs are still too scarce and wages are still too low; where schools are underfunded and violence is pervasive; where too many of our men spend their youth not behind a desk in a classroom, but hanging out on the streets or brooding behind a jail cell.

[10] My job, as President, is to advocate for policies that generate more opportunity for everybody—policies that strengthen the middle class and give more people the chance to climb their way into the middle class. Policies that create more good jobs and reduce poverty, and educate more children, and give more families the security of health care, and protect more of our children from the horrors of gun violence. That's my job. Those are matters of public policy, and it is important for all of us—black, white and brown—to advocate for an America where everybody has got a fair shot in life. Not just some. Not just a few. (Applause.)

[11] But along with collective responsibilities, we have individual responsibilities. There are some things, as black men, we can only do for ourselves. There are some things, as Morehouse Men, that you are obliged to do for those still left behind. As Morehouse Men, you now wield something even more powerful than the diploma you're about to collect—and that's the power of your example. So what I ask of you today is the same thing I ask of every graduating class I address: Use that power for something larger than yourself. Live up to President Mays's challenge. Be "sensitive to the wrongs, the sufferings, and the injustices of society." And be "willing to accept responsibility for correcting [those] ills."

Watch this video by AP Teacher Beth Hall (Coach Hall) on how to select evidence for rhetorical analysis essays (tinyurl.com/2z2a2d8z). Then review your evidence choices and make any changes that might improve your selection.

What's the Point? In one sentence, explain how this lesson can help you on the AP English Language and Composition exam.

_____

_____

_____

LESSON RA.10 Analyzing Word Choice and Tone

Eyes on the Exam

Exam readers will reward efforts to demonstrate your understanding of a writer's or speaker's **tone,** or **attitude** toward the subject, and writing style. Explaining how **word choice** contributes to a tone or style is one way to demonstrate that understanding.

LEARN

Words can convey many ideas as they reach an audience. They convey their **denotations,** or dictionary definitions. They also convey **connotations,** or shades of meaning, that can be positive or negative. Word choice can also convey a writer's or speaker's **perspectives** and biases, prejudices in favor of or against a position.

Consider, for example, the words Reagan chose to highlight the workers and their workplaces.

They worked in our factories, on ships and railroads, in stores, and on road construction crews. They were teachers, lumberjacks, seamstresses, and journalists.

The chart below shows what a few of those words might convey.

factories	lumberjacks
Denotation: a workplace where goods are manufactured, often with the help of machines	**Denotation:** workers who cut down trees and take them to mills
Connotation: neutral or positive (in contrast to *sweatshops*)	**Connotation:** often positive, possibly associated with the American tall tale character Paul Bunyan
Perspective: Making things helped build the United States, and workers played a key role in that nation-building.	**Perspective:** Workers who cut down trees provided building materials for homes and other projects. Resources such as trees are to be used for progress.

A rhetorical analysis essay might well point out how those words convey a tone of respect for the value of workers who helped build the country.

Here are some other examples from a different part of the speech:

For love of liberty, those who came before us tamed a vast wilderness and braved hardships which, at times, were beyond the limits of human endurance.

Consider what the words *tamed* and *wilderness* convey.

tamed	wilderness
Denotation: brought something wild under control	**Denotation:** uncultivated and uninhabited stretch of land
Connotation: usually positive (in contrast to *overpowered*)	**Connotation:** often positive today with conservation advocates; often negative in history as full of dangers
Perspective: The land needed to be brought under the control of settlers.	**Perspective:** The land needed to be settled with Americans to make it useful.

One way to interpret Reagan's choice of "tamed" and "wilderness" is to note that these words convey a tone of national pride. They reflect the belief that Americans had a right and duty to turn the wilderness into settlements and make the land productive, and they did so out of a love of liberty. That was and still is a popular perspective, but not all people share it. For example, Native Americans already living in North America had found a way to live in harmony with the land. They believed and continue to believe that nature should be preserved rather than "tamed." And to Native Americans, the land was not "wilderness"—not uninhabited—because they had lived there for thousands of years.

Understanding these words in the historical context may also provide insight. For example, in 1986, the idea of climate change was not as widely familiar as it is now. Several later presidents, both Democratic and Republican, set aside millions of acres of "wilderness" for preservation—the opposite of "taming"—in part to address concerns about factors contributing to climate change.

KEY POINT: Word choice is a window into a speaker's or writer's mind and viewpoints and may reflect **perspectives** tied to the historical context. Analyzing word choice is one strategy for understanding tone and rhetorical choices.

PRACTICE

Review the pieces of evidence you selected from the Morehouse speech in the Practice section of the previous lesson on page 147, and underline key words or phrases within them that stand out from the rest.

WRITE

Write a brief explanation of why the words or phrases you underlined are significant to the passage. Consider why Obama chose these precise words to help motivate the Morehouse graduates. You may want to make a chart like the one below to examine all that the words convey. Use as many rows as you need.

Word Choice	Denotation	Connotation	Perspective or Bias

Watch this video (tinyurl.com/mwe4fxfb) for more on denotation and connotation and the power of words to convey tone.

What's the Point? In one sentence, explain how this lesson can help you on the AP English Language and Composition exam.

_____

_____

_____

LESSON RA.11 Embedding Evidence

Eyes on the Exam

Your rhetorical analysis essay will be stronger and smoother if you **embed** your quotes into your sentences and seamlessly **weave in** your paraphrased evidence.

LEARN

When you are at the point of starting to embed quotes and paraphrases in your sentences, stand back and review for a few minutes how you got here and where you are going. So far you have

- Read the prompt and understood exactly your precise task.
- Read the passage, annotating it for "what" and "why" examples.
- Divided the passage into beginning, middle, and end.
- Formulated a thesis statement that includes two to three rhetorical choices and ties them to the message of the speaker (or the purpose or argument in other possible prompts). That thesis statement presents the rhetorical choices in the order in which you will cover them in your essay, typically, though not necessarily, the same order in which they appear in the text.
- Written topic sentences for each body paragraph, guided by your thesis statement, which is the road map to your essay.
- Marked the passage for textual evidence you may quote or paraphrase in support of the reasoning in each topic sentence.
- Analyzed word choice to examine tone and perspective and highlighted key words.

At this point, you know the passage very well. You have all the "raw materials" to build your essay. In the next few steps, you will be assembling the pieces you have gathered into a preliminary draft. In that draft, you will present claims (in your thesis statement and topic sentences) and then smoothly work into your sentences the evidence you will later explain to justify those claims.

This is the framework developed so far for an essay in response to the Reagan prompt.

Thesis Statement: In his July 3, 1986, speech at the Statue of Liberty, President Reagan lists diverse immigrants, repeats key words and ideas, and stirs patriotic emotions to convey the message that Americans share a love of liberty that improves their lives, guides national policy, and creates a bond of unity despite differences.

Topic sentence for the first body paragraph: President Reagan offers diverse examples of Americans from all walks of life to emphasize the ties that unify Americans despite their differences. (This relates to lists.)

Topic sentence for the second body paragraph: President Reagan repeats key words and ideas to highlight the love of liberty that unites Americans. (This relates to repetition.)

Topic sentence for the third body paragraph: As he concludes his speech, President Reagan stirs listeners with the moving ideals of liberty and each person's responsibility to keep it safe. (This relates to the appeal to emotions.)

Following is one way you can fill that framework in with quoted or paraphrased textual evidence. The body paragraphs are labeled BP1, BP2, and BP3. The supporting sentences that embed quoted material as evidence in each paragraph below are in italic type.

Thesis: In his July 3, 1986, speech at the Statue of Liberty, President Reagan lists diverse immigrants, repeats key words and ideas, and stirs patriotic emotions to convey the message that Americans share a love of liberty that improves their lives, guides national policy, and creates a bond of unity despite differences.

BP1: President Reagan offers diverse examples of Americans from all walks of life to emphasize the ties that bind them despite their diversity. *In plain language, he lists everyday Americans, "teachers, lumberjacks, seamstresses, and journalists," who "passed through this harbor" and "looked up at [the Statue of Liberty's] torch," imagining and then achieving a better life for themselves and their families.*

BP2: President Reagan highlights through repetition the love of liberty that unites Americans. *Reagan repeats the word "bond" several times and then defines it as a shared and "abiding love of liberty." The phrase "love of liberty" echoes through this section of his speech as he explains it was the motivation behind key events that shaped the nation's history—the war for independence, the westward movement and "taming of a vast wilderness," a terrible civil war, and the involvement in overseas wars in the name of freedom—all for "love of liberty."*

BP3: As he concludes his speech, President Reagan stirs listeners with the moving ideals of liberty and each person's responsibility to keep it safe. *He invokes the blessings of God, appealing to listeners' religious values, and calls on listeners "to keep alive the dream" that drew so many immigrants here. He reminds listeners of the stirring words by Emma Lazarus dedicated to the Statue of Liberty, and at just that point, a chorus begins singing those words, further lifting the emotions of the listeners. Reagan chooses words with strongly positive connotations, such as "beacon of hope" and "light unto the nations," adopting an almost biblical tone. After touching listeners' emotions, Reagan ends by asking everyone to share in the "symbolic act of faith" of lighting the Statue of Liberty's torch.*

Notice that the quotations are smoothly embedded in the sentences. One way to accomplish this flow is to follow the pattern of **ICE: I**ntroduce, **C**ite, **E**xplain. To *introduce* a quote, make sure there is at least one word before the quote. The quote itself is the *cite* part of ICE. To *explain*, you will provide commentary that ties the quote and evidence to your claims by explaining how that evidence supports your thinking—or reasoning—that justifies the claims. The next two lessons will explain how to add commentary.

When you're first learning how to integrate evidence into a sentence, you might use phrases such as "the author states" and "for example" to lead into your evidence. While these phrases are acceptable, examples in the body paragraphs above provide more advanced techniques for embedding evidence.

Notice where the quotes fall in this sentence. They can work effectively in the middle and at the end of sentences to complete a thought. Think of how you might express the thought without the quote, and then substitute your words with a quote to work them in smoothly. For example, you might write, "To emphasize what holds together diverse Americans . . . ." You can substitute "diverse Americans" with a quote that expresses the same thought:

To emphasize what holds together these "profoundly different people" . . .

You may sometimes have to adjust a quote to make it work in your sentences. You may need to change a word to make the sentence read more clearly or correctly, especially tenses of verbs and pronouns. In these cases, put brackets around the word you changed.

Example of changed wording with brackets: By mentioning that the immigrants "looked up at [the Statue of Liberty's] torch," Reagan reminds the audience that Lady Liberty served as a symbol of the American Dream for so many who saw her as they entered the United States.

KEY POINT: Make sure to have at least one word before the quoted evidence and remember that **shorter quotes are often easier to embed.**

PRACTICE

Embed the following quotes from Obama's 2013 Morehouse commencement speech into a sentence of your own. Remember to use brackets if you need to adjust the verbs or pronouns in the quote. Consider using the provided sentence starters as needed.

1. "Morehouse Mystique"
2. "an unknown, undersized, unassuming young freshman"
3. "the power of your example"

Sentence Starters

By noting that ["..."] Obama ....

By referencing [" ..."] Obama ....

Mentioning [" ..."] allows Obama to ....

Referencing [" ..."] helps Obama motivate the graduates because ....

WRITE

Using additional evidence you selected from Obama's 2013 Morehouse commencement speech in the previous lessons, write three new, separate sentences, each with its own embedded evidence. Be sure they relate to a claim you could make about that speech.

Check out these tips (tinyurl.com/46594zmt) from the University of Indiana Bloomington about using evidence effectively. Scroll down to read the short section called Using Quotations: A Special Type of Evidence. Then consider revising your sentences to apply the tips from the post.

What's the Point? In one sentence, explain how this lesson can help you on the AP English Language and Composition exam.

_____

_____

_____

LESSON RA.12 Commentary Part 1: Commentary Language

Eyes on the Exam

Evidence alone does not support a claim. A big part of your score will be based on how well you provide *commentary* that explains to the reader the **significance of your evidence.**

LEARN

Textual detail from your reading is not evidence in an essay until your **commentary** explains the way you are thinking about it and how it justifies the claims you make. Commentary may seem hard to grasp at first, but consider this simple example:

Claim: Chocolate cake is not a very healthy food.

Evidence: A slice of frosted chocolate cake has a high fat content (22 grams) and also a high level of refined carbohydrates (58 grams).

While the evidence may *seem* to support the claim, there is actually a missing link. Commentary needs to explain what those high levels of fat and refined carbohydrates have to do with healthy food.

Commentary: Foods that are high in fat and refined carbohydrates are known to have a harmful effect on health, increasing the chances of obesity, heart disease, and diabetes.

Commentary is a crucial component of a rhetorical analysis essay because the commentary *is* your analysis. It's where you explain the significance of your evidence by answering "why," "how," or "so what?" In the chocolate cake example, the commentary answered "why." A strong rhetorical analysis essay will have more commentary than evidence in each of the body paragraphs.

Here is an example of how commentary provides analysis in a possible first body paragraph (BP1) in the response to the Reagan speech. The evidence is in italics. The commentary is in bold type.

Thesis: In his July 3, 1986, speech at the Statue of Liberty, President Reagan lists diverse immigrants, repeats key words and ideas, and stirs patriotic emotions to convey the message that Americans share a love of liberty that improves their lives, guides national policy, and creates a bond of unity despite differences.

Topic Sentence for BP1 (claim): President Reagan offers examples of Americans from all walks of life to emphasize the ties that bind them despite their diversity.

Evidence: *In plain language, he lists everyday Americans, "teachers, lumberjacks, seamstresses, and journalists," who "passed through this harbor" and "looked up at [the Statue of Liberty's] torch," imagining and then achieving a better life for themselves and their families.*

Commentary: The mention of specific workplaces and specific workers, all having entered the country looking up at the Statue of Liberty, all reaching toward the same goal, <u>demonstrates</u> Reagan's claim that Americans, different though they are, share fundamental experiences and values. Naming their specific occupations and the places these Americans worked, Reagan helps listeners, many of whom have similar jobs, feel the very connection with their fellow Americans that Reagan is describing. The lists <u>emphasize</u> the unity Americans feel even through their differences and across time.

The underlined words are examples of verbs that can help you develop your commentary. The chart on the next page lists other verbs you can use to develop commentary.

Commentary Language: Verbs	
conveys	portrays
demonstrates	presents
emphasizes	reveals
exemplifies	signifies
highlights	showcases
illustrates	suggests
implies	underscores

While these words are synonyms for "shows," select the most precise verb for the specific sentence you are writing.

Other words can help you introduce your commentary. Consider the possibilities in the second body paragraph.

Topic sentence for BP2: President Reagan repeats key terms to highlight the love of liberty that unites Americans. **<u>Since</u> he is emphasizing unity,** *Reagan repeats the word "bond" several times and then defines it as a shared and "abiding love of liberty." The phrase "love of liberty" echoes through this section of his speech as he explains it was the motivation behind key events that shaped the nation's history—the war for independence, the westward movement and "taming of a vast wilderness," a terrible civil war, and the involvement in overseas wars in the name of freedom—all for "love of liberty."*

Commentary Language: Cause and Effect	
Because . . .	In this way,
Since . . .	Furthermore,
As such,	Thus, if . . .
Consequently,	Therefore,
For this reason,	

KEY POINT: Think carefully to provide **commentary that explains the significance of your evidence** to your claim. Commentary language helps you effectively convey your analysis of the evidence.

PRACTICE

Circle the commentary language in the examples below:

1. By mentioning that the "Morehouse Mystique" still endures, Obama honors the college's prestigious legacy while simultaneously praising the graduates. (Since) the graduates are the next generation of Morehouse Men, they likely feel compelled to draw upon the knowledge and skills they've gained at Morehouse to effect social change.

2. President Obama (emphasizes) the impact a Morehouse education can have on a young man. By noting that King began his journey as "an unknown, undersized, unassuming young freshman," President Obama (highlights) the transformation Dr.

King experienced, (since) Morehouse was where he learned the ideals that later helped him fight valiantly for social justice.

3. President Obama calls on the Morehouse graduates to use "the power of their example" to serve their brothers who have been left behind and inspire the change for the next generation. (Thus, if) these graduates apply the skills they learned in college, they will be able to effect change in their future careers. While they might not gain the same notoriety as Dr. King, these men are an important part of the Morehouse legacy.

WRITE

Select two examples of embedded evidence from your work in the previous lesson. Rewrite the embedded evidence and add commentary. Then circle your commentary language.

Watch this video (tinyurl.com/26k2jv6y) from Timm Freitas (the instruction begins at 00:49) and consult this verb list (tinyurl.com/3nzk4jar). Then consider revising your sentences to incorporate the knowledge you've gained from these additional resources.

Watch Beth Hall discuss limited commentary using the Reagan liberty speech prompt at the companion website (tinyurl.com/2mrx3r99) for this book. There you will find other videos by the authors as well as all the links included in the lessons in this book.

What's the Point? In one sentence, explain how this lesson can help you on the AP English Language and Composition exam.

_____

_____

_____

TEAM UP

In his video, Timm Freitas notes that commentary can shed light on evidence by addressing assumptions, stereotypes, and connotations. In a small group, as your teacher directs, review the sample commentary in the Practice section to identify assumptions and connotations in all three examples. Do the same with the commentary you wrote in the Write section.

- Look for assumptions the author makes about the audience's values, opinions, or knowledge, as well as assumptions about the topic itself.
- Connotations are the emotional meaning of words. Names have connotations as well. Look for the emotional connections of the words chosen in the commentary.

After identifying any assumptions and connotations, explain the effect they have on the commentary.

Using insights you may have gained from this activity, revise your commentary to build on connotative meanings and explore assumptions.

LESSON RA.13 Commentary Part 2: Connecting to the Rhetorical Situation

Eyes on the Exam

Commentary that explains your reasoning is essential. **Connecting your commentary to the rhetorical situation** provides solid opportunities to develop commentary.

LEARN

Recall the elements of the rhetorical situation from Lesson RA.2:

- **Exigence** (the impetus of or reason for the text)
- **Purpose** (the goals the writer or speaker wants to achieve)
- **Audience** (receivers of the message, who often have a variety of values and beliefs)
- **Writer or speaker** (a unique voice with values and beliefs)
- **Context** (the time, place, and occasion)
- **Message** (the substance of the writer's or speaker's main points)

Analyzing why a speaker or writer makes a particular choice for a specific audience on a specific occasion will help you generate good commentary. Focusing on the description of the rhetorical situation in the prompt is essential, but as you will learn in later lessons (RA.16 and RA.18), try to understand an even broader context as well as multiple purposes and multiple audiences the text may have. For example, in 1986, the United States, led by President Reagan, and the Soviet Union, led by Mikhail Gorbachev, were opponents in the Cold War (1947–1991). Reagan promoted democracy and capitalism, the economic engine of the nation, while Gorbachev promoted communism and the command economy that gave the power of economic decisions to the government. In some places around the world, military conflict, supported by both sides in the Cold War, was underway to determine which system of government and economy would prevail. So, while Reagan's immediate audience was certainly the people of the United States, the larger audience of his televised speech may have been the whole rest of the world, and his larger purpose may have been to convince people everywhere of the superiority of democratic capitalism.

The sentence frames below provide some possible ways to connect to the rhetorical situation in your commentary.

Sentence Frames for Commentary Connecting to the Rhetorical Situation	
To connect to the . . .	
Speaker	1. Given that (or Since) [SPEAKER] is [role or credentials], they must . . . because . . . . 2. Considering that [SPEAKER] seeks to [GOAL or PURPOSE], they . . . because . . . . 3. Given that [SPEAKER] values [X,] they . . . because . . . .
Audience	4. Knowing that s/he is speaking to [AUDIENCE], [SPEAKER] specifically emphasizes . . . because . . . . 5. Given that [AUDIENCE] likely values [X], [SPEAKER] . . . in order to . . . .

Sentence Frames for Commentary Connecting to the Rhetorical Situation	
Context and Exigence	6. Aware that [relevant context], [SPEAKER] . . . . 7. Given that at the time of the speech [reference to relevant fact or event], [SPEAKER] . . . in order to . . . . 8. Considering s/he is speaking at [event], [SPEAKER] must . . . because . . . .
Purpose	9. Clearly, [SPEAKER] aims to [PURPOSE]. Therefore, they . . . . 10. Since [SPEAKER] ultimately seeks to [PURPOSE], they . . . . 11. In an effort to [PURPOSE], [SPEAKER] . . . because . . . .
Message	12. In testament to the importance/value of [topic/issue], [SPEAKER] . . . because . . . . 13. To develop the message that . . . , [SPEAKER] . . . in order to . . . . 14. Considering that the audience is . . . , the message of [X] would resonate with them because . . . .

You can adapt these sentence frames to fit a variety of prompts and writing styles. These frames are a starting point to help you articulate your ideas.

Following are examples of those sentence frames in response to the Reagan prompt.

Exigence	(6.) Aware that liberty has been an American ideal since the nation's founding, Reagan quotes Thomas Jefferson to emphasize the importance of this "gift."
Context	(8.) Considering he is speaking at a landmark that quickly came to symbolize the American Dream to those who passed through Ellis Island, Reagan honors the tireless dedication the immigrants exhibited for the betterment of their families.
Message	(12.) In testament to the value of liberty, Reagan symbolically lights the "beacon of hope."

KEY POINT: Strong commentary often **connects the evidence to elements of the rhetorical situation,** especially the message, purpose, or argument.

PRACTICE

Read the following sentences and indicate which element of the rhetorical situation the commentary connects to (speaker, audience, context, exigence, purpose, or message). Some sentences may connect to more than one component of the rhetorical situation. If so, write both answers. You can indicate your answer by **writing S** for speaker, **A** for audience, **C** for context, **E** for exigence, **P** for purpose, or **M** for message **after each sentence.**

1. Given that he is speaking at the 2013 Morehouse commencement, President Obama references Dr. Martin Luther King, a famous alumnus, to remind the graduates that they are part of a legacy of Morehouse Men. *C, E*

2. As the first Black president of the United States, President Obama seeks to inspire the graduates to use the knowledge they have gained at Morehouse to help their brothers who have been left behind. *S, P*

3. Knowing that the United States has made considerable progress since the time of Dr. King yet there is still more progress to be made, Obama challenges the presumably excited and slightly nervous graduates to lead by example.

WRITE

Review the list of sentence frames on pages 158 and 159, and select three sentence frames to practice with for this activity. On separate paper, do your best to write a sentence using each of the sentence frames you selected to develop commentary for your response to Obama's Morehouse speech. You may embed evidence if needed. For this activity, the commentary sentences you write do not have to be in chronological order.

 Watch this video (tinyurl.com/33kx6kt8) by Beth Hall (Coach Hall) about her best tip for rhetorical analysis commentary. Then review your work and try to make improvements.

What's the Point? In one sentence, explain how this lesson can help you on the AP English Language and Composition exam.

_____

_____

_____

TEAM UP

In small groups, as your teacher directs, share the work you did in the Write section. Then develop some fluency in using these sentence frames for commentary connected to the rhetorical situation by completing this activity.

Take turns completing the sentence frames in the charts on pages 158-159 with specifics from your response to Obama's Morehouse speech. One person begins by stating a completed sentence frame based on the pattern in the first numbered frame in the chart. A second person continues by stating a completed frame based on the second numbered frame. Continue until all group members have had a chance to provide a completed frame. If there are remaining numbered items, repeat the process.

When you have completed the activity, return to the work you did in the Write section and strengthen the commentary you wrote.

LESSON RA.14 Including Quotes in Commentary

Eyes on the Exam

Embedding quotes from the passage into your commentary may make your analysis more complex as you combine your thinking with the thinking and ideas from the text. Complex writing generally earns higher points than simpler responses.

LEARN

As you can see, the process you are learning for writing rhetorical analysis essays is *layering*. From simple "what/why" notes to a tentative thesis statement and then to topic sentences, evidence, and commentary, each step adds another layer of development. You have already read about embedding quotes as evidence (Lesson RA.11). This lesson layers on the idea of using quotes in your *commentary*.

The following example comes from previous lessons, but it has been revised to include quotes in the commentary. The added quotes are in bold type.

> *[Topic Sentence]* President Reagan offers examples of Americans from all walks of life to emphasize the ties that bind them despite their diversity. *[Evidence]* In plain language, he lists everyday Americans, "teachers, lumberjacks, seamstresses, and journalists," who "passed through this harbor" and "looked up at [the Statue of Liberty's] torch," imagining and then achieving a better life for themselves and their families. *[Commentary]* The mention of specific workplaces and specific workers, all having entered the country looking up at the Statue of Liberty, all reaching toward the same goal, demonstrates Reagan's claim that Americans, though **"profoundly different,"** share fundamental experiences and values. Naming their specific occupations and the places these Americans worked—**"in our factories, on ships and railroads, in stores, and on road construction crews"**—Reagan helps listeners, many of whom have similar jobs, feel the very connection with their fellow Americans that Reagan is describing. The lists emphasize the unity Americans feel even through their differences and across time.

> **KEY POINT: Embedding short quotes from the passage into your commentary** can help you engage with the text and elevate the quality of your commentary.

PRACTICE

Select one of the examples below from a possible response to Obama's Morehouse speech. Revise your selected example to include at least one short quote integrated into the commentary. You may add more commentary if needed, but do your best to stay true to the intent of the original example.

1. President Obama emphasizes the impact a Morehouse education can have on a young man. By noting that King began his journey as "an unknown, undersized, unassuming young freshman," President Obama highlights the transformation Dr. King experienced, since Morehouse was where he learned the ideals that later helped him fight valiantly for social justice.

2. President Obama calls on the Morehouse graduates to use "the power of their example" to serve their brothers who have been left behind and inspire the change for the next generation. Thus, if these graduates apply the skills they learned in college, they will be able to effect change in their future careers. While they might not gain the same notoriety as Dr. King, these men are an important part of the Morehouse legacy.

WRITE

Select two examples of commentary from your analysis of Obama's Morehouse speech in previous lessons, and integrate at least one short quote into your existing commentary.

 This link (tinyurl.com/2szbnrk7) to the website of the San José State University Writing Center takes you to an explanation of several very clear techniques for working in quoted material.

What's the Point? In one sentence, explain how this lesson can help you on the AP English Language and Composition exam.

_____

_____

_____

TEAM UP

The document in the link above describes three ways of embedding quotations: setting them off, building them in, and introducing them with a colon. At the end of that document are a few sentences for practicing each type. Look those over, as well as the possible answers provided. Then work in small groups as your teacher directs to complete the following activity.

The sentences below are from an article in *The Washington Post* by Gillian Brockell, dated May 23, 2019, about the opening of a new Statue of Liberty museum.

1. "[The new museum] revives an aspect of the statue's long-forgotten history: Lady Liberty was originally designed to celebrate the end of slavery, not the arrival of immigrants."

2. "An early model, circa 1870, shows Lady Liberty with her right arm in the position we are familiar with, raised and illuminating the world with a torch. But in her left hand she holds broken shackles, an homage to the end of slavery."

3. "In the final model, Lady Liberty holds a tablet inscribed with the Roman numerals for July 4, 1776. The broken chains are still there though, beneath her feet . . . ."

Using the models on the linked document, with your group create six new sentences that include quotes from the sentences above. Create two sentences for each method of embedding quotes. Take care to avoid ambiguous pronouns and floating quotations (see link). Share your work with the whole class when everyone has finished.

LESSON RA.15 Writing an Effective Conclusion

Eyes on the Exam

While conclusions are not required in a rhetorical analysis essay on the AP English Language and Composition exam, knowing how to write an effective conclusion will help you gather your ideas and look back over your essay to be sure you accomplished what you set out to do.

LEARN

On the AP English Language and Composition exam, the bulk of your rhetorical analysis essay score will come from your evidence and commentary. So, if you are pressed for time, focus on your body paragraphs. However, if you do have time to write a conclusion on exam day, you should do so to prevent your essay from ending abruptly. Writing an effective conclusion is also a valuable writing skill for essays beyond the exam.

So, how do you write an effective conclusion?

Many students like to summarize their main points. While this can be an effective way to begin a conclusion, a strong conclusion will be more than just a summary. A strong conclusion will also examine the broader significance of a passage.

At some point in your education, you've likely been told to avoid starting your final paragraph with the phrase "in conclusion," and you might have wondered what to write instead.

Consider the following sentence frame and the corresponding examples to give you better ideas for the first sentence of the conclusion.

Sentence Frame: Taken together, the evidence clearly *demonstrates/suggests* that . . . .

Example 1: Taken together, the evidence clearly demonstrates that Reagan's use of repetition and unifying diction proudly highlights aspects of the nation that set it apart from other countries, its commitment to liberty, and the strong bond that commitment creates among a richly diverse people.

In this format, the example sentence restates the rhetorical choices mentioned in the thesis.

Following is a variation on this frame, one of many.

Sentence Frame Variation: Considering [some key aspect of the subject], it becomes clear that . . . .

Example 2: Considering the prominence of the Statue of Liberty, it becomes clear that Reagan is not only highlighting Lady Liberty as a symbol of the American Dream but also that immigrants have become an integral part of the "fabric" of America.

After writing a summary sentence that either restates the rhetorical choices and/or analyzes the message of the passage, do your best to examine the broader significance of the topic or passage.

These questions can help you home in on the significance.

1. To what extent is this message significant today?

2. What is the historical significance of this passage?

Here's what answers to these questions might look like in response to the Reagan liberty prompt.

1. Although America has made great strides in embracing diversity, immigration remains a contentious topic in America because some citizens wish for America to remain a respite for those seeking a better life, whereas other citizens demonstrate a concern regarding the limits of the country's continued growth.

2. Since its restoration in the 1980s, the Statue of Liberty has remained an iconic symbol of the United States. It's nearly impossible to travel throughout New York City without seeing Lady Liberty shirts, hats, snow globes, and more. In the decades since Reagan's presidency, Americans have continued to debate immigration policy. Regardless of one's opinions on immigration, one fact remains clear: America would not be the prosperous, powerful nation it is today without the invaluable contributions of generations of immigrants.

While these questions can help you determine the broader importance of the passage, they may not be equally relevant to all prompts. In some instances, you may wish to answer both questions (if applicable) to further develop your conclusion. In other instances, one of the questions might be a better fit than the other.

KEY POINT: An effective conclusion will examine **the broader implications** of the passage rather than merely summarize the main points of the essay.

PRACTICE

Experiment with each of the sentence frames on the previous page to write two possible strong first sentences for your concluding paragraph.

WRITE

On separate paper, write the first draft of a full concluding paragraph in response to the Obama Morehouse prompt (page 120). Use the sentence frames and questions provided in the Learn section of this lesson as a guide.

For more tips on writing an effective conclusion, check out this blog (tinyurl.com/5d6x7evm) from Grammarly. After reading it, make any revisions to your concluding paragraph that are likely to improve it.

What's the Point? In one sentence, explain how this lesson can help you on the AP English Language and Composition exam.

_____

_____

_____

Eyes on the Exam

Readers will score your evidence and commentary based on the criteria in Row B in the Rhetorical Analysis rubric.

LEARN

Carefully read each section of the Row B rubric and scoring guide.

- The first 5-column row, arranged from 0 points on the left to 4 points on the right, explains in general terms what criteria need to be met to achieve each score. Note that there are criteria for both evidence and commentary.

- The second 5-column row (next page) describes characteristics of essays earning each point. In both of those rows, key words have been printed in bold type to help you see the similarities and differences between the rankings.

- The final row provides additional clarifications for acceptable thesis statements.

Row B: Evidence AND Commentary (0-4 points), Scoring Criteria [1.A, 2.A, 4.A, 6.A–6.C]				
0 points	**1 point**	**2 points**	**3 points**	**4 points**
Simply **restates** thesis (if present), **repeats** provided information, or offers **information irrelevant to the prompt.**	EVIDENCE: Provides **evidence that is mostly general.** AND COMMENTARY: Summarizes the evidence but **does not explain how the evidence supports the student's argument.**	EVIDENCE: Provides **some specific relevant** evidence. AND COMMENTARY: Explains **how some of the evidence** relates to the student's argument, but **no line of reasoning** is established, or the **line of reasoning is faulty.**	EVIDENCE: Provides **specific evidence to support all claims in a line of reasoning.** AND COMMENTARY: Explains how **some of the evidence** supports a **line of reasoning.** AND Explains how **at least one rhetorical choice** in the passage contributes to the **writer's argument, purpose, or message.**	EVIDENCE: Provides **specific evidence to support all claims in a line of reasoning.** AND COMMENTARY: **Consistently explains how the evidence** supports a **line of reasoning.** AND Explains how **multiple rhetorical choices** in the passage contribute to the **writer's argument, purpose, or message.**

Decision Rules and Scoring Notes | Typical responses that earn

0 points:	1 point:	2 points:	3 points:	4 points:
Are **incoherent** or **do not address the prompt**. May be just **opinion with no textual references** or **references that are irrelevant**.	Tend to focus on **summary or description** of a passage rather than specific details or techniques. Mention **rhetorical choices with little or no explanation**.	Consist of a **mix of specific evidence and broad generalities**. May contain some **simplistic, inaccurate, or repetitive explanations** that don't strengthen the argument. May **make one point well,** but either **do not make multiple supporting claims** or **do not adequately support more than one** claim. Do **not explain the connections or progression** between the student's claims so a **line of reasoning is not clearly established**.	**Uniformly offer evidence** to support claims. Focus on the **importance of specific words and details** from the passage to build an argument. Organize an argument as a **line of reasoning composed of multiple supporting claims**. Commentary **may fail to integrate some evidence** or **fail to support a key claim**.	**Uniformly offer evidence** to support claims. Focus on the **importance of specific details** to build an argument. Organize and support an argument as a **line of reasoning composed of multiple supporting claims**, each with **adequate evidence that is clearly explained**. Explain how the **writer's use of rhetorical choices contributes to the student's interpretation** of the passage.

Additional Notes:

Writing that suffers from grammatical and/or mechanical errors that interfere with communication cannot earn the fourth point in this row. To earn the fourth point in this row, the response may observe multiple instances of the same rhetorical choice if each instance further contributes to the argument, purpose, or message of the passage.

Following are the skills from the Course and Exam Description that are assessed in Row B.

1.A Identify and describe components of the rhetorical situation: the exigence, audience, writer, purpose, context, and message.

2.A Write introductions and conclusions appropriate to the purpose and context of the rhetorical situation.

4.A Develop a paragraph that includes a claim and evidence supporting the claim.

6.A Develop a line of reasoning and commentary that explains it throughout an argument.

6.B Use transitional elements to guide the reader through the line of reasoning of an argument.

6.C Use appropriate methods of development to advance an argument.

PRACTICE

Complete the following activities and answer the questions about the Row B Evidence and Commentary rubric and scoring guide.

1. In your own words, explain two ways in which an essay scoring 3 points in Row B is similar to an essay earning 4.

2. The columns for a score of 3 and a score of 4 in Row B have one more category than do those for 0–2 scores. What is that category?

3. Describe the difference in evidence in an essay scoring a 1 in Row B and an essay earning a 2.

4. Can you discuss only one rhetorical choice in your essay and still earn a 4 in Row B? Explain your answer.

5. What would you say is the biggest difference between an essay earning a 2 in Row B and an essay earning a 3? Explain your answer.

6. If an essay adequately supports only one claim, what Row B score would it likely earn?

7. How can you meet all the criteria for 4 points and still not earn all 4?

You Be the Reader

Read sample essay RA.2.D in the appendix on page 279. Decide what score that essay earns in the Row B evidence and commentary category. Explain your answer.

Begin watching this video about the Rhetorical Analysis rubric from Marco Learning at 3:32 (tinyurl.com/3chsr9eh) to learn about a wall between score 2 and 3 and how to break past it.

Revise

Review the evidence and commentary you have developed in response to Obama's Morehouse speech. If you think it does not earn a 4 based on this rubric, revise as needed to raise your score. Even if you believe it earns 4 points as it is, revise your essay body to make it the best it can be.

Sophistication

LESSON RA.16 The Broader Context

Eyes on the Exam

Situating the text in a broader context can make your analysis more meaningful and help earn you an extra point on the exam.

LEARN

The College Board awards one point for sophistication on qualifying essays responding to the free-response questions. You can qualify for that point by doing at least one of the following:

1. Explaining the significance or relevance of the writer's rhetorical choices (given the rhetorical situation).

2. Explaining a purpose or function of the passage's complexities or tensions.

3. Employing a style that is consistently vivid and persuasive.

Further, a single strong sentence does *not* earn the sophistication point. Rather, you need consistent or multiple examples of complex and meaningful writing throughout the essay.

This lesson focuses on the first possibility (number 1 above), explaining why the rhetorical choices are important given the broader context of the rhetorical situation. Think about the broader concept as a "zooming out"—looking at the bigger picture. **Broader context** refers to the larger setting or background information surrounding the passage. This context can include historical, cultural, social, or political factors that influence the text and its effectiveness. Remember, the goal of a Rhetorical Analysis FRQ is to analyze not just *what* the text says, but *how* it says it and *why* those choices are significant. The broader context is a key part of that understanding.

For the broader context of a Rhetorical Analysis FRQ, think about the following:

1. **Historical Context:** What was happening in the world or in the specific region when the text was written? How might these events influence the content or the audience's reception of the text?

2. **Cultural/Social Context:** What were the leading cultural or social norms and values at the time? How do these norms and values influence the text's themes, language, and rhetorical strategies?

3. **Political Context:** Were there any significant political movements, figures, or events that could have influenced the text? How might the text be responding to or commenting on these political circumstances?

4. **Author's Background:** What do you know about the author's own life, beliefs, and experiences? How might these personal factors have shaped the writing?

5. **Audience:** Who is the intended audience of the text? How might the broader context affect how the audience receives or interprets the text?

In Lesson RA.15 on writing conclusions, you learned that you could ask yourself questions such as "To what extent is this message relevant today?" and "To what extent is this passage historically relevant?" While these questions are particularly helpful when trying to develop a conclusion paragraph, they can also be useful to develop sophistication in commentary in a body paragraph as well.

Following are a few ways you can refer to the broader context and add sophistication throughout your essay:

- In the introductory paragraph, if you know additional information about the speaker, audience, or context, you might include that information in the "context" portion of your introduction to help lead into your thesis.

- Within your body paragraphs, you might demonstrate a greater understanding of the rhetorical situation by integrating outside information about the speaker, audience, or context into your commentary.

In the examples below, the references to the broader context are underlined.

Introductory Paragraph with Broader Context Integrated

Some may think that our nation is more divided than united, that our differences create too wide a gulf to bridge. Political parties are miles apart. The gap between the pay of CEOs and workers has grown dramatically, in part because of a weakening of labor unions' power that started under President Reagan. Clashes about racial issues and immigration policies dominate headlines. However, the United States has a long history of strength through both unity and diversity, both in the spirit of liberty. This was the theme President Ronald Reagan chose to emphasize in his speech on July 3, 1986, at the lighting of the torch of the newly restored Statue of Liberty. President Reagan lists diverse immigrants, repeats key words and ideas, and stirs patriotic emotions to convey the message that Americans share a love of liberty that improves their lives, guides national policy, and creates a bond of unity despite differences.

You may not have the knowledge to add those particular contextual details, but stop and reflect on what you *do* know that can enrich your context. Maybe you are aware of differences between young people and older people that you can use as part of the context, or conflicts over what students can and cannot read. Or maybe you remember that Ronald Reagan was an actor before he went into politics, and you might include that information in part to explain his effectiveness at delivering a moving speech. Or maybe you remember the disagreements people had during the Covid pandemic about masking and vaccinations. Do your best to tie what you remember to the context established in the introduction.

Body Paragraph with Broader Context Integrated

President Reagan repeats key terms to emphasize the love of liberty that unites Americans. He repeats the word "bond" several times and then defines it as a shared and "abiding love of liberty." The phrase "love of liberty" echoes through this section of his speech as he explains it was the motivation behind key events that shaped the nation's history—the war for independence, the westward movement and "taming of a vast wilderness," a terrible civil war, and the involvement in overseas wars in the name of freedom—all for "love of liberty." The audience would have been well aware of the U.S. fighting in Latin America and the Middle East during Reagan's presidency to prevent the spread of communism during the Cold War, the period of tension between the United States and the Soviet Union.

Again, you may not have the knowledge of history to add this detail about what the audience of the time knew about foreign affairs. Whatever you can think of to add about the speaker, audience, and context will add depth and sophistication to your essay.

KEY POINT: Situating the text in **a broader context** can help you analyze the rhetorical situation of the passage more thoroughly and with greater sophistication.

PRACTICE

Below is a draft of a body paragraph in response to the Reagan prompt. Identify an example of analyzing the broader context of the rhetorical situation.

Reagan begins his speech by acknowledging the contributions of immigrants in order to emphasize the crucial role they have played in American history. These men and women "came from every land" and toiled as "teachers, lumberjacks, seamstresses, and journalists," all so their children could have a better life. In short, they completed a weeks-long, arduous journey across the Atlantic, cold and cramped aboard the ship but hopeful of the life that awaited them beyond the shores, beyond the Statue of Liberty. Given that he is speaking at a landmark that quickly came to symbolize the American Dream to those who passed through Ellis Island, Reagan honors the tireless dedication the immigrants exhibited not just for the betterment of their families but also for the betterment of their new nation. As these immigrants with "an abiding love of liberty" settled into their new homeland, they worked diligently to contribute to the country that had given them a renewed sense of hope and a newfound freedom. Whether it was working in factories, or, as Reagan notes, serving as tradesmen or educators, those who immigrated to the United States in the late 1800s and well into the 20th century became integral threads woven into the fabric of America.

WRITE

Write a well-developed body paragraph that attempts to address the broader context of Obama's Morehouse speech. You may use work from previous lessons. Then underline the sentences (or parts of the sentence) that you believe address the broader context.

Although you won't have access to outside sources on exam day, use these resources now to gain knowledge you can use to situate Obama's speech in a broader context. Then use that knowledge in the essay you have been developing in response to the Morehouse prompt.

The History of Historically Black Colleges and Universities (tinyurl.com/3f4nprwc)

The Legacy of Dr. Martin Luther King, Jr. (tinyurl.com/3p3sa92h)

Martin Luther King at Morehouse College (tinyurl.com/3ub748zc)

What's the Point? In one sentence, explain how this lesson can help you on the AP English Language and Composition exam.

LESSON RA.17 Vivid and Persuasive Style

Eyes on the Exam

Another way to earn the sophistication point is to use a **vivid and persuasive writing style** to help you construct a more thoughtful and strong rhetorical analysis essay.

LEARN

Following a few suggestions for your word choice, sentence structure, and punctuation can go a long way to helping you employ "a writing style that is consistently vivid and persuasive," as the rubric explains it.

Tip 1: Replace words like "good," "bad," "thing," and other overly general words with a more precise synonym.

Weak: Reagan <u>says</u> that the immigrants had a <u>good</u> impact on America.

Stronger: Reagan <u>applauds</u> the immigrants' <u>crucial</u> role in American history.

Tip 2: Avoid trite expressions.

Weak: Reagan paints a picture in the audience's mind when he describes the immigrants passing by the Statue of Liberty.

Stronger: The images Reagan creates of the immigrants passing by the Statue of Liberty show both the hardship of the voyage and the determination to achieve a better life.

("Paints a picture in the audience's mind," "to get his point across," and "to open their eyes" are overused expressions that often lead to limited commentary and are better expressed with more specific language.)

Tip 3: Add adjectives and adverbs for more precise writing.

Weak: America, the land of opportunity, gave these families hope.

Stronger: America, the land of opportunity, <u>bountifully</u> gave these <u>struggling</u> families a <u>steadfast</u> hope for the future

Tip 4: Add information through phrases and clauses.

Weak: The Statue of Liberty has become an iconic symbol of the American Dream.

Stronger: The Statue of Liberty, <u>sometimes known as Lady Liberty</u>, has become an iconic symbol of the American Dream. (The underlined part is an *appositive phrase*.)

Also Stronger: The Statue of Liberty, <u>which has welcomed newcomers for more than a century</u>, has become an iconic symbol of the American Dream. (The underlined part is a *nonrestrictive clause*.)

Both *appositive phrases* and *nonrestrictive clauses* are set off by commas (one before and one after) if they are in the middle of a sentence.

Tip 5: Combine sentences using coordination and subordination to clearly show relationships among ideas and create sentence variety.

Weak: Reagan appeals to his listeners' patriotism by quoting Thomas Jefferson. He appeals to their even loftier spiritual values when he mentions God.

Using Coordination: Reagan appeals to his listeners' patriotism by quoting Thomas Jefferson, <u>and</u> he appeals to their even loftier spiritual values when he mentions God. (These two sentences are roughly equal in importance. They are joined by the coordinating conjunction *and* to show that relationship. Other coordinating conjunctions are *but* and *or*.)

Using Subordination: While Reagan appeals to his listeners' patriotism by quoting Thomas Jefferson, he appeals to their even loftier spiritual values when he mentions God. (Now the sentences are combined to put the emphasis on the references to God. The first sentence has been turned into a *dependent* or *subordinate clause*, which cannot stand alone and does not carry as much importance as the second sentence, which remains an *independent clause*. The subordinating conjunction *while* signals that the idea that follows is going to be overshadowed by the idea in the independent clause. Other subordinating conjunctions include *although*, *because*, *before*, and *unless*.)

Showing relationships among ideas increases your persuasive power by leading your reader to see your reasoning,

Tip 6: Add meaningful advanced punctuation.

Semicolons

Semicolons join two independent clauses.

Example: The voyage from Europe to Ellis Island could last up to two weeks; once there, immigrants underwent an hours-long inspection process to make sure their paperwork was in order and that they were in good health.

Dashes

A *dash* can be used to add extra information to the end of an independent clause.

Example: When immigrants entered New York Harbor, the sight of the Statue of Liberty told them they had arrived—they were home.

A *pair of dashes* can be used to offset extra information in a sentence.

Example: When speaking at the torch-lighting ceremony—a symbolic celebration of freedom—Reagan eloquently articulates the integral role of liberty within American history.

Colons

A *colon* can be used to add extra information to the end of an independent clause. In many cases, it serves as an equal sign.

Example: These men and women journeyed to the U.S. with one goal in mind: freedom. (one goal in mind=freedom)

The advanced punctuation tips also provide tools to increase your persuasive impact, once again by showing how you establish connections among ideas.

The final tip reminds you that you yourself are in a rhetorical situation when you are writing your essay.

Tip 7: Make rhetorical choices.

The writers you study make rhetorical choices. As a writer, you get to make rhetorical choices to develop your argument too. As you develop your writer's voice, you might consider incorporating meaningful repetition, or perhaps you can include a meaningful comparison. Think of rhetorical choices that have had a persuasive impact on you and try to use them in your own writing.

KEY POINT: Precise wording, combined sentences to show relationships, and **meaningful punctuation** can help make a rhetorical analysis essay more vivid and persuasive.

PRACTICE

Below is a draft of a body paragraph. Identify at least two instances of vivid and persuasive style.

Reagan begins his speech by acknowledging the contributions of immigrants in order to emphasize the crucial role they have played in American history. These men and women "came from every land" and toiled as "teachers, lumberjacks, seamstresses, and journalists," all so their children could have a better life. In short, they completed a weeks-long, <u>arduous</u> journey across the Atlantic, cold and cramped aboard the ship <u>but hopeful</u> of the life that awaited them beyond the shores, beyond the Statue of Liberty. Given that he is speaking at a landmark that quickly came to symbolize the American Dream to those who passed through Ellis Island, Reagan honors the tireless dedication the immigrants exhibited not just for the betterment of their families but also for the betterment of their new nation. As these immigrants with "an abiding love of liberty" settled into their new homeland, they worked diligently to contribute to the country that had given them what they wanted: a renewed sense of hope and a newfound freedom. Whether they worked in factories, which steadily turned out the tools that helped build the nation, or served as tradesmen or educators, those who immigrated to the United States in the late 1800s and well into the 20th century became integral threads woven into the fabric of America.

WRITE

Review your paragraph from the previous lesson. Identify any instances of a vivid and persuasive style already present in your paragraph. Revise to incorporate the tips above where appropriate.

Read this blog (tinyurl.com/226sum2t) from University of the People to learn about advanced punctuation that you can use to elevate your writing style. Also, check out this blog post (tinyurl.com/mrxwy8yd) from Marco Learning for more tips about creating a sophisticated writing style. You may want to complete a chart like the one at the bottom of the page to count the words in your sentences and identify the types of sentences you used.

Watch Beth Hall demonstrate vivid and descriptive writing using the Reagan liberty prompt at the companion website (tinyurl.com/2mrx3r99) for this book. There you will find other videos by the authors as well as all the links included in the lessons in this book.

What's the Point? In one sentence, explain how this lesson can help you on the AP English Language and Composition exam.

_____

_____

_____

LESSON RA.18 Complexity and Tension

Eyes on the Exam

Examining the underlying complexities and tensions in the passage can yield a more interesting, thought-provoking analysis. You can earn one point for sophistication.

LEARN

Recall that the three ways to earn the sophistication point are

- Situating the passage in a broader context.
- Consistently using vivid and persuasive language.
- Explaining a purpose or function of the passage's complexities or tensions.

This final lesson on sophistication focuses on examining the complexities and tensions of the rhetorical situation or the passage itself to write a more complex and mature analysis. The work required for this point tests your ability to explore the nuanced or conflicting elements of a passage and explain how these elements contribute to the overall message, purpose, or effect of the text.

These questions can help you uncover complex elements:

- Is there any tension between the speaker and audience? If so, what is the cause of the tension, and how does the speaker make rhetorical choices to address this tension?
- Which, if any, social or political tensions are present in the passage or within the passage's context?
- Are there any contradictions in the text? If so, how can you explain them?
- Are there shifts in tone, and if so, what effect do they have on the text?
- What might the speaker leave unsaid?

Consider the excerpt on the following page of Reagan's speech at the Statue of Liberty torch-lighting ceremony. The first column includes the text; the second offers explanations of possible tensions and complexities.

Passage	Implied Tension
What was it that tied these profoundly different people together? What was it that made them not a gathering of individuals, but a nation? That bond that held them together, as it holds us together tonight, that bond that has stood every test and travail, is found deep in our national consciousness: an abiding love of liberty. For love of liberty, our forebears—colonists, few in number and with little to defend themselves—fought a war for independence with what was then the world's most powerful empire. For love of liberty, those who came before us tamed a vast wilderness and braved hardships which, at times, were beyond the limits of human endurance. For love of liberty, a bloody and heart-wrenching civil war was fought. And for love of liberty, Americans championed and still champion, even in times of peril, the cause of human freedom in far-off lands.	This portion of the text leads to possible complexities and tensions because the language is highly patriotic, yet some people might object to Reagan's portrayal of American history as it ignores the underlying tensions present during those key moments within American history. In Lesson RA.10, the tension about westward expansion was explored by examining the word choice of "tamed a vast wilderness." The championing of freedom in far-off lands might represent another source of complexity and tension. The memory of the war in Vietnam was no doubt still fresh in listeners' minds, and during Reagan's administration, military actions in Central America and the Middle East were divisive political issues. These military actions were related to Cold War tensions between the United States and the Soviet Union.
"The God who gave us life," Thomas Jefferson once proclaimed, "gave us liberty at the same time." But like all of God's precious gifts, liberty must never be taken for granted. Tonight we thank God for the many blessings He has bestowed on our land; we affirm our faithfulness to His rule and to our own ideals; and we pledge to keep alive the dream that brought our forefathers and mothers to this brave new land.	This quote is a possible source of tension or complexity. While Christianity was the dominant religion during Jefferson's time, American citizens have a wide array of religious beliefs and thus would likely have differing reactions to this quote. Furthermore, although Jefferson acknowledges liberty, his political legacy is complicated by his use of enslaved people on his properties. Throughout American history, marginalized groups have not experienced equal liberties.
We are the keepers of the flame of liberty. We hold it high tonight for the world to see, a beacon of hope, a light unto the nations. And so with joy and celebration and with a prayer that this lamp shall never be extinguished. I ask that you all join me in this symbolic act of faith, this lighting of Miss Liberty's torch.	The notion that America is a "beacon of hope" is a potential source of complexity and tension within the passage. As president, Reagan upholds the notion that America is a "light unto the nations." However, some people might disagree with this statement. Additionally, while some people still chase the American Dream, others believe it is an empty promise.

Now think about how you can incorporate what you have found into your essay. Since throwing a line in here or there will not be sufficient to earn the point, think about how you can weave an idea through your essay.

You may want to begin at the beginning. Consider how an acknowledgment of tension and complexity might appear in the introduction.

Some may think that our nation is more divided than united, that our differences create too wide a gulf to bridge. However, the United States has a long history of strength through both unity and diversity, both in the spirit of liberty. This was the theme President Ronald Reagan chose to emphasize in his speech on July 3, 1986, at the lighting of the torch of the newly restored Statue of Liberty. President Reagan lists diverse immigrants, repeats key words and ideas, and stirs patriotic emotions to convey the message that liberty is one of the most important values Americans share. In so doing, he implicitly criticizes as inferior the Communist Soviet Union and its allies, opponents of the United States in the lingering Cold War.

How might that concept be woven into a body paragraph? Here's one way.

President Reagan offers diverse examples of Americans from all walks of life to emphasize the ties that bind them despite their diversity. In plain language, he lists everyday Americans, "teachers, lumberjacks, seamstresses, and journalists," who "passed through this harbor" and "looked up at [the Statue of Liberty's] torch," imagining and then achieving a better life for themselves and their families. With this thought, Reagan may also be reminding his global listeners that the opportunity to improve one's economic situation through hard work is not available in communist economies, though many listeners would know that moving out of poverty into wealth is far from easy even in the United States. The mention of specific workplaces and specific workers, all having entered the country looking up at the Statue of Liberty, all reaching toward the same goal, demonstrates Reagan's claim that Americans, though "profoundly different," share fundamental experiences and values. Naming their specific occupations and the places these Americans worked—"in our factories, on ships and railroads, in stores, and on road construction crews"—Reagan helps listeners, many of whom have similar jobs, feel the very connection with their fellow Americans that Reagan is describing. The lists emphasize the unity Americans feel even through their differences and across time.

The underlined sentence above achieves two results: it situates the remarks in the context of the Cold War and also highlights a tension by noting that the United States has economic inequities that some Communist countries do not.

KEY POINT: Articulating possible **tensions and complexities** in your essay will raise the level of interest and engagement readers experience.

PRACTICE

Read the selections of Obama's Morehouse speech below, and on separate paper identify the implied complexity or tension.

1. Dr. King was just 15 years old when he enrolled here at Morehouse. He was an unknown, undersized, unassuming young freshman who lived at home with his parents. And I think it's fair to say he wasn't the coolest kid on campus—for the suits he wore, his classmates called him "Tweed." But his education at Morehouse helped to forge the intellect, the discipline, the compassion, the soul force that would transform America. It was here that he was introduced to the writings of Gandhi and Thoreau, and the theory of civil disobedience. It was here that professors encouraged him to look past the world as it was and fight for the world as it should be. And it was here, at Morehouse, as Dr. King later wrote, where "I realized that nobody . . . was afraid."

2. Now, think about it. For black men in the '40s and the '50s, the threat of violence, the constant humiliations, large and small, the uncertainty that you could support a family, the gnawing doubts born of the Jim Crow culture that told you every day that somehow you were inferior, the temptation to shrink from the world, to accept your place, to avoid risks, to be afraid—that temptation was necessarily strong.

3. So the history we share should give you hope. The future we share should give you hope. You're graduating into an improving job market. You're living in a time when advances in technology and communication put the world at your fingertips. Your generation is uniquely poised for success unlike any generation of African Americans that came before it.

4. But that doesn't mean we don't have work—because if we're honest with ourselves, we know that too few of our brothers have the opportunities that you've had here at Morehouse. In troubled neighborhoods all across this country—many of them heavily African American—too few of our citizens have role models to guide them. Communities just a couple miles from my house in Chicago, communities just a couple miles from here—they're places where jobs are still too scarce and wages are still too low; where schools are underfunded and violence is pervasive; where too many of our men spend their youth not behind a desk in a classroom, but hanging out on the streets or brooding behind a jail cell.

5. My job, as President, is to advocate for policies that generate more opportunity for everybody—policies that strengthen the middle class and give more people the chance to climb their way into the middle class. Policies that create more good jobs and reduce poverty, and educate more children, and give more families the security of health care, and protect more of our children from the horrors of gun violence. That's my job. Those are matters of public policy, and it is important for all of us—black, white and brown—to advocate for an America where everybody has got a fair shot in life. Not just some. Not just a few.

WRITE

Select one rhetorical choice from Obama's Morehouse commencement speech. Then do your best to write a paragraph in which you analyze the implied complexities or tensions within your commentary.

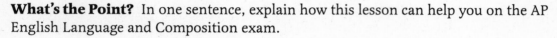 For more information on the sophistication point, here are two excellent videos, each about 15 minutes long.

Garden of English (Timm Freitas): <u>How to Write for SOPHISTICATION (Get That Point!)</u> (tinyurl.com/45kayhfx)

Coach Hall Writes (Beth Hall): <u>Sophistication Point AP Lang</u> (tinyurl.com/2jpbz5jv)

What's the Point? In one sentence, explain how this lesson can help you on the AP English Language and Composition exam.

_____

_____

_____

TEAM UP

In his video, Timm Freitas explains that while identifying fallacies can add sophistication, being overly critical of the writer or speaker is unwise. Neither speech you have been studying in these lessons contains logical fallacies, but fallacies have been noted in another excellent speech known for its inspiring message. That speech is the famous "Stanford Commencement Speech" delivered in 2005 by Steve Jobs, co-founder of Apple Inc. In his speech, Jobs shares three personal stories about "connecting the dots," "love and loss," and "death." While the overall message is motivational, encouraging graduates to pursue their passions and see opportunities in life's setbacks, some might argue that certain aspects of his narratives could be subjected to fallacies or over-simplifications.

Working in small groups as your teacher directs, watch or read the speech <u>here</u> (tinyurl.com/59vjupcn), keeping a critical eye out for what aspects of the speech may contain fallacious reasoning. (You can review fallacies at the <u>Purdue Online Writing Lab</u> (tinyurl.com/493b4res). Work with your group to find possible fallacies, and then share your findings with the whole class.

It's important to note that the intention of Jobs's speech was to inspire and motivate, and it has been widely celebrated for its powerful and positive messages. The identification of potential fallacies or contradictions is not to diminish its value but to highlight how even well-received and influential speeches can contain elements that warrant critical analysis.

RHETORICAL ANALYSIS Sophistication Review (Row C)

Eyes on the Exam

Whether you receive a point for sophistication depends on how well your essay meets the criteria in Row C of the rubric.

LEARN

Carefully read each section of Row C.

- The first row describes in general terms what the essay must demonstrate to earn the sophistication point.
- The second row describes characteristics of essays missing or earning the sophistication point. It also provides specific examples and criteria.
- The final row provides additional clarifications for earning the sophistication point.

Row C: Sophistication (0-1 points), Scoring Criteria [2.A, 4.C, 6.B, 8.A, 8.B, 8.C]	
0 points	**1 point**
Does not meet the criteria for one point.	Demonstrates sophistication of thought and/or develops a complex understanding of the rhetorical situation.
Responses that do not earn this point: Attempt to contextualize the text, but such attempts consist predominantly of sweeping generalizations (*"No President has an easy job . . ."* OR *"From the founding days of our nation . . ."*). Only hint at or suggest other arguments (*"Not all people see things as Reagan does . . ."* OR *"Most people in the country think . . ."*). Examine individual rhetorical choices but do not examine the relationships among different choices throughout the text. Oversimplify complexities in the text. Use complicated or complex sentences or language that is ineffective because it does not enhance the analysis.	**Responses that earn this point may demonstrate sophistication of thought and/or a complex understanding of the rhetorical situation by doing any of the following:** *Explaining the significance or relevance of the writer's rhetorical choices (given the rhetorical situation).* *Explaining a purpose or function of the passage's complexities or tensions.* *Employing a style that is consistently vivid and persuasive.*
Additional Notes: This point should be awarded only if the sophistication of thought or complex understanding is part of the student's argument, not merely a phrase or reference.	

Following are the skills from the Course and Exam Description that are assessed in Row C.

2.A Write introductions and conclusions appropriate to the purpose and context of the rhetorical situation.

4.C Qualify a claim using modifiers, counterarguments, or alternative perspectives.

6.B Use transitional elements to guide the reader through the line of reasoning of an argument.

8.A Strategically use words, comparisons, and syntax to convey a specific tone or style in an argument.

8.B Write sentences that clearly convey ideas and arguments.

8.C Use established conventions of grammar and mechanics to communicate clearly and effectively.

PRACTICE

Complete the following activities and answer the questions about the Row C Sophistication rubric and scoring guide.

1. Which of the following do you need to do to earn the sophistication point?
   - Explain the significance or relevance of the writer's rhetorical choices (given the rhetorical situation).
   - Explain a purpose or function of the passage's complexities or tensions.
   - Employ a style that is consistently vivid and persuasive.

2. What should you avoid when trying to contextualize a text?

3. What kind of language should you use for your best chance at earning the sophistication point?

4. Why might efforts to add complexities in a few places fail to earn the sophistication point?

5. How important are counterarguments in earning the sophistication point?

You Be the Reader

Read sample essay RA.2.C in the Appendix on page 277. Decide whether the essay earns a sophistication point. Explain your answer.

Watch this video (tinyurl.com/2jpbz5jv) by Beth Hall in which she reviews the sophistication point and how to earn it.

Revise

Review the efforts you have made to achieve sophistication in your essay in response to Obama's Morehouse speech. Revise as needed to make sure your efforts are woven throughout your essay.

LESSON RA.19 Sample Essay: From a 3 to a 4

Eyes on the Exam

Exam readers score essays on the standard rubric that allows each essay to score up to 6 total points. Up to 1 point is awarded for a thesis that responds to the prompt. Up to 4 points are awarded for effectively including evidence and sufficiently developing commentary. Up to 1 point is awarded for sophistication. Before continuing with this lesson, review the entire rhetorical analysis rubric at this link (tinyurl.com/yckwdjj9). Scroll down to Scoring Rubric for Question 2: Rhetorical Analysis.

LEARN

The following essay is a student draft in response to the Reagan liberty prompt on page 115. (**Task:** After reading President Reagan's speech, write a well-developed essay in which you analyze how President Reagan makes rhetorical choices to convey his message about American values.)

This student earned a total score of 3 out of 6 points. The score breakdown is as follows (the points for each row are in bold type):

Row A: Thesis	0				**1**
Row B: Evidence and Commentary	0	1	**2**	3	4
Row C: Sophistication	**0**				1
Total			**3/6**		

PRACTICE

Look closely at the first two paragraphs of this essay, which have been annotated below. Text from the essay is in the middle column. The left column provides thoughts an exam reader might have, and the right column provides several suggestions for improving the essay. Read the comments and advice carefully to be sure you understand them. In the Write activity that follows, you will be asked to make changes based on advice.

Comments	Essay	Advice
Stronger verbs needed	**(1)** Since its beginning, America has prided itself on being a place where people could get a fresh start. **(2)** During the late 1800s and early 1900s, the American Dream was alive and well. **(3)** Thousands of people immigrated to the U.S. in hopes of a better life. **(4)** For many, seeing the Statue of Liberty was a sign they'd made it. **(5)** Because of this, Lady Liberty has come to symbolize freedom. **(6)** In his 1986 speech at the Statue of Liberty torch-lighting ceremony, Ronald Reagan uses repetition, questions, and unifying diction to convey his message about the importance of liberty in American history.	Work rhetorically accurate verbs into sentence 6.
	(7) Reagan begins his speech by repeating "they" when talking about the immigrants. **(8)** For example, he says	

Comments	Essay	Advice
Avoid saying *says*.	"they were the men and women who labored all their lives" so that their children would have better lives. **(9)** This quote shows that the immigrants worked hard. **(10)** This is important because America wouldn't be what it is today without their hard work. **(11)** Reagan also says that "they worked in factories, on ships and railroads, in stores, and on road construction crews." **(12)** He then adds that "they were teachers, lumberjacks, seamstresses, and journalists." **(13)** By saying "they," he emphasizes that we owe a lot of gratitude to the people who immigrated here and worked hard because they are a huge part of the reason why America is what it is today. **(14)** This repetition is important to help Reagan convey his message.	Reword the sentence to avoid using the word *says*, perhaps by integrating the direct quote more seamlessly.

KEY POINT: A number of **small but meaningful changes** can work together to raise the score of a rhetorical analysis essay.

WRITE

Read the full student draft below. Then respond to the questions provided so that you can help this draft increase in score by at least one point in the evidence and commentary row. The changes you are asked to make address words, phrases, and whole sentences. You will also be asked to increase the coherence and cohesion of the whole essay's line of reasoning.

[1] Since its beginning, America has prided itself on being a place where people could get a fresh start. [2] During the late 1800s and early 1900s, the American Dream was alive and well. [3] Thousands of people immigrated to the U.S. in hopes of a better life. [4] For many, seeing the Statue of Liberty was a sign they'd made it. [5] Because of this, Lady Liberty has come to symbolize freedom. [6] In his 1986 speech at the Statue of Liberty torch-lighting ceremony, Ronald Reagan uses repetition, questions, and unifying diction to convey his message about the importance of liberty in American history.

[7] Reagan begins his speech by repeating "they" when talking about the immigrants. [8] For example, he says "they were the men and women who labored all their lives" so that their children would have better lives. [9] This quote shows that the immigrants worked hard. [10] This is important because America wouldn't be what it is today without their hard work. [11] Reagan also says that "they worked in factories, on ships and railroads, in stores, and on road construction crews." [12] He then adds that "they were teachers, lumberjacks, seamstresses, and journalists." [13] By saying "they," he emphasizes that we owe a lot of gratitude to the people who immigrated here and worked hard because they are a huge part of the reason why America is what it is today. [14] This repetition is important to help Reagan convey his message.

[15] Reagan also poses questions. [16] "What was it that tied these profoundly different people together?" [17} He does this to show that liberty has always been important to U.S. citizens: it's an ideal the country was founded on. [18] This question helps further his message and is important because he is at the Statue of Liberty.

[19] Reagan concludes his speech by repeating the word "we" to unite Americans. [20] By saying "we are the keepers of the flame of liberty" and "we hold it high tonight for the world to see," Reagan invigorates a sense of pride in his American audience. [21] This leads to his call to action. [22] He asks the audience to join him in the symbolic lighting of the torch. [23] This act will remind people that the ideal of freedom is alive and well in the United States.

[24] When considering the topic of liberty in the United States, it is clear that freedom has been important since the country's beginning and remains important today, decades after Reagan's 1986 speech.

As you answer the questions, focus on providing specific and precise changes that consider the context of what is written so that your recommended changes can be substituted into the essay and it will read smoothly. You may try to make changes that will help this paper earn the sophistication point; however, your focus should be making changes that will raise the score in Row B of the scoring rubric.

1. The writer wants to revise the thesis (sentence 6) to include rhetorically accurate verbs. Rewrite the thesis to do so. **(Lesson RA.6)**

2. The writer wants to revise the topic sentence of the first body paragraph (sentence 7) to include a "why" (reason) to better establish a line of reasoning. **(Lesson RA.8)**

3. The writer wants to revise sentence 13 to include more precise language instead of "a lot" and "huge." Revise the sentence to include more advanced word choice. **(Lesson RA.17)**

4. The writer wants to revise the concluding sentence of body paragraph 1 (sentence 14) to include a specific message emerging from the passage. Identify a possible message from the passage and revise that sentence accordingly. **(Lesson RA.2)**

5. The writer wants to refine the topic sentence of body paragraph two (sentence 15) to create a more effective transition and strengthen the line of reasoning by more clearly establishing the reason for the rhetorical choice. Revise the sentence to do so. **(Lesson RA.8)**

6. The writer wants to embed the quote or a portion of the quote in sentence 16 to better connect their own reasoning with the information from the passage. Rewrite the sentence with embedded evidence. **(Lesson RA.11)**

7. The writer wants to expand the commentary in sentence 18 to connect to the rhetorical situation. Revise the sentence to include a reference to the specific message. **(Lesson RA.13)**

8. The writer wants to combine sentences 21 and 22 to emphasize Reagan's call to action. Combine these sentences using a colon. **(Lesson RA.17)**

9. The writer wants to add more commentary to body paragraph 3 to better justify the claim given the evidence from the passage. Write detailed commentary that explains the evidence in paragraph 3. **(Lessons RA.12 and 13)**

10. The writer wants to develop a stronger, more specific conclusion for the essay. Write a conclusion that meets the following criteria:

- Situates the issue in a broader context by addressing how the topic or message is relevant to American history and/or society today **(Lessons RA.16 and 18)**
- Incorporates advanced punctuation, such as a colon or dashes **(Lesson RA.17)**

What's the Point? In one sentence, explain how this lesson can help you on the AP English Language and Composition exam.

_____

_____

_____

TEAM UP

Work independently to answer the questions that follow the sample essay. When you are finished, and as your teacher directs, break into small groups and compare your answers question by question.

- Note the similarities and differences among the answers.
- Evaluate the effectiveness of each change.
- Discuss questions that were especially challenging to you. Try to articulate what made them challenging. Seek and give feedback to help group members overcome any challenges.

This activity should help you see that there are many different ways to revise that would enhance the score of this essay.

LESSON RA.20 Sample Essay: From a 4 to a 5

Eyes on the Exam

Exam readers score essays on the standard rubric that allows each essay to score up to 6 total points. Up to 1 point is awarded for a thesis that responds to the prompt. Up to 4 points are awarded for effectively including evidence and sufficiently developing commentary. Up to 1 point is awarded for sophistication.

You may want to review the entire rhetorical analysis rubric at this link (tinyurl.com/yckwdjj9). Scroll down to Scoring Rubric for Question 2: Rhetorical Analysis.

LEARN

The following essay is a student draft in response to the Reagan liberty prompt on page 115. (**Task:** After reading President Reagan's speech, write a well-developed essay in which you analyze how President Reagan makes rhetorical choices to convey his message about American values.) This student earned a total score of 4 out of 6 points. The score breakdown is as follows (the points for each row are in bold type).

Row A: Thesis	0				**1**
Row B: Evidence and Commentary	0	1	2	**3**	4
Row C: Sophistication	**0**				1
Total			4/6		

PRACTICE

Look closely at the first paragraph and part of the second paragraph of this essay, which have been annotated below. Text from the essay is in the middle column. The left column provides thoughts that an exam reader might have, and the right column provides several suggestions for improving the essay. Read the comments and advice carefully to be sure you understand them. In the Write activity that follows, you will be asked to make changes based on advice.

Comments	Essay	Advice
Introduction might benefit from a hook, though that is not required Identify speaker's credentials.	[1] In his 1986 speech at the Statue of Liberty torch-lighting ceremony, Ronald Reagan not only acknowledges the contributions of immigrants but also underscores the importance of liberty. [2] In doing so, he conveys the continued significance of both freedom and the American Dream.	Might consider a meaningful fragment, universal truth, or other hook strategies Provide some more information about who Reagan is

Comments	Essay	Advice
First quote not really embedded Stronger rhetorical verb would be better than *states*	[3] In order to ultimately convey that the U.S. remains a beacon of hope, Reagan begins his speech applauding the often underacknowledged hard work of those who immigrated to America. [4] He states, "They worked in our factories, on ships and railroads, in stores, and on road construction crews." [5] He also states that "they were teachers, lumberjacks, seamstresses, and journalists" who "came from every land." [6] By listing the roles of these immigrants, Reagan emphasizes how important these men and women were to society: they filled important jobs that helped society function and grow.	Avoid using whole sentences as quotes. Work shorter sections into your own sentences. Look for stronger synonym for *states*

KEY POINT: Spend the most time on exam day **making your evidence and commentary the best they can be.**

WRITE

Read the full student draft below. Then, respond to the questions provided so that you can help this draft increase in score by at least one point in the evidence and commentary row. The changes you are asked to make address words, phrases, and whole sentences. You will also be asked to increase the coherence and cohesion of the whole essay's line of reasoning.

[1] In his 1986 speech at the Statue of Liberty torch-lighting ceremony, Ronald Reagan not only acknowledges the contributions of immigrants but also underscores the importance of liberty. [2] In doing so, he conveys the continued significance of both freedom and the American Dream.

[3] In order to ultimately convey that the U.S. remains a beacon of hope, Reagan begins his speech applauding the often underacknowledged hard work of those who immigrated to America. [4] He states, "They worked in our factories, on ships and railroads, in stores, and on road construction crews." [5] He also states that "they were teachers, lumberjacks, seamstresses, and journalists" who "came from every land." [6] By listing the roles of these immigrants, Reagan emphasizes how important these men and women were to society: they filled important jobs that helped society function and grow. [7] As Reagan notes, these men and women left their lives behind and worked diligently so that "their children would be well fed, clothed, and educated." [8] By paying homage to the immigrants who passaged through Ellis Island—the ones whose first sight of the U.S. was likely the very statue at which Reagan is delivering his speech—Reagan underscores the value of the American Dream: it drew people to America, and without their efforts, our country would not be what it is today.

[9] Next, Reagan expounds upon the importance of liberty. [10] To show the importance of liberty in American history, Reagan references several key events. [11] These examples prove that liberty is not a new concept. [12] It's a core ideal of the nation that has been of the utmost importance for generations. [13] He also quotes Thomas Jefferson, one of the nation's founding fathers, to support his message about the importance of liberty. Jefferson

referred to liberty as a God-given gift, implying that it is precious. [14] For this reason, Reagan claims that "liberty must not be taken for granted." [15] Given that he is speaking during the 1980s, amidst the end of the Cold War and rise of communism, his American audience would likely find his message important. [16] Therefore, they'd be more receptive to his call for America to continue to be a "beacon of hope" that will "never be extinguished."

[17] In conclusion, Ronald Reagan acknowledges the immigrants' hard work and examines the role of liberty throughout American history to convey the value of the American Dream. [18] While the American Dream drove thousands of people to start a new life in America, for many, it was just that: a dream.

As you answer the questions, focus on providing specific and precise changes that consider the context of what is written so that your recommended changes can be substituted into the essay and it will read smoothly. You may try to make changes that will help this paper earn the sophistication point; however, your focus should be making changes that will raise the score in Row B of the scoring rubric.

1. The writer would like to develop the introduction to include an appropriate hook and context before the thesis statement. Revise the introduction to accomplish this goal. **(Lesson RA.7)**

2. The writer would like to revise the thesis (sentence 1) to include the speaker's credentials. Revise sentence 1 to accomplish this goal. **(Lesson RA.2)**

3. To remove any unnecessary repetition, the writer wants to combine sentences 4 and 5 and embed the evidence more effectively by omitting the phrase "He states" and shortening the quotes. Revise sentences 4 and 5 to accomplish this goal. **(Lesson RA.11)**.

4. The writer wants to better develop the reasoning in the first body paragraph by including additional commentary after sentence 7. Revise the paragraph to accomplish this goal. **(Lessons RA.12 and 13)**

5. The writer wants to revise the topic sentence of body paragraph 2 to create a more effective transition that more clearly establishes a line of reasoning. Revise sentence 9 to accomplish this goal. **(Lesson RA.8)**

6. The writer would like to select and embed evidence to better support the reasoning in sentence 10. Write one to two sentences that would achieve this outcome. **(Lessons RA.9, 10, and 11)**

7. The writer would like to strengthen the commentary in sentences 11 and 12, ensuring that it effectively explains the significance of the evidence. Revise these sentences to provide specific, developed commentary for the evidence you added in question 3. **(Lessons RA.12 and 13)**

8. The writer wants to develop the commentary in sentence 15 to clarify why, given the context, the audience would find the message important. Write additional commentary to accomplish this goal. **(Lessons RA.13 and 16)**

9. The writer wants to improve the style of the essay by elevating the word choice. Make three separate revisions to help the writer make progress in achieving this goal. Your revisions can include elevating the word choice, adding adjectives or adverbs, or incorporating advanced punctuation. **(Lesson RA.17)**

10. The writer wants to revise the conclusion to further analyze the broader context and the complexity of the message. Write additional sentences to accomplish this goal. **(Lessons RA.15, 16, and 18)**

What's the Point? In one sentence, explain how this lesson can help you on the AP English Language and Composition exam.

_____

_____

_____

TEAM UP

Work independently to answer the questions that follow the sample essay. When you are finished, and as your teacher directs, break into small groups and compare your answers question by question.

- Note the similarities and differences among the answers.
- Evaluate the effectiveness of each change.
- Discuss questions that were especially challenging to you. Try to articulate what made them challenging. Seek and give feedback to help group members overcome any challenges.

Then, using the **Rhetorical Analysis Key Point Review** on the next two pages, collaborate with your group members and briefly talk through each lesson's Key Point. Try to say as many things as you remember about each point. If you need a refresher, refer back to the page number indicated after the Key Point to review the lesson.

After you talk through each section (Prompt, Thesis, Evidence and Commentary, and Sophistication), pause and as a group try to come up with the single most important thing you should remember about that section. Then move on to the next section.

After you complete the Rhetorical Analysis Key Point Review, complete the self-evaluation that follows it. When everyone has finished, regroup and share your evaluations. Ask for feedback on areas that concern you, and give feedback when you can to help others.

****

After completing the Free-Response Practice Question: Rhetorical Analysis on page 191, and if your teacher directs, meet with your group and read your responses to the rhetorical analysis prompt. Then partner up and use the rubrics for Row A (page 143), Row B (page 165), and Row C (page 179) to evaluate your partner's essay. Discuss the evaluations and articulate what you learned that will help you when exam day comes.

RHETORICAL ANALYSIS Key Point Review

PROMPT

RA.1 A rhetorical analysis prompt contains **three main parts: background** on the reading passage, **directions** for writing an essay analyzing the passage, and the **reading passage** itself. (page 115)

RA.2 Adding labels or notes can help you remember to connect the rhetorical choices to the rhetorical situation when you begin planning and writing. (page 118)

RA.3 "What/Why" annotations help you engage with the passage as you reread. These annotations will help you with future steps in the writing process. (page 122)

RA.4 Determine the **line of reasoning** by dividing the text into different sections and identifying the key idea of each section. Use this analysis to write claims about what happens in the beginning, middle, and end of the text. (page 128)

RA.5 Review your knowledge of **rhetorical choices** and *devices* so you can efficiently analyze how and why a writer or speaker makes or uses them. (page 131)

THESIS

RA.6 Your prompt will include one of the following phrases: convey a message, develop an argument, or achieve a purpose. To truly answer the prompt, **your thesis should include the specific message, argument, or purpose.** (page 134)

RA.7 Introductory paragraphs commonly contain three parts: **hook, context, and thesis.** For timed essays, a hook is optional. However, do include appropriate specifics about the rhetorical situation and a defensible thesis to avoid a jarringly abrupt introduction. (page 137)

RA.8 Look to your **thesis statement** for the **main ideas and order of your topic sentences.** Link them with **transitions** that show how your ideas are moving from the beginning of the speech to the end. (page 141)

EVIDENCE AND COMMENTARY

RA.9 Choose **specific, clear evidence** from your text to support your reasoning and justify the claim each topic sentence asserts about rhetorical choices the speaker or writer makes. When selecting direct quotes as evidence, look for short quotes (roughly 3–12 words). (page 146)

RA.10 Word choice is a window into a speaker's or writer's mind and viewpoints and may reflect **perspectives** tied to the historical context. Analyzing word choice is one strategy for understanding tone and rhetorical choices. (page 150)

RA.11 Make sure to have at least one word before the quoted evidence and remember that **shorter quotes are often easier to embed.** (page 152)

RA.12 Think carefully to provide **commentary that explains the significance of your evidence** to your claim. Commentary language helps you effectively convey your analysis of the evidence. (page 155)

RA.13 Strong commentary often **connects the evidence to elements of the rhetorical situation,** especially the message, purpose, or argument. (page 158)

RA.14 **Embedding short quotes from the passage into your commentary** can help you engage with the text and elevate the quality of your commentary. (page 161)

RA.15 An effective conclusion will examine **the broader implications** of the passage rather than merely summarize the main points of the essay. (page 163)

SOPHISTICATION

RA.16 **Situating the text in a broader context** can help you analyze the rhetorical situation of the passage more thoroughly and with greater sophistication. (page 168)

RA.17 **Precise wording, combined sentences** to show relationships, and **meaningful punctuation** can help make a rhetorical analysis essay more vivid and persuasive. (page 171)

RA.18 Articulating possible **tensions and complexities** in your essay will raise the level of interest and engagement readers experience. (page 174)

SAMPLE ESSAYS

RA.19 A number of **small but meaningful changes** can work together to raise the score of a rhetorical analysis essay. (page 181)

RA.20 Spend the most time on exam day **making your evidence and commentary the best they can be.** (page 185)

SELF-EVALUATION

In the space below, evaluate your readiness for answering the Rhetorical Analysis Free-Response Question.

What are your strengths? What part(s) of the rhetorical analysis essay do you feel confident about?

In what aspects of writing the rhetorical analysis essay do you need more practice and guidance?

What are three steps you can take for getting that additional practice and guidance?

Free-Response Practice Question: Rhetorical Analysis

Suggested time—40 minutes

(This question counts as one-third of the total essay section score.)

The following speech was delivered on December 8, 2001, by Condoleezza Rice, former Secretary of State to George W. Bush and the first African American female to hold the position. At the time of the address, she was accepting the Mary McLeod Bethune Award from the National Council of Negro Women, an organization that seeks to empower African American women and promote education and leadership. Read the excerpt carefully. Write an essay in which you analyze the rhetorical choices Rice makes to convey her message about education.

In your response you should do the following:
- Respond to the prompt with a thesis that analyzes the writer's rhetorical choices.
- Select and use evidence to support your line of reasoning.
- Explain how the evidence supports your line of reasoning.
- Demonstrate an understanding of the rhetorical situation.
- Use appropriate grammar and punctuation in communicating your argument.

[1] I could not be more honored than to receive the Bethune Award because I feel a great kinship with Mary McLeod Bethune and I think we all do. . . . [2] It's extraordinary to think that at the time that Dr. Bethune lived, she was asked by a president of the United States to go to Liberia, in 1952, on a diplomatic mission. [3] It's extraordinary that she was invited to the White House in 1928. [4] It's extraordinary that a young, black woman from South Carolina could found a college and be its president for almost four decades. [5] It's extraordinary, not because she wasn't talented enough to do it, but because she lived and toiled at a time when to do that as an African-American woman was extraordinary.

[. . .]

[6] I also feel, of course, a great, great kinship with this wonderful organization. [7] It's been a part of our lives and a part of our histories from the time that any of us could remember. [8] It is an organization that stands for the best in America because it stands for opportunity, and it stands for hope, and it stands for belief. It stands for . . . the tremendous gains that we as African-Americans, and African-American women, have made in these many years. . . .

[9] I also feel a great kinship to Dr. Bethune and to this organization because we share a passion for education. . . . [10] I'm a living example of what education can mean, because it goes back a long way in my family. . . .

[11] Maybe some of you've heard me tell the story of Granddaddy Rice, a poor sharecropper's son in Ewtah[,] Alabama, who, somehow, in about 1919 decided he was going to get book learning.

[12] And so he asked people . . . how a colored man could get to college. [13] And they said to him, "Well you see there's this college not too far away from here called Stillman College, and if you could get there, they take colored men into college." . . .

[14] My grandfather understood something, and so did my grandmother and my mother's parents, and that is that higher education, if you can attain it, is transforming. [15] You may come from a poor family, you may come from a rural family, you may be first-generation college-educated, but once you are college-educated, the most important thing about you,

in many ways, is that you're a college graduate and you are transformed. [16] And I have to tell you that if I have a concern at all today in America, it is that we have got to find a way to pass on that promise to children, no matter what their circumstances, because it's just got to be the case in America that it does not matter where you came from, it only matters where you're going.

. . . [17] But we have a hard job ahead of us if that promise is going to continue to be fulfilled. [18] We've got an educational system that is, frankly, not living up to the demands of today to educate our children.

[. . .]

[19] Now, there's another message that we need to deliver to our kids. [20] It's that educational excellence is key, but so are limitless educational horizons.

[21] You know, I didn't start out to be a Russian specialist. [22] I'm not Russian, in case you haven't noticed. [23] And so I went to college to be a concert pianist. [24] I could read music before I could read. [25] But, about my sophomore year in college, I started to encounter those kids who could play from sight everything that it had taken me all year to learn. [26] And I thought, I'm in trouble. . . .

. . . [27] I was already now a junior in college. . . . [28] [F]ortunately, in the spring quarter of my junior year, I wandered into a course in international politics taught by a Soviet specialist . . . . [29] And suddenly, I'd found love. . . .

[30] And, so, I studied Russia. [31] And I studied Russian. [32] And I became proficient at what I did and I went off to teach. [33] And President Bush, the first, asked me to come and be his specialist for Soviet affairs. [34] And, in June 1990, I found myself in a helicopter taking off with Mikhail Gorbachev, Raisa Gorbachyova,[1] me and the Secret Service, and I thought to myself, "I'm really glad I changed my major."

[35] For me, the passion came in something quite unusual. [36] We have to tell our kids, too, that it's okay for your passion to come in something that's not expected of you. [37] If you can be excellent at something, if you love something, go and do it. [38] And then provide them the education to do so. [39] That, in many ways, is our most important value as Americans . . . .

[. . .]

[40] Ladies and Gentlemen, it was the way that Mary McLeod Bethune believed, it has been the way that this great organization has believed, it is what we, as Americans, believe.

---

1 Mikhail Gorbachev was a leader of the Soviet Union for many years, including as President from 1990–1991. Raisa Gorbachyova was his wife, known for her Soviet activism and philanthropy.

LESSON ARG.1 The Argument Prompt

Eyes on the Exam

Remember the saying, "AP really means **a**nswer the **p**rompt." Exam readers will look for how effectively your respond to the specific tasks required in the prompt.

LEARN

The Argument Free-Response Question on the AP Language and Composition exam prompts you to make an effective argument about something you've probably not given much thought. That argument relies on only your knowledge and experience, including how you understand the topic and task from the prompt.

Read the prompt below, which we will call Prompt A. The parts of the prompt are labeled below, but they will not be labeled on the exam.

[Introduction]

At a ceremony to recognize the academic achievements of middle school students, a speaker encouraged students to "take the hard classes; don't just chase A's and a high GPA (Grade Point Average)—the challenges will benefit you more later."

[Task]

Write an essay that argues your position on the value to students of taking challenging classes.

[Directions]

In your response you should do the following:

- Respond to the prompt with a thesis that presents a defensible position.
- Provide evidence to support your line of reasoning.
- Explain how the evidence supports your line of reasoning.
- Use appropriate grammar and punctuation in communicating your argument.

The **introduction** gives you a context (a quote, topic, or a concept) to consider. The **task** then begins with "write an essay that **argues** your **position**." All argument prompts will have that wording. The two key words in the first part of the task are *argues* and *position*. *Argues* means something very different from *explain* or *summarize* or *describe*. As everyone who has had an argument with a friend or sibling knows, the task of arguing assumes that there are differences in viewpoints. So, built into your task is the concept that you might meet resistance to your ideas. *Position* means the stand you take on the topic. Those who hold different positions may disagree with yours. To argue effectively, you need to provide convincing evidence that your position is reasonable.

The next part of the task has two variations. Prompt A shows one of them. You are asked to argue your position "on the value" of something specific related to the introduction, in this case taking challenging classes. On exam day, you might get a variation on that prompt that asks you to argue your position on the "extent to which" something about the topic matters. Your **position**—what you think about the topic—should drive all of the choices you make in your argument.

The "**value**" of something is how useful or important you believe it is, while the "**extent to which**" is the level at which or how much something is true or useful in your view.

While the first two parts change with each exam, the **specific directions** always remain the same. Remember, the parts of the prompt will not be labeled on the exam.

[Introduction]

At a ceremony to recognize the academic achievements of middle school students, a speaker encouraged students to "take the hard classes; don't just chase A's and a high GPA (Grade Point Average)—the challenges will benefit you more later."

[Task]

Write an essay that argues your position on the *extent to which* taking challenging classes benefits students.

[Directions]

In your response you should do the following:

- Respond to the prompt with a thesis that presents a defensible position.
- Provide evidence to support your line of reasoning.
- Explain how the evidence supports your line of reasoning.
- Use appropriate grammar and punctuation in communicating your argument.

KEY POINT: An argument prompt contains three main parts: the **introduction** of a topic and situation gives you context to consider, the **task** explains the topic for your argument, and the **directions** provide essential specific guidance for your essay.

PRACTICE

You will learn more about each section of the prompt and the argument essay in the lessons that follow. For now, do your best to complete these activities.

Part 1: Reread the prompt above on challenging classes and reflect on what you just learned. Then, on separate paper, respond to the following:

[handwritten margin note: benefits of students taking challenging classes]

1. In your own words, identify and explain the topic of the prompt. You might want to begin your sentence with "The topic of the prompt is . . . ."

[handwritten margin note: challenging classes are good, kids should focus on it and not high GPA]

2. List and be ready to explain two to three different viewpoints people might have on the topic.

3. Write down and explain your initial reaction to the task. (You are not committed to this view; these are just your first thoughts.) *[handwritten: Students should be challenged]*

Part 2: In your own words, describe what the first three bullet points in the directions ask you to do. *[handwritten: Write a defensible thesis, give good evidence for a line of reasoning, provide commentary for your evidence]*

WRITE

Read the prompt below on boredom and creativity. Notice that this prompt uses the "extent to which" wording. Then follow the directions below it.

> Technology allows us to fill our free time in ways never before imagined. However, a recent study finds that the constant distractions we experience today "could be preventing our minds from settling into a deeper, more complete feeling of boredom. . . . [w]hich is a shame, given complete boredom can be fertile grounds for innovation."
>
> Write an essay that argues your position on the extent to which boredom is necessary for creativity and innovation.
>
> In your response you should do the following:
> - Respond to the prompt with a thesis that presents a defensible position.
> - Provide evidence to support your line of reasoning.
> - Explain how the evidence supports your line of reasoning.
> - Use appropriate grammar and punctuation in communicating your argument.

Spend five minutes writing during which you:
- Describe your understanding of the introduction.
- State two to three different perspectives or positions on the ideas in the introduction.
- Write about a life experience you have had that may explain why you feel the way you do (for example, a time you and your brother were bored and decided to make a music video).

Watch this video (tinyurl.com/53szehrk) by AP teacher Timm Freitas about the AP argument prompt. After watching, look back over Prompts A and B to find the springboard into the prompts.

Watch Brandon Abdon discuss the wording of argument prompts using the challenging classes prompt at the companion website (tinyurl.com/2mrx3r99) for this book. There you will find other videos by the authors as well as all the links included in the lessons in this book.

What's the Point? In one sentence, explain how this lesson can help you on the AP English Language and Composition exam.

_____

_____

_____

NOTE: The links included in these lessons have been coded to be ad free. Occasionally you may see a message saying that a video is not available. In that case, just refresh your browser and the video will load.

LESSON ARG.2 Unpacking the Task

Eyes on the Exam

The better you **understand** the task, the better you will be able to **complete** it in your essay.

LEARN

The **introduction** part of the prompt serves mainly to get you thinking about a context. The heart of the prompt is the **task**. Recall that in Prompt A, the following is the task:

> Write an essay that argues your position on the value to students of taking challenging classes.

That sounds straightforward: What benefits do students get from taking hard classes? However, some of the words do raise questions. Thinking through those questions will help you get a deeper understanding of the topic, including how others may think about the words in the task. For example, if you unpack the different ways someone might understand the prompt, you might find these questions in the task.

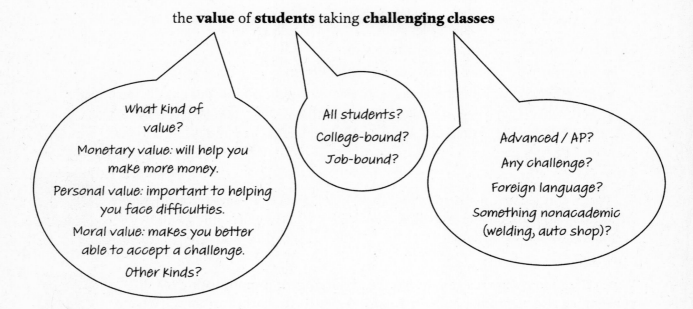

the **value** of **students** taking **challenging classes**

What kind of value?
Monetary value: will help you make more money.
Personal value: important to helping you face difficulties.
Moral value: makes you better able to accept a challenge.
Other kinds?

All students?
College-bound?
Job-bound?

Advanced / AP?
Any challenge?
Foreign language?
Something nonacademic (welding, auto shop)?

With those questions in mind, following are reasonable ways you might express a position on the value of challenging classes:

1. College-bound students should take any kind of challenging class because it will prepare them for the difficult material they will see in college.

2. All students should take something that challenges them because it will build their character and help them learn to accept the challenges in life.

3. College-bound students should avoid too many challenging classes because they may lower your GPA and affect college applications.

4. Taking challenging classes would likely benefit most people because we tend to avoid difficult things.

Any of these ways would work in response to this prompt because each is based on a reasonable understanding of the language in the task.

> **KEY POINT:** The first step in responding to the prompt is **identifying key words and the questions they might raise**. Your response must be reasonable based on possible understandings of the key words.

PRACTICE

Read Prompt B below.

> Technology allows us to fill our free time in ways never before imagined. However, a recent study finds that the constant distractions we experience today "could be preventing our minds from settling into a deeper, more complete feeling of boredom. . . . [w]hich is a shame, given complete boredom can be fertile grounds for innovation."
>
> Write an essay that argues your position on the <u>extent to which boredom is necessary for creativity and innovation</u>.
>
> In your response you should do the following:
>
> - Respond to the prompt with a thesis that presents a defensible position.
> - Provide evidence to support your line of reasoning.
> - Explain how the evidence supports your line of reasoning.
> - Use appropriate grammar and punctuation in communicating your argument.

Part 1: On separate paper, copy the underlined portion of the task. Then make notes on it like those on the previous page about Prompt A. Identify questions the words may raise and the different possible understandings those questions reflect. *what kind of boredom, for what people? all?, what kind of creativity*

Part 2: Considering the different possibilities you've uncovered, write three to five different reasonable initial responses.

WRITE

Choose one of your initial responses from the Practice section above. In a few sentences, explain the thinking that led you from your first reading of the task through your unpacking of the language and then to the response you chose. Also write about a life experience or something you have learned that may relate to the topic, and explain why you took the position you did.

Watch <u>this video</u> (tinyurl.com/5an2zxsd) from an AP English teacher and the test preparation experts at Marco Learning.

What's the Point? In one sentence, explain how this lesson can help you on the AP English Language and Composition exam.

_____

_____

LESSON ARG.3 Big Ideas in the Prompt

Eyes on the Exam

Identifying and understanding the **bigger ideas** related to the specific prompt will give you tools to develop your essay effectively.

LEARN

Arguments focus on a certain topic, such as challenging classes, but they are also always about some bigger concept or idea, such as self-improvement. Here are some other examples.

- An argument about building a new highway through farmland is not merely about the farmland. It is also about the big ideas that the farmland and the highway might represent: *progress*, *personal rights*, *government*, and *nature*, for example.

- An argument about what time to start school isn't just about time. It is also about **big ideas** related to school start times: *mental and physical health*, *family*, *safety*, and *economics*.

On exam day, you will have to build an understanding of the prompt very quickly. Looking *for* and thinking *about* big ideas related to the topic of the prompt may help you better frame your argument.

Big ideas are also often called abstract ideas or universal ideas. **Abstract ideas,** unlike specific things, do not exist in the physical world—they exist only in minds. The concept of abstract ideas may help you remember that every real problem is about something more— an abstraction, an idea. **Universal ideas** are those that apply in a wide variety of contexts. Readers may be more engaged in your argument if you find an idea that touches all people's experiences in some way—some universal experience.

In Prompt A, for example, several bigger abstract ideas appear directly in the introduction and task: *recognition*, *achievement*, *encouragement*, *value*, and *challenge*. The words pointing to those ideas are underlined below.

> At a ceremony to <u>recognize</u> the academic <u>achievements</u> of middle school students, a speaker <u>encouraged</u> them to "take the hard classes; don't just chase A's and a high GPA— the challenges will benefit you more later."
>
> Write an essay that argues your position on the <u>value</u> of students taking <u>challenging</u> classes.

Still other abstract ideas may come to mind from reflecting on the information in the prompt: *maturity*, *confidence*, *difficulty*, *risk*, *success*, *failure*, and *strength*, for example.

To write well, you usually need to feel a connection to the topic. If you have trouble connecting to the topic of the prompt, you can usually find a related big idea that *does* interest you and then connect the topic of the prompt to that big idea.

For example, you may not care much or know enough to encourage students to take challenging classes. However, you may want to write about the abstract and universal idea of taking risks because you believe taking risks makes people stronger.

All of the following are reasonable ways of initially responding to the task by *looking beyond it* to a bigger idea. The words on the next page in bold type are the bigger ideas. The underlined parts relate specifically to the topic of the prompt.

1. Taking **risks,** like <u>challenging yourself with a difficult class</u>, often make us stronger.

2. <u>Challenging yourself with a difficult class</u> helps you really know you earned your **achievements.**

3. <u>Difficult classes</u> only set people up for **failure.**

4. People feel the most **successful** when they have faced something difficult and come out on top, <u>like passing a class that was particularly difficult</u>.

Connecting to big ideas gives you a tool for broadening the scope of your writing. Placing the topic in a broader context is one way to earn the sophistication point. (See pages 240–241.)

> **KEY POINT:** Considering **big ideas** related to the topic of the prompt can deepen your understanding of that topic and lead to a better argument.

PRACTICE

Review the introduction and task of Prompt B below.

> Technology allows us to fill our free time in ways never before <u>imagined</u>. However, a recent study finds that the <u>constant distractions</u> we experience today "could be <u>preventing</u> our minds from settling into a deeper, more <u>complete feeling of boredom</u>. . . . [w]hich is a shame, given complete boredom can be fertile grounds for <u>innovation</u>."
>
> Write an essay that argues your position on the <u>extent</u> to which boredom is necessary for <u>creativity</u> and <u>innovation</u>.

Part 1: Underline the words in the prompt that represent a big idea. Then make a list of those ideas. Add abstract or universal ideas that you think may relate to the topic of the prompt.

Part 2: Use this list to write two to three responses to the prompt that address a big idea.

WRITE

Choose one of your initial responses from the Practice section. Write a few sentences that explain the thinking that led you from your first reading of the task through the possible big ideas and then to your initial response. Then write about a life experience related to the big idea (not just the topic) that may explain why you feel the way you do.

Watch <u>this video</u> (tinyurl.com/yc6j5f5k) by AP teacher S. Abuel explaining **SOMA** (**S**elf, **O**thers, **M**atrix, and **A**bstract) as domains in which ideas and examples for arguments are found, After watching, review your work and try to make additions to your list in Practice Part 1.

What's the Point? In one sentence, explain how this lesson can help you on the AP English Language and Composition exam.

_____

_____

_____

LESSON ARG.4 Selecting Good Examples as Evidence

Eyes on the Exam

In the argument essay, you will use your **experience** and **knowledge** when providing evidence to support your position.

LEARN

Just as you might give reasons to show why you're right in an argument with a friend, you will need to defend your position in the argument essay and show why your position is reasonable. There is no right or wrong in the argument essay as long as you have good evidence and reasoning. You will support your position on the topic (and maybe the big ideas related to it) with **examples** from your own life and the **knowledge** you have acquired and explain reasonably how they **justify,** or help prove, your point.

Review the introduction to Prompt A below.

> At a ceremony to recognize the academic achievements of middle school students, a speaker encouraged them to "take the hard classes; don't just chase A's and a high GPA—the challenges will benefit you more later."

You may have experience with this exact scenario. Maybe you took a very difficult math class and made a B or a C but recognized that it made you better at math. Maybe you had a teacher who encouraged you to take AP Physics, but you decided not to because you were afraid of it. Maybe now you wish you had because you know you'll have to take it in college anyway. Either of those examples from **personal experience** would be useful in your response.

But you may not have similar experiences. Even if you do, you will likely need other examples to help your argument. Connecting to "worlds" or "domains" beyond the prompt itself might help you generate ideas. These connections depend on **general knowledge** you have acquired. The chart provides examples of these domains and how they can be connected to the prompt.

Connections to Worlds or Domains		
Initial Response / Claim	Taking difficult classes is valuable for making people stronger learners.	
World or Domain	**Example**	**Connection to Prompt**
Current Events	Jeff Bezos's quote: "You earn a reputation by trying to do hard things well."	As the owner of one of the largest companies in the world, Bezos explains that he built Amazon by doing hard things and doing them well. So he gained the respect of others and trust in both him and his company.
Personal Experience	My own fear of taking Algebra I	I was in 7th grade when my math teacher encouraged me to take Algebra I in 8th grade. My parents and counselor made me do it, but I did pretty well, and now I am going to major in math and engineering. I feared the challenge and the mistakes I knew I would make.

History	President Kennedy's speech about going to the moon	President Kennedy's 1962 speech kicked off the American race to the moon by explaining that the reason to do it was because it was hard. He was implying that if it had been easy, then it may not have been worth doing.
Literature/Arts	?	
Politics	?	
Pop Culture	Rapper Jay-Z failing when he was young	When Jay-Z was first starting out, he couldn't get a record company to even listen to him, so he sold his own CDs and tapes out of his car until he got so popular he couldn't be ignored. He eventually made enough money to start his own record label and is now a billionaire.
Science	Psychology of facing difficult experiences	In AP Psych, we have learned about people who are both better able to do new things and are more confident in themselves after facing difficult experiences.
Sports	Professional surfer Bethany Hamilton having her arm bitten off by a shark	Hamilton was 13 in 2003 when she lost her left arm in a shark attack. Within a <u>month</u>, she was surfing again and continues to surf professionally today, winning many events throughout her career.

The more specific your examples are, the easier your reader will be able to see and understand the connections and how they support your argument. However, the examples alone do not "prove" or justify your argument. You will need to clearly explain why each example you use in your essay supports your argument. Future lessons will offer instruction in those explanations.

Notice that not every row of the chart is filled out. You may not have enough time to get solid examples for each world/domain. Aim for getting a few examples you know you can use to show and support your thinking as you justify your response.

KEY POINT: Connecting to worlds or domains beyond the prompt will give you a chance to **tap into your knowledge** and find interesting examples to support your argument.

PRACTICE

Review the introduction and task of Prompt B below. Then complete the activities on the next page.

> Technology allows us to fill our free time in ways never before imagined. However, a recent study finds that the constant distractions we experience today "could be preventing our minds from settling into a deeper, more complete feeling of boredom. . . . [w]hich is a shame, given complete boredom can be fertile grounds for innovation."
>
> Write an essay that argues your position on the extent to which boredom is necessary for creativity and innovation.

Part 1: Recreate the three-column framework of the chart called Connections to Worlds or Domains on the previous pages. Write your initial position on Prompt B at the top of the chart and copy the worlds or domains into the first column. Then think of as many examples as you can and write them in the second column. In the third column, briefly explain the connection each has to the prompt.

Part 2: With a classmate, share your initial position and one of the connections you made and explain how your chosen example supports or justifies your argument.

WRITE

Choose one of your examples from the Practice activity above. Write for five minutes. In that writing, state your initial position, provide your specific example, and then explain how that example supports your thinking about the topic and justifies your position.

Watch this video (tinyurl.com/v7xxvy28) by AP teacher Timm Freitas about specific examples as evidence in the argument essay.

You may also watch this video (tinyurl.com/3kcsrdeu) by AP teacher Crystal Laliberte about using personal examples in your argument essay.

What's the Point? In one sentence, explain how this lesson can help you on the AP English Language and Composition exam.

_____

_____

_____

TEAM UP

You now have at least two ways to record examples for argument essays: the "Connections to Worlds or Domains" chart in this lesson and the "Universal Evidence Logs" chart in the first video, with columns for Personal Experience, Acquaintance Experience, Media Knowledge, and Cultural Knowledge. Although each of you has plenty of knowledge and experiences to provide good examples for your argument essays, sometimes you might need a little help tapping into those. Talking with peers can help bring those to mind.

Work in small groups as your teacher directs. Begin by sharing personal experiences that might be good examples of some bigger idea. Ask, "what stands out in my memory as an experience I learned from? What did I learn?" Take turns answering those questions. Chances are group members will think, "that reminds me of a time I . . . ." Keep notes of examples you think of or examples you might use as "acquaintance experiences." Be sure to identify the big idea associated with each example. Continue talking until everyone has had at least one time to talk. If time permits, go another round.

Thesis

LESSON ARG.5 Claim and Thesis

Eyes on the Exam

Your argument essay must explicitly **state a claim that can be defended.**

LEARN

The most essential part of any argument is the **claim,** a statement that asserts your position on the topic.

Review Prompt A below.

> At a ceremony to recognize the academic achievements of middle school students, a speaker encouraged students to "take the hard classes; don't just chase A's and a high GPA—the challenges will benefit you more later."
>
> Write an essay that argues your position on the value to students of taking challenging classes.
>
> In your response you should do the following:
>
> - Respond to the prompt with a thesis that presents a defensible position.
> - Provide evidence to support your line of reasoning.
> - Explain how the evidence supports your line of reasoning.
> - Use appropriate grammar and punctuation in communicating your argument.

Claims

Recall that a **claim** is a statement asserted to be true. It is different from a fact, which, by definition, *is* true. A claim makes a statement that others might not agree with—it is only *said to be true.*

Claims must be **defensible,** meaning they must require some evidence and explanation and not be too obvious or factual. Consider the following possible claims for Prompt A.

Difficulties change people.

Some classes are more difficult than others.

Taking a risk is risky.

These are not defensible because they mainly state facts that do not require evidence and explanation. While each may *seem* to suggest a response to the prompt, they leave no room for disagreement. An actual defensible claim must directly address the topic and explicitly state a position on it. Consider these examples:

Challenging classes *are good*.

Some difficult classes *can be helpful*.

Taking a risk on a difficult class *may interfere with your dreams*.

These are better: they directly **address the topic** of the prompt (underlined) and state a **specific perspective** (*italics*). However, the position each claim states leaves a reader asking questions: why they "are good," how they "can be helpful," or how they "may interfere with your dreams." A better claim (on its way to a thesis statement) would offer specific reasons.

Reasons are the "why" behind a position. **Reasoning** is the process of developing the grounds for "why" and logically connecting them to a position. The thinking you have done to explain your claim using those reasons is your **line of reasoning**, the trail of thinking you've followed to justify your claim about the topic.

Thesis Statements

As you move from a claim to a statement that also gives the "why" or "how" for your claim, you are getting closer to a **thesis statement,** an explicit and concise statement of the claim and related parts of the argument, including examples and/or parts of your reasoning. Verbs in a good thesis statement are stronger than just *are* or *can be* (as they were in the claims) as they become more specific to your thinking.

A thesis statement is a promise to your reader: "Here is my topic, here is my position, and here is a reason (or a few reasons) why I believe the way I do about it." The rest of the essay then does the explaining.

The following possible claims for Prompt A have now evolved into thesis statements because they directly address the topic of the prompt (underlined) while also providing a reason in the claim (*italics*) that relies on stronger verbs that help show the attitude toward the topic. These examples are ***open* thesis statements** because they do not name the specific examples that will help explain the line of reasoning to the reader.

<u>Challenging classes</u> *strengthen students.*

Taking <u>difficult courses</u> *benefits students in the future.*

<u>Difficult courses</u> *prove more harmful than helpful.*

Thesis statements that suggest or name the specific examples that will support the line of reasoning are called ***closed* thesis statements.** For example, the following are effective *closed* thesis statements. (The specific examples are numbered.)

<u>Challenging classes</u> *strengthen students* since they (1) encourage them to see failure as opportunity and (2) help students develop perseverance.

<u>Difficult courses</u> *prove more harmful than helpful* because they can (1) lower GPA and (2) bring down your confidence.

These are closed because they state exactly what the essay will cover. While an open thesis leaves room for other examples, the closed thesis limits the examples that will be discussed.

Both examples of a closed thesis above are acceptable because they explicitly state the claim related directly to the topic (underlined), assert a position (*italics*), and then provide specific examples of how or why the claim might be true (numbered).

Connected Thesis Statements

Another approach to developing a thesis can involve either an open or a closed thesis. A **connected thesis statement** will either list or suggest some connections beyond the topic itself that relate directly to a big idea. (See Lessons ARG. 3 and ARG.4.) Revising some examples from above, we might end up with these thesis statements:

Closed and connected: **Intentionally facing difficult situations,** like taking challenging classes, strengthens people, as shown by (1) the <u>failure of young Jay-Z</u> to get a record contract and (2) <u>my own experience</u> with Algebra I.

Open and connected: **Choosing to accept difficult challenges,** like taking difficult courses, often benefits people by helping them overcome failure and fear of mistakes.

Notice that the big idea—the idea related to the topic—is in bold in each of these. The thesis statement is no longer just about challenging classes; it's about facing any kind of difficulty. This approach allows you to connect to the world beyond school and use any example of anyone facing difficulty and then succeeding. Notice, however, that one of the examples in each is directly about school. This tie to the prompt will prevent the essay from veering too far off the topic of challenging classes.

In each thesis, the essay might use the same examples (underlined), but in the second thesis, the writer is either not sure of what examples to use or wants to leave room to change while writing. And even though the first thesis promises to address Jay-Z and Algebra I and must do that, the writer might still add other connections too (for example, the number of rejections J. K. Rowling got before she found a publisher for her Harry Potter books).

Which type of thesis you use comes down to what you have time for, what you understand about the topic, and what you (and your teacher and class) have done to prepare.

KEY POINT: Your thesis must have a **defensible claim** and should **suggest a line of reasoning** that shows your thinking about the topic and claim.

PRACTICE

Review Prompt B below. Notice the bullet point requiring a defensible position (in bold).

> Technology allows us to fill our free time in ways never before imagined. However, a recent study finds that the constant distractions we experience today "could be preventing our minds from settling into a deeper, more complete feeling of boredom. . . . [w]hich is a shame, given complete boredom can be fertile grounds for innovation."
>
> Write an essay that argues your position on the extent to which boredom is necessary for creativity and innovation.
>
> In your response you should do the following:
>
> - **Respond to the prompt with a thesis that presents a defensible position.**
> - Provide evidence to support your line of reasoning.
> - Explain how the evidence supports your line of reasoning.
> - Use appropriate grammar and punctuation in communicating your argument.

Part 1: Make a chart like the one below to develop your response to Prompt B from your initial claim to an open thesis and a closed thesis.

From Claim to Thesis		
Initial Claim:	Topic:	Simple Position (good, bad):
	Write it:	
Open Thesis:	Topic:	Position (with stronger verb) and Reasoning:
	Write it:	
Closed Thesis:	Topic:	Position (with stronger verb) and Reasoning:
	Specific Reason 1:	Specific Reason 2:
	Write it:	

Part 2: With a classmate or family member, share your open or closed thesis and explain how your reasoning leads to your position. Ask for feedback on what makes sense and what does not. Make note of what you need to clarify.

WRITE

Using the open or closed thesis you drafted in the Practice section, write for five minutes, explaining the reasoning that leads to your claim.

 Watch this video (tinyurl.com/4ucexc64) by popular YouTube teacher Brian Tolentino. In this video, he discusses other approaches to the open and closed thesis statements.

What's the Point? In one sentence, explain how this lesson can help you on the AP English Language and Composition exam.

_____

_____

_____

TEAM UP

Promises play a role in almost all human interactions. You promise your parent or guardian you will be home by 10:00 p.m. They might promise you that they'll pick you up in time for soccer practice. Politicians promise voters they will enact certain policies, and voters expect them to keep their promises. Many businesses provide guarantees of satisfaction—a promise you will be happy with their product or you'll get your money back.

Writers make promises, too, as you read in this lesson. "Here is my topic, here is my position, and here is a reason (or a few reasons) why I believe the way I do about it." Breaking that promise may not be as consequential as breaking other promises, such as to your family or friends, but it is a broken promise to your reader all the same.

Work in small groups as your teacher directs. Then take turns articulating the promise you are making in the thesis statement you worked with in the Write activity above. Say it just like the quoted "promise" sentence. For example, you might say, "Here is my topic: taking risks. Here is my position: unless you know the result is worth the risk, don't do it. Here are a few reasons I believe the way I do about it: (1) I wanted to take horseback riding lessons, but I was afraid of being on the horse. I forced myself to do it and never had any fun. I realized what I really liked was just being around horses and grooming them. (2) My family moved here from Guatemala before I was born. They took a huge risk when they left for an unknown future. But they were leaving a place with too much violence, and their life in the United States is now good. That was a risk worth taking."

After each person articulates a thesis promise, provide feedback on whether the reasons offered sound convincing. Right now those reasons are just preliminary thoughts, but feedback will help each writer achieve a stronger, clearer thesis statement.

LESSON ARG.6 Thesis Statement and Introduction

Eyes on the Exam

You may not always need a full introduction, because your thesis is the most important part of the start of your essay. However, an introduction may provide your reader a good lead in to your thesis.

LEARN

Write your claim and thesis before writing the **introduction**. Your thesis is a very specific and focused statement and the destination of your introduction. When you begin to write the sentences that precede your thesis statement, think broadly. Then gradually sharpen your focus until you get to your thesis statement. Picture the introduction as an inverted triangle.

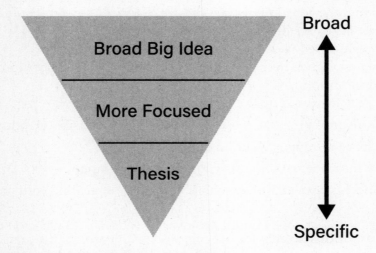

Here is a possible closed thesis statement for Prompt A:

> Challenging classes *strengthen* students since they *encourage* them to see *failure* as *opportunity* and help students develop *perseverance*.

The topic of this prompt (students taking challenging classes) is directly addressed in the underlined portion, while the big ideas emerging in the thesis include strength, encouragement, failure, opportunity, and perseverance (italicized). An introduction that leads into this thesis would do well to introduce and briefly discuss one or more of these big ideas and their importance to the topic. The chart below shows the movement from broad to narrow and the repetition of *failure*, the big idea.

Narrowing an Introduction	
Broad Big Idea ↓ People & Failure ↓ Schools & Failure ↓ Effect on Students ↓ Thesis Statement Tied to Big Idea	*Failure* happens. The most successful people have often been those who also *failed* at something. They had to *fail* first so they would know what it means to succeed. But in schools, *failure* is almost always a bad word. Too many students learn to fear taking risks because *failure* is unacceptable. Many never develop *perseverance* because they never had to struggle through something difficult. This is why it is important for students to take tough classes. <u>Challenging classes</u> strengthen students since they encourage them to see *failure* as opportunity, and they help students develop <u>perseverance</u>.

In this example, an argument about students taking challenging classes is really an argument about the importance of failure in developing perseverance. Since everyone has had some experience with failure, readers can relate to this universal idea even if they are not especially interested in challenging classes for students.

> **KEY POINT:** An **introduction,** though not required, may help focus your argument and also help the reader connect to it.

PRACTICE

Review Prompt B below.

> Technology allows us to fill our free time in ways never before imagined. However, a recent study finds that the constant distractions we experience today "could be preventing our minds from settling into a deeper, more complete feeling of boredom. . . . [w]hich is a shame, given complete boredom can be fertile grounds for innovation."
>
> Write an essay that argues your position on the extent to which boredom is necessary for creativity and innovation.
>
> In your response you should do the following:
> - Respond to the prompt with a thesis that presents a defensible position.
> - Provide evidence to support your line of reasoning.
> - Explain how the evidence supports your line of reasoning.
> - Use appropriate grammar and punctuation in communicating your argument.

Part 1: Draft a thesis for this prompt (or use one already drafted from a previous lesson). Then underline the topic of the prompt (as in the "Narrowing an Introduction" chart on the previous page). Circle the big ideas in your thesis.

Part 2: Using the paragraph in "Narrowing an Introduction" as a model, draft a possible introduction for Prompt B that ends with your thesis statement. Circle the big ideas.

WRITE

Carefully read over the draft of your introduction. Then write for five minutes, explaining how your examples both support your argument and also relate to the big idea(s) in your introduction.

 Watch this video (tinyurl.com/5n82398m) from Tolentino Teaching, which recommends spending no more than five minutes on an introduction and gives you a chance to practice five introductions. Give it a try!

What's the Point? In one sentence, explain how this lesson can help you on the AP English Language and Composition exam.

_____

_____

_____

LESSON ARG.7 Thesis and Opposing Views

Eyes on the Exam

The best arguments might include and **respond to other possible arguments.** The better you handle differing viewpoints, the better your argument essay will be.

LEARN

Arguments arise because people have different experiences, and people see things through the lens of their own experiences. These different ways of seeing are **alternative perspectives.** (The word *perspective* derives from the Latin word *specere,* which means "to look at." The word *spectacles*—"glasses"—has the same root.)

A claim reflects *your* perspective on a topic based on *your* experiences. In an argument, you are entering a conversation with others who have different experiences and perspectives. As you begin forming, stating, and then developing and supporting your argument, you should consider how others might offer a **counterargument** to yours. Failure to think about and address a counterargument might leave you arguing with only yourself.

Recall the possible closed thesis for Prompt A:

<u>Challenging classes</u> *strengthen* students since they *encourage* them to see *failure* as *opportunity* and help students develop *perseverance.*

Clearly the writer of this thesis will argue that challenging classes have positive effects on students. However, to build a strong argument, the writer should consider alternative perspectives and address those ideas as well.

While there are multiple ways to insert an alternative perspective—or counterargument— one of the most effective is to express the alternative view in a **subordinate clause.** Think of clauses as thoughts. A sentence is a complete thought. It has at least one independent clause. A subordinate clause, in contrast, cannot stand alone as a complete thought. As its name suggests, its importance is "below" (*sub-*) that of the independent clause it leans on.

Independent Clause: Challenging classes strengthen students. (complete thought)

That sentence can stand alone. However, that statement would immediately drop to a lower level of importance and stop being independent if it were introduced with a **subordinating conjunction,** such as *although.*

Dependent or Subordinate Clause: *Although* challenging classes strengthen students . . .

That thought is not complete. *Although* makes the reader expect something that will finish the thought. That something is an independent clause (in bold in the sentence below).

Although challenging classes strengthen students, **they may cause stress.**

However, you will want *your* viewpoint, not an alternative point, to take the strong position in the sentence in the independent clause. You can introduce an alternative viewpoint without taking the emphasis away from your perspective by introducing the *alternative* through a subordinate clause.

<u>*Although*</u> *some students claim that difficult classes create too much additional* **stress,** *those classes and the* **stress** *they create actually* strengthen students since they encourage them to see failure as opportunity and help students develop perseverance.

With the change to the thesis in italics, you can that see the subordinate clause (with the underlined subordinating conjunction) at the beginning introduces a possible alternative perspective: the reasonable idea that challenging classes create stress for students. The thesis now also includes a reference to that stress in the main claim (in bold) so that it directly addresses the opposing concern.

Subordinating conjunctions not only make the clause that follows subordinate, but they also suggest a relationship between the main claim and the alternative perspective. The alternative viewpoint is presented as an idea to be moved beyond or to be put in service of the main claim.

The following subordinating conjunctions are especially good for introducing a counterargument.

Select Subordinating Conjunctions for Counterarguments	
Although	Though
Even if	Whereas
Even though	While
Rather than	

By this point, you may have all the parts you need to write a thesis statement that can serve as an outline for your entire essay. Consider this fully developed thesis:

Even though the pain of failure and difficulty prevents many people from taking risks, intentionally facing difficult situations, such as taking challenging classes, strengthens people, as shown by the initial failure of young Jay-Z to get a record contract but finally succeeding and my own experience with Algebra I, ultimately proving that accepting challenges helps us begin to see difficulty as opportunity.

Thesis Outline Organizer		
Counterargument	*Even though the pain of failure and difficulty prevents many people from taking risks,*	
Topic and Claim	*. . . intentionally facing difficult situations, such as taking challenging classes, strengthens people . . .*	
Reasons *. . . as shown by . . .*	1) *the <u>initial failure of young Jay-Z</u> to get a record contract . . .* *and*	2) *<u>my own experience</u> with Algebra I,*
Big Idea Statement (what it's really about)	*. . . ultimately proving that accepting challenges helps us begin to see difficulty as opportunity.*	

That's a very long sentence. You can, in fact, spread your thesis over several shorter sentences if you prefer. You can move the parts around, but these are the essential parts to organize everything you need to write an effective argument essay.

PRACTICE

Read the following possible alternative perspectives on taking difficult classes. Choose one and then revise the thesis on the previous page to include it. **Include a subordinate clause** and **revise the claim** in the thesis to account for the new clause.

1. Taking difficult classes can damage someone's GPA and affect college prospects.

2. Some parents want their students to make straight A's.

KEY POINT: Effective arguments address **alternative perspectives** without taking the focus away from the main perspective.

WRITE

Review Prompt B below.

> Technology allows us to fill our free time in ways never before imagined. However, a recent study finds that the constant distractions we experience today "could be preventing our minds from settling into a deeper, more complete feeling of boredom. . . . [w]hich is a shame, given complete boredom can be fertile grounds for innovation."
>
> Write an essay that argues your position on the extent to which boredom is necessary for creativity and innovation.
>
> In your response you should do the following:
>
> - Respond to the prompt with a thesis that presents a defensible position.
> - Provide evidence to support your line of reasoning.
> - Explain how the evidence supports your line of reasoning.
> - Use appropriate grammar and punctuation in communicating your argument.

Draft a thesis for this prompt (or revise one already drafted from a previous lesson) that includes a **subordinate clause** introducing an **alternative perspective** and **addressing that counterargument** in the claim.

👆 Watch <u>this video</u> (tinyurl.com/3x4d9zwk) by Beth Hall starting at 7:23. The video provides a sentence frame for a thesis statement that includes opposing views.

What's the Point? In one sentence, explain how this lesson can help you on the AP English Language and Composition exam.

_____

_____

_____

LESSON ARG.8 Thesis and Topic Sentences

Eyes on the Exam

Topic sentences for paragraphs can be the key to establishing a **line of reasoning,** which is required in higher-scoring essays.

LEARN

You may remember from earlier lessons that a thesis statement is a promise to your reader: "Here is my topic, here is my position, and here is a reason (or a few reasons) why I feel the way I do about it." The rest of the essay then does the explaining.

The paragraphs in the rest of the essay might start with topic sentences that relate directly to the reasons given in the thesis. In this sense, the thesis can also be thought of as a road map for your argument: the topic is where you're **starting,** the reasons are the **directions,** and the claim is your **destination.**

Review the introduction and task in Prompt A below.

> At a ceremony to recognize the academic achievements of middle school students, a speaker encouraged students to "take the hard classes; don't just chase A's and a high GPA—the challenges will benefit you more later."
>
> Write an essay that argues your position on the value to students of taking challenging classes.

One possible (closed) thesis for this prompt follows:

Challenging classes strengthen students since they <u>encourage them to see failure as opportunity</u> and <u>help students develop perseverance.</u>

The reasons for the claim—the "directions" in the road map—are underlined. Because this is a closed thesis, it lays out explicitly what the paragraphs in the essay body will address and in what order. The chart below shows some very basic, but useful, topic sentences. Read across the columns for the complete sentences.

Basic Topic Sentences Created from a Closed Thesis Statement #1			
Paragraph #	Topic	Claim	Reasons
1.	Challenging classes . . .	. . . encourage students...	. . . to see failure as opportunity.
2.	Challenging classes . . .	. . . help students...	. . . develop perseverance.

In a timed essay, these types of topic sentences will provide what you need for your paragraphs.

Following is another example of a closed thesis that makes specific connections to the reasons (underlined) and states a claim ("strengthens people") about a bigger idea (bold) related to the specific topic from the prompt (italicized).

Intentionally **facing difficult situations,** like *taking challenging classes,* strengthens people, as shown by (1) <u>the failure of young Jay-Z to get a record contract but finally succeeding</u> and (2) <u>my own experience with Algebra I.</u>

Basic Topic Sentences Created from a Closed Thesis Statement #2			
Paragraph #	Topic	Claim	Reasons
1.	**Difficult situations . . .**	. . . strengthen people . . .	<u>as demonstrated by Jay-Z going from selling CDs from his trunk to becoming a multibillionaire.</u>
2.	**Difficult situations . . .**	. . strengthen people . . .	<u>as I learned when I was pushed to take Algebra I in middle school.</u>

As long as the topic, claim, and reasons are all represented, you could write the sentences in different ways. For example, the following all work as topic sentences for the same paragraph.

Difficult situations strengthen people, as demonstrated by Jay-Z going from selling CDs from his trunk to becoming a multibillionaire.

Billionaire Jay-Z's early struggles as a rapper demonstrate how difficult situations often make people stronger.

People often grow stronger when they are faced with difficult situations, as when billionaire Jay-Z failed to get a record contract when he was young but chose to sell CDs from his car instead of quitting.

An open thesis will also work for this topic and claim. One possible open thesis for this prompt follows:

Choosing to accept difficult challenges, like taking difficult courses, often benefits people by <u>helping them overcome failure</u> and <u>fear of mistakes.</u>

The reasons (underlined) do not speak for themselves. They will need specific examples in the paragraphs. When mapping out the topic sentences, think of examples you could use and list them.

Basic Topic Sentence Created from an Open Thesis			
Paragraph #	Topic	Claim	Reasons
1.	*Difficult challenges . . .*	*. . . benefit people by* <u>*helping them . . .*</u>	<u>*. . . overcome failure.*</u> Examples in paragraph: – Jay-Z – others
2.	*Difficult challenges . . .*	*. . . benefit people by* <u>*helping them . . .*</u>	<u>*. . . overcome fear of mistakes.*</u> Examples in paragraph: – my experience in Algebra I – others

PRACTICE

Review Prompt B below.

> Technology allows us to fill our free time in ways never before imagined. However, a recent study finds that the constant distractions we experience today "could be preventing our minds from settling into a deeper, more complete feeling of boredom. . . . [w]hich is a shame, given complete boredom can be fertile grounds for innovation."
>
> Write an essay that argues your position on the extent to which boredom is necessary for creativity and innovation.
>
> In your response you should do the following:
>
> - Respond to the prompt with a thesis that presents a defensible position.
> - Provide evidence to support your line of reasoning.
> - Explain how the evidence supports your line of reasoning.
> - Use appropriate grammar and punctuation in communicating your argument.

Part 1: Draft a thesis for this prompt (or use one already drafted from a previous lesson).

Part 2: Using one of the Basic Topic Sentences tables on previous pages as a model, write topic sentences related to your thesis from Part 1. List all the specific examples you would use.

WRITE

Examine one of the topic sentences you just developed. Then answer the questions.

1. What might the paragraph that follows that topic sentence contain?
2. How would you explain the specific example you use?
3. How does it help demonstrate your claim?

Watch this video (tinyurl.com/mxntbpur) by AP teacher Beth Hall about different ways to approach topic sentences.

What's the Point? In one sentence, explain how this lesson can help you on the AP English Language and Composition exam.

_____

_____

_____

Eyes on the Exam

Readers will score your thesis based on Row A in the Argument rubric.

LEARN

Carefully read each section of the Row A rubric and scoring guide.

- The first row under "Row A: Thesis . . ." explains in general terms how a response can fail to receive the point (first column). The second column explains, also in general terms, what a response needs to do to earn the point.
- The row beneath that provides *general examples* of ways to miss or earn the point.
- The second to the last row provides *specific examples* of the items in the previous row.
- The final row provides additional clarifications for acceptable thesis statements.

Row A: Thesis (0-1 points), Scoring Criteria [4.B]	
0 points	**1 point**
For any of the following: There is no defensible thesis. The intended thesis only restates the prompt. The intended thesis provides a summary of the issue with no apparent or coherent claim. There is a thesis, but it does not respond to the prompt.	Responds to the prompt with a thesis that presents a defensible position.
Decision Rules and Scoring Notes	
Responses that do not earn this point:	**Responses that earn this point:**
Only restate the prompt. Do not take a position, or the position is vague or must be inferred. State an obvious fact rather than making a claim that requires a defense.	Respond to the prompt rather than restate or rephrase the prompt. Clearly take a position on the value (or harm) of taking difficult classes and/or facing other challenges

Examples that do not earn this point:	**Examples that earn this point:**
Do not take a position	**Present a defensible position that responds to the prompt**
"Nobody likes hard classes, but some students take them."	*"By definition, challenges require a level of effort and anxiety that set them apart from other pursuits, whether those challenges relate to taking difficult classes in school, trying to win a high score in an athletic competition, or going on a wilderness discovery trip. Although it may be exhausting, a well-chosen challenge can boost confidence and help prepare you for other challenges that will surely arise in the future."*
Address the topic of the prompt but are not defensible—it is an obvious fact stated as a claim	
"Everyone has a lazy side, but in the end people all have to work at something."	*"Like many other people, I tended to steer clear of challenging tasks for a long time, but two key experiences in my life—horseback riding and interning at our local newspaper—have shown me the value tackling challenges can offer, including turning my life in an entirely new direction."*
	"While some may argue that focusing on securing high grades and a strong GPA is crucial for academic and career prospects, taking challenging classes is inherently more valuable for students because it fosters critical thinking and problem-solving skills and prepares them for real-world challenges, ultimately contributing to a more profound and comprehensive educational experience."

Additional Notes:

The thesis may be more than one sentence, provided the sentences are in close proximity.

The thesis may be anywhere within the response.

The thesis *may* establish a line of reasoning that structures the essay, but it needn't do so to earn the thesis point.

A thesis that meets the criteria can be awarded the point whether or not the rest of the response successfully supports that line of reasoning.

PRACTICE

Complete the following activities and answer the questions about the Row A Thesis rubric and scoring guide.

1. In your own words, explain three problems that could keep you from earning the thesis point.

2. Explain whether restating the prompt in different words is a useful strategy. Identify the part of the prompt that addresses that.

3. Can a thesis statement stretch out in separate sentences over several paragraphs? Identify the part of the rubric that answers that question.

4. Does a thesis statement need to be closed? Identify the part of the rubric that answers that question.

5. Will you miss the point if you save your thesis statement for the final paragraph? Identify the part of the rubric that answers that question.

You Be the Reader

Read sample essay ARG.3.B in the Appendix on page 281. Decide whether that essay earns the thesis point. Explain your answer.

 Watch as Beth Hall describes a formula for writing an effective thesis statement (tinyurl.com/2s4hhhp9). Then try using that formula to revise the thesis in the sample essay ARG.3.B.

_____

_____

_____

Revise

Review the thesis statement you have developed in response to Prompt B about boredom and creativity. If you think it does not earn the thesis point based on this rubric and Beth Hall's explanations, revise as needed to correct that. Even if you believe it earns the thesis point, revise your thesis to make it the best it can be.

Evidence and Commentary

LESSON ARG.9 Specific Examples as Evidence

Eyes on the Exam

To write a strong argument, use very **specific examples and details** and explain them throughout the paragraphs.

LEARN

In the argument essay, your evidence comes from your **experiences** and **knowledge:** what you have read, watched, been taught, and discussed, for example. However, your perspective on those matters may differ from others' perspectives. For this reason, you must explain your examples well enough for your audience to understand how the examples support your argument. Your readers will understand best if your examples are very **specific**—clearly defined and explained—and detailed. The more detailed and specific your examples are, the less likely readers with experiences different from yours will question what you mean or why you included those examples.

Recall the closed thesis statement below in response to Prompt A:

Intentionally facing difficult situations, like taking challenging classes, strengthens people, as shown by (1) the rapper <u>Jay-Z when he was young</u> and (2) <u>my own experience</u> with Algebra I, ultimately proving that accepting challenges helps us begin to see difficulty as opportunity.

This thesis mentions two types of examples: one is a connection to the domain of popular culture; the other is your personal experience. For both types of examples, first identify **what** you are talking about and then provide specific details to show **why** you are using that example.

The first example offered is Jay-Z. Although your readers likely know about Jay-Z from their own knowledge of popular culture, you still need to provide specific details about him and explain his connection to your main claim.

Read the following drafts of sentences about Jay-Z as an example to meant to support the argument about facing difficult situations.

Example 1: Jay-Z was a poor kid from the Bronx who *had to sell CDs out of his car* before he got famous.

Example 2: When the **rapper Jay-Z** was first starting out, he *couldn't get a record company to even listen to him,* so he *sold his own CDs and tapes out of his car* until he got so popular he couldn't be ignored. He *eventually made enough money to start his own record label* and is *now a billionaire.*

Example 3: Today, **Jay-Z is a well-known rapper and producer,** but when he was starting out, he *couldn't get a record company to even listen to his music.* <u>He took that challenge and made it into an opportunity</u> when he *started selling his own CDs and tapes out of his car.* Eventually, he got so popular that *he made enough money to start his own record label* and is *now a billionaire.*

You can probably see that ***Example 1*** is the least effective. It assumes that the reader knows exactly who Jay-Z is and will be able to connect the idea that Jay-Z "had to sell CDs out of his car" to the argument. Remember, though, that the reader is not in your head—you must provide the details and make the connections that help the example work in your argument.

Example 2 does a better job providing details. This draft at least tells the reader that Jay-Z is a rapper. It then provides some specific details about his experience that relate directly to difficulties he faced, how he overcame them, and how he has succeeded.

Example 3 improves on Example 2. It explains who Jay-Z is with enough detail that even readers who haven't heard of him will know he is famous. Importantly, in the underlined portion, the writer connects the example to the **language of the prompt and the thesis** ("challenge" and "opportunity"). It also includes very specific details showing what Jay-Z went through in facing challenges and succeeding.

The second example cited in the thesis statement on the previous page is the writer's fear of taking Algebra I. Readers will most certainly *not* know about that personal experience with algebra, so the writer will need to provide enough information to make the experience clear but not so much that the essay drifts off the topic.

When using your personal experiences as examples, watch out for two common problems:

1. Incorrectly assuming the reader will understand the details because those details are so familiar to you

2. Mistakenly providing *so* much detail that you go off topic because you want the reader to completely understand

Following are examples of each type of problem:

Example 4: When I was in 7th grade, my school wanted me to take Algebra I as an 8th grader. My parents and counselor agreed, so I took it as an 8th grader, and it was very hard. Now, I want to be a math or engineering major because of that class.

Example 5: When I was in 7th grade, I did well with math, and my teacher regularly gave me things to challenge me and even asked me to be on the academic team as the math person. That was the most encouraging teacher I had ever had to that point. I was afraid of Algebra I, though, and my parents knew it. Things had been rough at home, and my parents didn't really understand me then, so when they pushed me to take Algebra I in 8th grade— after my school had recommended it—I was very reluctant. After my counselor met with me, I went for it, and I have never looked back. Yes, it was hard, but I learned I had to work and study and ask the teacher questions. These things made me a better student in general so that when I went to high school, I took Algebra II, Calculus, and Physics, and still had to work hard. My physics teacher was not very good, so I had to do a lot of work with my classmates and look up a lot of things on the Internet. That was frustrating because we were pretty much teaching ourselves, but we worked hard. Now I plan on either being a math major or an engineering major when I get to college, but I need to start applying right now.

Example 4 does identify the example (the "what") but doesn't show anything about how it relates to the claim in the thesis. Also, the writer makes a giant leap from taking Algebra 1 and finding it hard to deciding to major in math. The reader may be able to make the connection, but that is the writer's job.

Example 5 obviously provides way more information than needed, much of it unrelated to the focus of the paragraph.

> **KEY POINT:** Supporting examples need **specific details** that help the reader understand why each example helps support your argument.

PRACTICE

Revise **Example 5** on the previous page to provide enough information for a reader to understand, removing unnecessary information. Also, make clear the example's tie to the claim in the thesis.

WRITE

Reread Prompt B below.

> Technology allows us to fill our free time in ways never before imagined. However, a recent study finds that the constant distractions we experience today "could be preventing our minds from settling into a deeper, more complete feeling of boredom. . . . [w]hich is a shame, given complete boredom can be fertile grounds for innovation."
>
> Write an essay that argues your position on the extent to which boredom is necessary for creativity and innovation.
>
> In your response you should do the following:
> - Respond to the prompt with a thesis that presents a defensible position.
> - Provide evidence to support your line of reasoning.
> - Explain how the evidence supports your line of reasoning.
> - Use appropriate grammar and punctuation in communicating your argument.

Choose an example you might use to support an argument about this prompt (or use a thesis from a previous lesson). Then, using **Example 3** on page 218 as a model, provide the necessary detail to identify "what" your example is and to demonstrate "why" or "how" it relates to the claim you are making.

Watch this video (tinyurl.com/42sc5j76) by AP teacher Timm Freitas with an outstanding strategy for identifying and understanding your own experiences so you can use them effectively on the exam.

Watch Brandon Abdon discuss audience and assumptions using the prompt on challenging classes at the companion website (tinyurl.com/2mrx3r99) for this book. There you will find other videos by the authors as well as all the links included in the lessons in this book.

What's the Point? In one sentence, explain how this lesson can help you on the AP English Language and Composition exam.

_____

_____

_____

LESSON ARG.10 Commentary: Explanation of Examples

Eyes on the Exam

The exam reader is not in your head: you must **explain how your examples relate to your claim**.

LEARN

You may recall from other lessons that reasons are the "why" behind a belief. **Reasoning** is the process of thinking about reasons and logically connecting them to that belief. The thinking you have done to explain your claim using those reasons is your **line of reasoning:** the trail of thinking you've followed to develop your claim about the topic.

In the argument essay, you make your claim, state examples that will help you make your argument about that claim, and then explain *how* those examples help you make that argument. You explain the thinking that led you to your claim and to the examples you identify to support that thinking. Your examples (evidence) support your reasoning, which then justifies your claim. The step that often gets skipped—or assumed—is showing how the examples support the *reasoning* and how the reasoning justifies the claim.

That is **commentary:** your explanation about how the examples (and their specific details) lead to and support your thinking (reasoning) about the claim.

For example, a thesis for Prompt A may look like this:

Intentionally **facing difficult situations, like taking challenging classes, strengthens people,** as shown by (1) the rapper <u>Jay-Z facing failure when he was young</u> and (2) <u>my own fear of taking</u> Algebra I, ultimately proving that accepting challenges helps us begin to see difficulty as opportunity.

This thesis promises that the two numbered and underlined examples will support the writer's thinking that led to the claim (in bold). Details for the first example that may appear in a paragraph could look like this:

When the **rapper Jay-Z** was first starting out, he *couldn't get a record company to even listen to him*, so he *sold his own CDs and tapes out of his car* until he got so popular he couldn't be ignored. He *eventually made enough money to start his own record label* and is *now a billionaire*.

The details alone, however, are never enough. You must explain *how* those details relate to the topic and claim with your commentary. In the paragraph below, the commentary is underlined.

When the rapper Jay-Z was first starting out, he couldn't get a record company to even listen to him, so he sold his own CDs and tapes out of his car until he got so popular he couldn't be ignored. He eventually made enough money to start his own record label and is now a billionaire. <u>Because</u> *he* faced these **challenges,** *he* <u>probably became more successful than if he had been</u> *signed to a record label* <u>early on.</u> *Those early* **difficulties** <u>may cause many people to just give up. Instead,</u> *he* <u>saw it as an</u> **opportunity** <u>and a</u> **challenge** <u>to be</u> **overcome.** *If he had just been signed to a record label,* <u>then</u> *he* <u>may not have learned the value of</u> **working as hard** <u>as</u> *he had to.* <u>[Ultimately, this illustrates how facing difficult situations, like taking challenging classes, makes people stronger and creates opportunities for success.]</u>

The chart on the next page lists a few characteristics of strong commentary.

Characteristics of Effective Commentary
1. Commentary should be as long as or longer than the details that come before it. The commentary is the brain of the essay and should be given plenty of room.
2. Commentary should address both the example and the argument. The sample on the previous page discusses *both* Jay-Z *and* **challenges and difficulties.** (The words in bold type relate to the argument, and the words in italics relate to the example.) If you find you are talking only about Jay-Z, then you are probably summarizing the example. If you find you are talking only about the claim or topic, then you may not be including enough details about the example.
3. The final sentence—in brackets in the example—should link back to **the topic** of the prompt, **the claim of the thesis**, and **the big ideas** at the end of the thesis. Those links connect the example and the explanation directly to what the prompt demands.

KEY POINT: Commentary is your **analysis, interpretation, or explanation of the examples** you have chosen as evidence and how those examples support your reasoning and claim.

PRACTICE

The thesis on the previous page introduces a personal example related to the writer's experiences in Algebra I. You have probably had a similar personal experience.

Identify a personal experience during which you faced a challenge, overcame it, and became stronger. It can be any experience—no matter how large or small you feel it was. Write about that example and how it may help to support the thinking behind the claim in the thesis on the previous page. Then, using the chart above as a guide, check your details and your commentary to confirm they are effective. If they are not, revise. To help you stay on track,

- Circle words you use to connect directly to the thesis.
- Put boxes around words and phrases in the commentary that tie directly to the example.

Be ready to share with a partner or the class.

WRITE

Review Prompt B below. Then complete the activity that follows.

Technology allows us to fill our free time in ways never before imagined. However, a recent study finds that the constant distractions we experience today "could be preventing our minds from settling into a deeper, more complete feeling of boredom. . . . [w]hich is a shame, given complete boredom can be fertile grounds for innovation."

Write an essay that argues your position on the extent to which boredom is necessary for creativity and innovation.

In your response you should do the following:

- Respond to the prompt with a thesis that presents a defensible position.
- Provide evidence to support your line of reasoning.
- Explain how the evidence supports your line of reasoning.
- Use appropriate grammar and punctuation in communicating your argument.

Choose an example you might use to support a claim about Prompt B (or use a thesis from a previous lesson). Then develop that example in writing and provide commentary with the characteristics shown in the chart on the previous page.

Watch this video (tinyurl.com/2mtkvj6x) by AP teacher Beth Hall with some similar advice for writing commentary (and some additional help, too).

What's the Point? In one sentence, explain how this lesson can help you on the AP English Language and Composition exam.

_____

_____

_____

TEAM UP

Following are a thesis and three pieces of evidence. Work together in small groups as your teacher directs to develop and write commentary explaining how each piece of evidence supports the argument. Remember to link the commentary to both the evidence *and* the thesis. When you're done, compare your group's commentary with that of other groups.

Thesis: Board games play a crucial role in developing social skills and fostering interpersonal relationships.

Evidence 1: A study in the "Journal of Leisure Research" indicates that playing board games leads to increased verbal communication and collaboration among players.

Evidence 2: Research highlighted in "Social Development" shows that children who regularly engage in board game play exhibit higher levels of empathy and understanding of social cues.

Evidence 3: A survey conducted by the National Board Game Association found that regular board game players report stronger family bonds and friendships.

Here's an example of commentary using a different piece of evidence about board games and children's anxiety.

Research from the "American Journal of Play" sheds light on the psychological benefits of board games, particularly for children who experience social anxiety. This study suggests that board games are a gentle and enjoyable way for anxious children to engage in social interaction. The structured nature of these games provides a less intimidating social environment, allowing children to interact with peers without the uncertainties in other social settings. Consequently, playing board games can make it easier for children to develop confidence and comfort in social interactions. This evidence further supports the claim that board games are not just recreational activities but also valuable tools for overcoming social challenges and enhancing social competence.

LESSON ARG.11 Commentary: Signal Words

Eyes on the Exam

Your use of certain words and phrases will help a reader follow your argument.

LEARN

An argument makes your claim about a topic, explains the thinking that led you to that claim, and provides examples to show why you think the way you do.

Signal words are specific words or phrases that indicate the structure of the argument and guide a reader through the logic or progression of your thinking. These words can signal different aspects of an argument, such as introducing a point, showing a cause-and-effect relationship, adding more information, contrasting ideas, or concluding a point.

Signal Words to Guide Readers	
Cause and Effect	because, consequently, so, so that, thus, since, for this reason, as a result, therefore, accordingly, due to, if . . . then . . .
Addition	furthermore, moreover, in addition, also, second
Comparison/Contrast	however, on the other hand, unlike, in contrast
Decisive Language (indicates a statement the writer does not want argued)	ultimately, clearly, categorically, consequently, crucially, critically, unequivocally (Make sure statements following this language match what the decisive conjunction describes.)

Read the possible thesis and first example paragraph for Prompt A. In the example paragraph, the commentary is underlined.

Thesis: Intentionally **facing difficult situations, like taking challenging classes, strengthens people,** as shown by (1) the rapper Jay-Z facing failure when he was young and (2) my own fear of taking Algebra I, ultimately proving that accepting challenges helps us begin to see difficulty as opportunity.

First example paragraph: When the rapper Jay-Z was first starting out, he couldn't get a record company to even listen to him, so he sold his own CDs and tapes out of his car until he got so popular he couldn't be ignored. He eventually made enough money to start his own record label and is now a billionaire. **Because** he faced these challenges, he probably became more successful than if he had been signed to a record label early on. Those early difficulties may cause many people to just give up. Instead, he saw it as an opportunity and a challenge to be overcome. **If** he had just been signed to a record label, **then** he may not have learned the value of working as hard as he had to. [Ultimately, this example illustrates how facing difficult situations, like taking challenging classes, makes people stronger and creates opportunities for success.]

Notice the cause-and-effect language (in bold). It signals to the reader that the commentary is explaining how the example caused or led the writer to arrive at the essay's thesis.

The last sentence (in brackets) links the example and commentary to the original prompt about taking challenging classes and to the bigger idea of finding opportunity in difficulty. Starting that sentence with the decisive word *Ultimately* signals to readers that the analysis of the example is conclusive.

Using sentence frames for each sentence in your commentary may help you organize your thinking about each of your examples. Using the frames in the order presented below will reflect a logical progression of your thoughts.

You may remember from previous lessons the advice about using strong verbs. You will see that advice worked into the sentence frames along with cause-and-effect signal word suggestions. The signal words are in bold.

Sentence Frames for Argument Commentary
Commentary Sentence 1 This example [**choose one strong verb:** *proves, illustrates, supports, confirms, refutes, disproves, shows the limitations of, suggests, implies*] [insert reference to the claim from the thesis] **because** [explain how your example relates to the claim]. **Example:** This example [suggests] that [facing difficult situations strengthens people] **because** [Jay-Z clearly saw the difficulties of rejection and struggle as opportunities for success.]
Commentary Sentence 2: Consequently, [**choose one:** *if/since*] [insert assumption about relationship between the example and argument], [finish sentence by explaining the logical outcome of the assumption]. **Example: Consequently,** [since] [he eventually became one of the most successful rappers and musical artists of all time], [he clearly was strengthened by his struggles in a way that he would not have been had he simply been signed early on.]
Commentary Sentence 3: [**Choose one:** *Therefore, Thus*] [articulate logical outcome and make sure to include either the word *since* or a phrase starting with *because* at some point in this sentence]. **Example:** [**Thus,**] [if he had not faced the difficulties that he did, then he may not have become as famous as he is **because** he did not have to work as hard].
Commentary Sentence 4 (The Link): [**Choose one:** *Ultimately, Clearly, Categorically, Consequently, Crucially, Critically, Unequivocally*] this example [choose one strong verb: *proves, illustrates, supports, confirms, refutes, disproves, shows the limitations of, suggests, implies*] [a statement linking the topic and claim to the big idea in the thesis]. **Example:** [**Ultimately,**] this example [illustrates] [how facing difficult situations, like taking challenging classes, makes people stronger and creates opportunities for success].

KEY POINT: Use words and phrases that **guide your reader's understanding** of how your examples relate to your thesis.

PRACTICE

Reread Prompt B on the next page. Pay special attention to the first three bullet points (in italics).

Technology allows us to fill our free time in ways never before imagined. However, a recent study finds that the constant distractions we experience today "could be preventing our minds from settling into a deeper, more complete feeling of boredom. . . . [w]hich is a shame, given complete boredom can be fertile grounds for innovation."

Write an essay that argues your position on the extent to which boredom is necessary for creativity and innovation.

In your response you should do the following:

- *Respond to the prompt with a thesis that presents a defensible position.*
- *Provide evidence to support your line of reasoning.*
- *Explain how the evidence supports your line of reasoning.*
- Use appropriate grammar and punctuation in communicating your argument.

Using work from previous lessons, choose an example you might use to support an argument about this prompt (or a thesis from a previous lesson). Provide the specific and detailed information for that example and then choose one of the following options:

Option 1

Write (or revise, if you are using work from a previous lesson) your commentary using cause-and-effect language and decisive-language **signal words** from the list above.

Option 2

Write (or revise, if you are using work from a previous lesson) your commentary following the **sentence frames** on the previous page.

In both options:

1. Underline cause-and-effect language and decisive-language signal words you use.
2. Share with a partner and be ready to explain what each signal word means to your argument.

WRITE

Choose another example that you might use to support an argument in response to Prompt B. Without looking at the list above or at any examples, explain the example you chose and provide commentary on it using cause-and-effect language, decisive language, and strong verbs. Write for about 10 minutes. You may be surprised by the result.

Watch this video (tinyurl.com/es8phsp6) by AP teacher Timm Freitas with some similar advice for writing commentary.

What's the Point? In one sentence, explain how this lesson can help you on the AP English Language and Composition exam.

_____

_____

_____

LESSON ARG.12 Paragraph Organization

Eyes on the Exam

The better structured your paragraphs are, the more likely you are to earn points in the Evidence and Commentary row of the rubric. You can earn up to four of the question's total six points by doing well in that row.

LEARN

Paragraphs are segments of text related to some part of your claim. Each represents a stage in the progression of your **line of reasoning.**

A useful pattern for constructing your paragraphs is **I**dentify, **E**xplain, **L**ink. You can remember that pattern by its letters: **IEL.**

Review the following possible thesis statement for Prompt A.

Intentionally **facing difficult situations, like taking challenging classes, strengthens people,** as shown by (1) the rapper Jay-Z facing failure when he was young and (2) my own fear of taking Algebra I, [ultimately proving that accepting challenges helps us begin to see difficulty as opportunity].

Here's how the IEL pattern might work out for the first body paragraph that goes with that thesis statement.

Paragraph Parts	Full Paragraph
Topic Sentence **I**dentify example and provide details **E**xplain how the example relates to the argument	***Difficult situations strengthen people,*** *as demonstrated by Jay-Z going from selling CDs from his trunk to becoming a multibillionaire.* When the rapper Jay-Z was first starting out, he couldn't get a record company to even listen to him, so he sold his own CDs and tapes out of his car until he got so popular he couldn't be ignored. He eventually made enough money to start his own record label and is now a billionaire. Because he faced **these challenges**, he probably **became more successful** than if he had been signed to a record label early on. Those **early difficulties** may cause many people to just give up. Instead, he saw it as an **opportunity** and a **challenge to be overcome**. If he had just been signed to a record label, then he may not have learned the **value of working as hard** as he had to.
[Link example back to bigger ideas]	[Ultimately, this example illustrates how facing **difficult situations**, like taking **challenging classes, makes people stronger and creates opportunities for success**.]

The topic sentence connects the claim (in bold) in the prompt and thesis to the specific example this paragraph examines. The remaining parts then **i**dentify the example in detail, **e**xplain (underlined) the thinking about how the example relates to the thesis, and then **l**ink (in brackets)—or connect—the entire paragraph back to the topic of the prompt and the bigger idea in the thesis.

Sometimes you may have more than one example that relates to the same part of your thesis. You do not *need* to include additional examples, but if you do, you can work in the new information as shown in the paragraph below. The sentences are numbered for easy reference.

[1] Difficult situations strengthen people, as demonstrated by Jay-Z going from selling CDs from his trunk <u>and Walt Disney originally going bankrupt</u>. [2] When the rapper Jay-Z was first starting out, he couldn't get a record company to even listen to him, so he sold his own CDs and tapes out of his car until he got so popular he couldn't be ignored. [3] He eventually made enough money to start his own record label and is now a billionaire. [4] Because he faced these challenges, he probably became more successful than if he had been signed to a record label early on. [5] Those early difficulties may cause many people to just give up. [6] Instead, Jay-Z saw it as an opportunity and a challenge to be overcome. [7] If he had just been signed to a record label, then he may not have learned the value of working as hard as he had to. [8] *Not only is Jay-Z an example of difficulty actually strengthening someone,* <u>*but so*</u> *is the world-famous Walt Disney.* [9] Disney's first animation studio was somewhat popular but failed to make much money. [10] He had to file bankruptcy, but soon he started over. [11] Having learned from his first failure, this time he managed money and work successfully as he made the first movie-length cartoon, *Snow White*. [12] Consequently, since the company he founded after bankruptcy now rules the entertainment industry, he clearly was strengthened by his struggles in a way that he would not have been had he given up after his bankruptcy. [13] Thus, if he had not faced those difficulties, then he may not have succeeded and his company may not have become the giant it is, because he did not learn important lessons. [14] Ultimately, these examples illustrate how facing failure and other difficult situations, like taking challenging classes, makes people stronger and creates opportunities for success.

Note the **sentence frame used to add the new example.** Note also the signal word for additional information: *also*.

Not only [something related directly to the claim and previous example], but [*also* or *so does*] [the new example and its connections to the claim].

PRACTICE

1. Write the sentence numbers that represent **I** (identify), **E** (explain), and **L** (link) in the section of the paragraph on Jay-Z.

2. Write the sentence numbers that represent **I** (identify), **E** (explain), and **L** (link) in the section of the paragraph on Walt Disney.

WRITE

Reread Prompt B below.

> Technology allows us to fill our free time in ways never before imagined. However, a recent study finds that the constant distractions we experience today "could be preventing our minds from settling into a deeper, more complete feeling of boredom. . . . [w]hich is a shame, given complete boredom can be fertile grounds for innovation."
>
> Write an essay that argues your position on the extent to which boredom is necessary for creativity and innovation.
>
> In your response you should do the following:
> - Respond to the prompt with a thesis that presents a defensible position.
> - Provide evidence to support your line of reasoning.
> - Explain how the evidence supports your line of reasoning.
> - Use appropriate grammar and punctuation in communicating your argument.

Using work from previous lessons, choose an example you might use to support an argument about this prompt (or a thesis from a previous lesson). Then complete the following activities:

1. Write a paragraph that follows the pattern in the "Full Paragraph" chart on page 227.

2. After writing, identify the parts of your paragraph by putting a wavy line under the *identification* of the example and details, underlining the *explanation* of the new example, circling words that tie back to the claim in the topic sentence and thesis, and then bracketing the *link* to the bigger idea.

3. Share your paragraph to get some feedback and opportunities to revise.

Visit this site (tinyurl.com/399ntp8e) for a similar model for organizing a paragraph but with different letters: PEEL. Watch the video on this site as well.

What's the Point? In one sentence, explain how this lesson can help you on the AP English Language and Composition exam.

_____

_____

_____

LESSON ARG.13 Essay Structure

Eyes on the Exam

Having an essay structure in mind on exam day will help you quickly plan and write your essay.

LEARN

Some patterns for structuring essays have proven effective. The most useful one on exam day resembles what is sometimes called the "classical" structure. It focuses on helping your reader understand your argument and then addresses and rebuts the most important possible alternative perspective and counterargument near the end.

Classical Essay Structure	
Introduction	Starts with the big idea beyond the topic of the prompt and then leads into a discussion of the topic. From there, it focuses on what you will claim, and it ends with the thesis. (You do not necessarily need a full introduction on the exam essays. You might just focus on having a strong thesis.)
Body	• Main Paragraphs: Identify the example(s) you will use to support your reasoning, then explain the details of the example before linking the example to your claim (and maybe to the bigger idea). • Counterargument: The last paragraph of the body addresses and rebuts a counterargument.
Conclusion	Starts narrow with the prompt topic and your claim before broadening out to express a reflection on the big idea (why everyone should care).

You might picture the shape of a classical essay this way.

Structure of "Classical" Essay

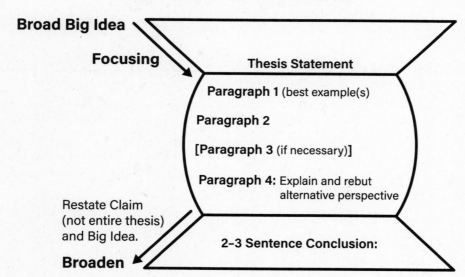

Another reliable essay structure is one in which

- A lead-in introduces the big idea before the introduction ends with the thesis.
- Each paragraph extends from the thesis as it develops the argument with examples.
- The counterargument connects back to the thesis as it addresses and rebuts an opposing viewpoint.
- The conclusion also links directly back to the thesis to express a reflection about the big idea (why everyone should care).

You might picture the shape of that essay structure as the organizer below shows.

Alternative Essay Structure

Introduction	} **Introduction**
Thesis	
Paragraph 1	
Paragraph 2	} **Body**
[Paragraph 3 (if necessary)]	
Address and Rebut Counterargument	
Conclusion	} **Conclusion**

In both structures, as you move from one paragraph to the next, use structural signal words so your reader knows where you are heading.

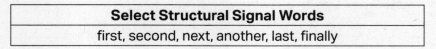

Select Structural Signal Words
first, second, next, another, last, finally

KEY POINT: Knowing a structure for your essay before the exam will help save you time. **Practice writing essays in one of these patterns often** so that it will be natural to you on exam day.

PRACTICE

Either on your own or collaboratively, read sample essay ARG.3.D in the Appendix on page 283 and complete the following activities.

1. Examine the diagram for a classical essay structure carefully until you are sure you understand it. Then label the parts of essay ARG.3.D as they align with the parts of the organizer.

2. Based on the essay and your examination of the organizer, identify two places in the essay you would suggest a revision. Explain your choices.

WRITE

Review Prompt B below.

> Technology allows us to fill our free time in ways never before imagined. However, a recent study finds that the constant distractions we experience today "could be preventing our minds from settling into a deeper, more complete feeling of boredom. . . . [w]hich is a shame, given complete boredom can be fertile grounds for innovation."
>
> Write an essay that argues your position on the extent to which boredom is necessary for creativity and innovation.
>
> In your response you should do the following:
> - Respond to the prompt with a thesis that presents a defensible position.
> - Provide evidence to support your line of reasoning.
> - Explain how the evidence supports your line of reasoning.
> - Use appropriate grammar and punctuation in communicating your argument.

On your own paper, recreate the organizer of the classical essay. Use a thesis statement and any other previous work you have done on this prompt. Then, plan an essay using that organizer just as you might on exam day.

Watch this video (tinyurl.com/3hzhsbu4) by AP teacher John Moscatiello from Marco Learning with some advice for planning the essay on exam day.

What's the Point? In one sentence, explain how this lesson can help you on the AP English Language and Composition exam.

_____

_____

_____

LESSON ARG.14 Subordinate Clauses and Opposing Viewpoints

Eyes on the Exam

Exam readers will expect you to **address opposing viewpoints** in your argument.

LEARN

A **subordinate clause** is not a complete thought and therefore cannot be the main clause of a sentence. (See Lesson ARG.7.) Since the ideas in a subordinate, or dependent, clause always take a back seat to the ideas in the main independent clause, using a subordinate clause is a good way of introducing an opposing view without taking the focus off *your* view.

Recall that subordinate clauses always begin with a subordinating conjunction. Common subordinating conjunctions are *although, while, though, whereas, even though, even if,* and *rather than.* All of these set up a contrast between two ideas. In an argument, those contrasting ideas are your claim and an alternative perspective.

An alternative perspective on Prompt A (facing difficulties) might be expressed this way:

Although some people would disagree, taking challenging classes actually benefits students.

While this statement has a subordinate clause (in italics) and a subordinating conjunction (underlined), it does not actually express an alternative perspective. It says only that some would disagree. Make sure that when you address alternative perspectives, you are specific, as in the example below:

Although some students claim that difficult classes create too much additional **stress***, those* classes *and the* **stress** *they create actually* strengthen students since they encourage them to see failure as opportunity and help students develop perseverance.

In this case, the subordinating clause (in italics) and the subordinating conjunction (underlined) immediately show that the writer has considered a specific alternative perspective: the reasonable idea that challenging classes make stress for students. The thesis now also includes a reference to that stress in the main claim (in bold) so that it directly addresses the opposing concern.

KEY POINT: You are always arguing with an alternative perspective. Introduce specific opposing views in a subordinate clause using a **subordinating conjunction.**

PRACTICE

Examine sample essay ARG.3.C in the Appendix on page 282.

1. Revise a sentence in one of the body paragraphs to include a subordinating clause that connects to the alternative perspective suggested in the thesis.

2. Write a new sentence with a subordinate clause that you could insert into one of the main body paragraphs.

3. Explain each choice you made and how you expect it to affect the argument.

WRITE

Review Prompt B below.

> Technology allows us to fill our free time in ways never before imagined. However, a recent study finds that the constant distractions we experience today "could be preventing our minds from settling into a deeper, more complete feeling of boredom. . . . [w]hich is a shame, given complete boredom can be fertile grounds for innovation."
>
> Write an essay that argues your position on the extent to which boredom is necessary for creativity and innovation.
>
> In your response you should do the following:
> - Respond to the prompt with a thesis that presents a defensible position.
> - Provide evidence to support your line of reasoning.
> - Explain how the evidence supports your line of reasoning.
> - Use appropriate grammar and punctuation in communicating your argument.

Make an initial claim for this prompt or use work from a previous lesson. Then complete the following activities.

1. Identify two or three specific alternative perspectives to your initial claim.
2. Develop two or three separate sentences using subordinate clauses to directly address those alternative perspectives. Then also address them in the claim.

Watch this video (tinyurl.com/2dkury53) from Khan Academy for some more thinking about subordinating conjunctions.

What's the Point? In one sentence, explain how this lesson can help you on the AP English Language and Composition exam.

_____

_____

_____

LESSON ARG.15 Rebuttal and Refutation of Opposing Viewpoints

Eyes on the Exam

Exam readers will look for your ability to respond to alternative perspectives.

LEARN

Including an alternative perspective will show that you have taken a differing viewpoint seriously. Briefly discussing it in your essay and demonstrating that you understand it may help you gain a reader's trust and respect.

One way to address an opposing view is to **rebut** it by making an opposite claim. When you go on to explain the argument behind that **rebuttal,** you are developing a **refutation.**

For the purposes of the exam, there are two trustworthy ways to include a rebuttal and refutation. Try to do at least one of these on exam day:

1. Include an entire paragraph that addresses an opposing view. (See Lesson ARG.13, Essay Structure.) Devoting a paragraph to an opposing view shows you have really put some thought into that alternative perspective. Also, offer a very short, new example that shows your reasoning about the rebuttal and refutation.

2. State it within a main body paragraph. This approach allows you to address any doubts you predict a reader may have about a specific example.

> **KEY POINT: Rebuttal** and **refutation** show thinking about alternative perspectives in relation to your claim and may elevate the quality of your essay.

PRACTICE

Part 1: Examine sample essay ARG.3.A in the Appendix on page 280.

1. Identify the paragraph that offers a rebuttal and refutation.

2. Identify and explain the claim being refuted. How does the example given help to support the refutation? How could it be improved?

Part 2: Review this paragraph from essay ARG.3.D in the Appendix on page 283.

[12] Fear of failure includes fear of mistakes that could lead to failure. [13] This specific kind of failure can still strengthen people, like I learned in middle school. [14] In 7th grade I did well in math. [15] The teacher told me and my parents that I should take Algebra I in 8th grade. [16] They signed me up for it and I was afraid all summer. [17] Once I was in the class I saw that making mistakes helped me to think different. [18] This example shows how accepting my mistakes made me stronger. [19] Though someone could argue that I was too young to see how these things really affected me, it's been three years and that is enough time to think about that experience and how it changed me. [20] Everybody makes mistakes, but those mistakes and challenges will make us better.

3. Identify the sentence that offers a rebuttal and refutation.

4. Identify and explain the claim being refuted and how it relates to the idea and example in the paragraph. How could it be improved?

WRITE

Review Prompt B below.

> Technology allows us to fill our free time in ways never before imagined. However, a recent study finds that the constant distractions we experience today "could be preventing our minds from settling into a deeper, more complete feeling of boredom. . . . [w]hich is a shame, given complete boredom can be fertile grounds for innovation."
>
>   Write an essay that argues your position on the extent to which boredom is necessary for creativity and innovation
>
> In your response you should do the following:
>
> - Respond to the prompt with a thesis that presents a defensible position.
> - Provide evidence to support your line of reasoning.
> - Explain how the evidence supports your line of reasoning.
> - Use appropriate grammar and punctuation in communicating your argument.

Make an initial claim for this prompt or use work from a previous lesson. Then complete the following activities:

1. Identify a specific alternative perspective to your initial claim.

2. Identify a new example beyond the essay itself that you could use to show your understanding of the alternative perspective.

3. Write a three- to five-sentence rebuttal and refutation of the alternative perspective using a subordinate clause and the example you identified.

Watch this brief video (tinyurl.com/yc6wype8) explaining how Supreme Court Justice Ruth Bader Ginsberg addressed a counterargument about affirmative action.

What's the Point? In one sentence, explain how this lesson can help you on the AP English Language and Composition exam.

_____

_____

_____

Eyes on the Exam

Readers will score your evidence and commentary based on the criteria in Row B in the Argument rubric.

LEARN

Carefully read each section of the Row B rubric and scoring guide.

- The first 5-column row, arranged from 0 points on the left to 4 points on the right, explains in general terms what criteria need to be met to achieve each score. Note that there are criteria for both evidence and commentary.

- The second 5-column row (next page) describes characteristics of essays earning each point. In both of those rows, key words have been printed in bold type to help you see the similarities and differences between the rankings.

- The final row provides additional clarifications for acceptable evidence and commentary.

Row B: Evidence AND Commentary (0-4 points), Scoring Criteria [2.A, 4.A, 6.A, 6.B, 6.C]				
0 points	**1 point**	**2 points**	**3 points**	**4 points**
Simply **restates** thesis (if present), **repeats** provided information, or offers **information irrelevant to the prompt.**	EVIDENCE: Provides **evidence that is mostly general.** AND COMMENTARY: Summarizes the evidence **but does not explain how the evidence supports the argument.**	EVIDENCE: Provides **some specific relevant** evidence. AND COMMENTARY: Explains how **some of the evidence** relates to the student's argument, but **no line of reasoning** is established, or the **line of reasoning is faulty.**	EVIDENCE: Provides **specific evidence to support all claims in a line of reasoning.** AND COMMENTARY: Explains how **some of the evidence** supports **a line of reasoning.**	EVIDENCE: Provides **specific evidence to support all claims in a line of reasoning.** AND COMMENTARY: **Consistently explains how the evidence** supports **a line of reasoning.**

Decision Rules and Scoring Notes		Typical responses that earn ...		
0 points:	**1 point:**	**2 points:**	**3 points:**	**4 points:**
Are **incoherent** or **do not address the prompt.** May be **just opinion with no evidence** or evidence that is **irrelevant.**	Tend to focus on **a summary of the evidence** rather than specific details.	Consist of a **mix of specific evidence and broad generalities.** May contain some **simplistic, inaccurate, or repetitive explanations** that don't strengthen the argument. May make one point well, but either **do not make multiple supporting claims** or **do not adequately support** more than one claim. Do not explain the connections or progression between the student's claims so **a line of reasoning is not clearly explained.**	**Uniformly offer evidence** to support claims. Focus on the **importance of specific details** to build an argument. Organize an argument as a **line of reasoning composed of multiple supporting claims.** Commentary **may fail to integrate some evidence or fail to support a key claim.**	Focus on the **importance of specific details** to build an argument. Organize and support an argument as a **line of reasoning composed of multiple supporting claims**, each with **adequate evidence that is clearly explained.**

Additional Notes:

Writing that suffers from grammatical and/or mechanical errors that interfere with communication cannot earn the fourth point in this row.

Following are the skills from the Course and Exam Description that are assessed in Row B.

2.A Write introductions and conclusions appropriate to the purpose and context of the rhetorical situation.

4.A Develop a paragraph that includes a claim and evidence supporting the claim.

6.A Develop a line of reasoning and commentary that explains it throughout an argument.

6.B Use transitional elements to guide the reader through the line of reasoning of an argument.

6.C Use appropriate methods of development to advance an argument.

PRACTICE

Complete the following activities and answer the questions about the Row B Evidence and Commentary rubric and scoring guide.

1. In your own words, explain two ways in which an essay scoring a 3 is similar to an essay earning a 4.

2. What is the highest score you can earn in Row B if your essay lacks a line of reasoning?

3. Describe the difference in evidence in an essay scoring a 1 and an essay earning a 2 in Row B.

4. What would you say is the biggest difference between an essay earning a 2 in Row B and an essay earning a 3? Explain your answer.

5. If an essay adequately supports only one claim, what Row B score would it likely earn?

6. How can you meet all the criteria for 4 points and still not earn all 4?

You Be the Reader

Read sample essay ARG.3.C in the Appendix on page 282. Decide what score that essay earns in the Row B evidence and commentary category. Explain your answer.

Review the sample essays <u>on this site</u> (tinyurl.com/2953ubar) and the scores and comments they received from exam readers. Pay special attention to the Row B score.

Revise

Review the evidence and commentary you have developed in response to Prompt B about boredom and creativity. If you think it does not earn a 4 based on this rubric, revise as needed to raise your score. Even if you believe it earns 4 points as it is, revise your essay body to make it the best it can be.

LESSON ARG.16 Joining the Conversation: The Broader Context

Eyes on the Exam

The best essays often **connect the argument** to ideas and conversations beyond the exam.

LEARN

Row C of the argument rubric identifies four ways an essay can earn the sophistication point:

- Articulate an argument's implications or limitations by setting it in a larger context.
- Create a nuanced argument by exploring complexities and tensions.
- Make effective rhetorical choices to strengthen the impact of an argument.
- Employ a vivid and persuasive style.

Recall from Lesson ARG.3 on big ideas that while arguments are about a specific topic, that specific topic also relates to bigger ideas beyond the argument itself—the **broader context.**

- An argument about building a new highway through farmland is not merely about the farmland or the highway. It is also about big ideas that the farmland and the highway might represent: progress, personal rights, government, and nature, for example.
- An argument about school starting time isn't just about time. It is also about big ideas related to it: learning, health, family, safety, and economics, to name a few.

Conversations about the values of highways and the rights of farmers have been ongoing since the government began building roads. In the same way, conversations about school schedules as they relate to students' families, lives, and health have been ongoing.

On exam day, focus on the topic from the prompt but recognize you are entering ongoing conversations on that topic and on bigger ideas related to that topic. Strengthen your argument by addressing the broader context of that conversation.

Example: Critically, the government's role in taking farmlands for public highway projects becomes part of an ongoing conversation about **individual rights** and **government overreach.**

This sentence tells the reader that the argument is important because it touches on aspects of life that affect everyone: individual rights and government overreach.

You can use a sentence frame like the following to place a topic in context.

Sentence Frame for the Broader Context

[**Choose one:** *Ultimately, Clearly, Categorically, Consequently, Crucially, Critically, or Unequivocally*] [the topic of the prompt or *this* if it's in the previous sentence] becomes part of an ongoing conversation about [big idea(s)].

Placing the topic in a larger context one time in the introduction or conclusion is a start, but to get closer to the sophistication point, you need to connect to the larger context in each paragraph. Further, as you respond to opposing views, acknowledge the limitations of each viewpoint in the conversation, including your own.

KEY POINT: Every argument enters a **broader, ongoing conversation** about a topic and other related topics, and each argument has both strengths and limitations. Pointing those out will show you are thinking critically about the topic.

PRACTICE

Part 1: Examine sample essays ARG.3.A and ARG.3.C in the Appendix on pages 280 and 282. They are in response to Prompt A.

1. Identify where in each the essay connects to the broader context of an ongoing conversation.

2. Explain the differences in how essays ARG.3.A and ARG.3.C address the larger context. How do the different approaches affect each essay?

Part 2: Examine sample essay ARG.3.B in the Appendix on page 281.

1. Where could you revise the essay to include a connection to an ongoing conversation?

2. Write what you would insert or revise in that spot and explain your choice.

WRITE

Review Prompt B below.

> Technology allows us to fill our free time in ways never before imagined. However, a recent study finds that the constant distractions we experience today "could be preventing our minds from settling into a deeper, more complete feeling of boredom. . . . [w]hich is a shame, given complete boredom can be fertile grounds for innovation."
>
> Write an essay that argues your position on the extent to which boredom is necessary for creativity and innovation.
>
> In your response you should do the following:
> - Respond to the prompt with a thesis that presents a defensible position.
> - Provide evidence to support your line of reasoning.
> - Explain how the evidence supports your line of reasoning.
> - Use appropriate grammar and punctuation in communicating your argument.

Make an initial claim for this prompt or use work from a previous lesson. Then complete the following activities:

1. Revise your claim to include a big idea and a connection to an ongoing conversation.

2. List two or three examples you might use to support the reasoning behind that claim, and then add a sentence for each explaining how it relates to the ongoing conversation.

Watch Brandon Abdon discuss the broader context using the challenging classes prompt at the companion website (tinyurl.com/2mrx3r99) for this book. There you will find other videos by the authors and other links included in this book.

What's the Point? In one sentence, explain how this lesson can help you on the AP English Language and Composition exam.

LESSON ARG.17 Rhetorical Moves

Eyes on the Exam

You can appeal to your reader using some of the same rhetorical choices in your argument that you explore in others' arguments.

LEARN

Effective arguments balance the message of the writer (you) with the needs of the reader. Certain choices you can make as you craft the message in your argument will engage the reader in particular ways.

You may have heard about different "appeals" you can make to a reader.

- Ethical appeal—showing your values so the reader can relate to you. This appeal helps address the question "Why should the reader trust you?"

- Emotional appeal—including information and discussion that evokes emotions (positive, negative, or some other) in the reader. This appeal helps address the question "Why should the reader care about this?"

- Logical appeal—offering explanations and statements that help the reader see the common sense reasoning in the argument, hoping they come to see that it "just makes sense." This appeal help address the question "Why should the reader believe you?"

You cannot actually "use" an appeal. Appeals are effects of other choices you make in your argument. The rhetorical choices you make will create and affect different appeals in different ways.

The table on the next page focuses on the rhetorical choices that often apply to the reasoning of an argument and methods of developing ideas. For each strategy, the bulleted explanation includes "what" to clarify the focus, provide examples, or suggest strategies; "why" so you understand the reasoning behind the move; and "how" to explain what to do. It also includes an example of an original "draft" and a "revised" version using the advice.

You may not have time to plan for these choices during your timed writing. Try to focus on two or three of these that come easiest to you and push yourself to think about how you can use them as you plan and write your argument.

Since you will not have time to revise on test day, you should practice these before the test so you can use them as you write. Try revising old essays with them.

Rhetorical Moves and Methods of Development	
Comparison **-Simile**	**Comparisons are rhetorical moves used to show similarities between things that are different in most ways.** **Simile** • **What:** Comparing something in the argument to something with which the audience may be familiar • **Why:** Help the reader better understand your perspective by comparing it to something they have experienced • **How:** Explain that some aspect of what you are saying is "like" (simile) or can be "compared" to something else and then explain how the two are alike. Be sure to use generally understood, fairly common comparisons. Using a comparison few understand will likely hurt your essay. • **Draft:** Signing up for Algebra turned out to be the thing that scared me all summer. • **Revised with simile:** At the time, signing up for Algebra felt like being in a haunted house and always being on guard, knowing that something scary could happen. I knew I couldn't avoid it, but I couldn't quit thinking about it. It ruined my summer. In this case, the simile attempts to connect to a similar situation that many people may have experienced in an attempt to help the audience better understand how the writer felt.
-Metaphor	**Metaphor** • **Draft:** Throughout history, the most successful people have often been those who also failed at something. But in schools, failure is almost always a bad word. • **Revised with metaphor:** Success is an onion because there are many layers to it. Each of those layers is a lesson learned from experience, sometimes success and sometimes failure. Throughout history, the most successful people have often been those who also failed at something. But in schools, failure is almost always a bad word. While failure—like an onion—may make you cry sometimes, it is still an essential layer to build toward success. Here, the writer compares success to an onion because of the many layers of experience that create it and because those experiences may sometimes bring us to tears. This comparison is general enough for readers to understand and helps them see the writer's perspective that all experience is essential to build toward success.

Contrasts	**Contrasts are rhetorical moves that emphasize or clarify differences.** • **What:** Set your example or claim against something similar (but slightly different) • **Why:** Illustrate how your example or claim is unique and nuanced compared to another • **How:** Introduce your example or claim and then a similar one. Explain that they are similar but then focus on how yours is different and more significant. As with comparisons, contrast your claim or example with something in some way familiar or common to a general audience. • **Draft:** Signing up for Algebra turned out to be the thing that scared me all summer. • **Revised:** Signing up for Algebra turned out to be the thing that scared me all summer. It wasn't just the uncertainty that comes sometimes with the beginning of a new school year; this was a real fear of going into something I knew I would fail. It was not something I would just get used to, like new teachers and a new schedule, but something that would ruin me for sure. Here the writer contrasts waiting to start Algebra with something most people have felt, a general unease about starting a new school year.
Narration **-Anecdotes**	**Narration is a rhetorical choice to tell a story that helps make a point.** • **What:** Tell a brief anecdote (real or fictional) related to the topic and possibly to your argument. • **Why:** Help your reader better connect to your perspective, the tone of the argument, and/or the rhetorical situation. • **How:** Include the necessary parts of a story: characters, conflict, and some action (at the least). You may include some dialogue and some other elements of a story if there is time. • **Draft:** Signing up for Algebra turned out to be the thing that scared me all summer. • **Revised:** On a June morning, a boy wakes up early when he would normally sleep in. This first day of summer vacation should be a day of catching up on sleep lost in the last nine months and getting ready for the coming summer, but the boy is just not there. Instead, he wakes to images in his head of his smiling math teacher. "I'm excited you'll be with us in Algebra I next year," she says sincerely, but then her face twists in the way that sometimes happens in movies to show an anxiety or confusion. This anxiety and even fear would cross the boy's mind nearly every day for the next eight weeks. This boy was me after I was pressed to take Algebra I as an eighth grader. I worried all summer. Little did I know that the challenge the class posed would motivate me to get even better at math, with plans now to become a mechanical engineer. Here, the writer uses the brief story to take the reader into the situation to see and even feel the emotions the writer felt.

Description	Description is a technique that evokes the readers' senses.
-Images and Imagery	• **What:** Include sensory details the reader will find familiar to establish and emphasize the mood of a setting or the tone (attitude) toward a topic.
	• **Why:** Connect with the reader's senses and even activate their emotions and improve their understanding.
	• **How:** Choose details relevant to the 5+1 senses (smell, taste, touch, sound, smell, and emotion) and include them in the description and commentary of your argument.
	• **Draft:** Signing up for Algebra made me uncomfortable because I had a fear of failure that overwhelmed me, and I couldn't quit thinking about it all summer long.
	• **Revised:** My hands were sweaty on the mouse pad as I clicked the checkbox next to "Algebra I," making my final course selection for the next year. As I moved the cursor toward the submit button, my fingers seemed to freeze. My hand was cold and wet and still. I knew then that fear smelled like the stale air in the media center as I looked around at the rest of the class at their screens, making their choices, smiling about band or laughing about their decision to take Mr. Barnes for PE for a third year. The sounds all faded. All I could hear was the deafening electronic "click" made by the computer as I tapped the mouse pad to hit submit. Few people seemed to notice as I quickly closed the laptop and took my first breath in what seemed like minutes. I had done it. Signing up for Algebra made me uncomfortable because I had a fear of failure that overwhelmed me, and I couldn't quit thinking about it all summer long.
	The writer here tells a story related to the topic but included a lot of sensory detail to communicate an attitude toward the event they are discussing.
Definition	Definition is a method of developing a topic by clarifying what it is.
	• **What:** Being specific about the meaning of something as you understand it
	• **Why:** Help the reader understand what you mean by the words you use and ideas you convey
	• **How:** Pause in the writing to specifically define something by telling what it means to you and possibly giving an example
	• **Draft:** I wasn't sure about signing up for Algebra. I was overwhelmed with a fear that I would fail. I couldn't quit thinking about it all summer.
	• **Revised:** I wasn't sure about signing up for Algebra. Most people probably think of fear in relation to something dangerous or deadly, but that's not how I saw Algebra. Instead, my fear was of the uncertainly of success and the certainty of pain. I couldn't quit thinking about it all summer.
	In this case, the writer takes one possible definition of fear and then provides a more clarified definition of fear as it relates to the situation.

Cause-Effect	Cause-effect is a method of development that shows how a cause, or driving force, leads to an effect, or result.
	• **What:** Show how some things cause or are the cause of others in a situation
	• **Why:** Help the reader recognize your understanding of how things relate to one another
	• **How:** Connect and explain how something is caused by or causes something else
	• **Draft:** I wasn't sure about signing up for Algebra. I was overwhelmed with a fear that I would fail. I couldn't quit thinking about it all summer.
	• **Revised:** I wasn't sure about signing up for Algebra. That uncertainty and the constant doubt I felt eventually made me fear the class. Specifically, I feared I would make too many mistakes that would lead to failing the class. I couldn't quit thinking about it all summer.
	Here, the writer saw a need to insert one cause-effect scenario: the causes are the "uncertainty" and "doubt" and their effect is "fear." The writer also revised and expanded the statement about feeling "overwhelmed" to create another cause-effect scenario: the cause being "too many mistakes" and the effect being "failing the class."
Call to Action	Call to action is a rhetorical move to persuade an audience to do something.
	• **What:** Tell your reader what they should do a result of your argument
	• **Why:** Gives your argument a purpose beyond itself
	• **How:** Include a significant step or steps that your audience could take as a result of your argument to further the purpose of the argument
	• **Draft:** Those kinds of challenges change people, even if they are painful and upsetting. Crucially, encouraging students to take more challenging classes becomes part of an ongoing conversation about the importance of failure and risk.
	• **Revised:** Those kinds of challenges change people, even if they are painful and upsetting. Crucially, we should both encourage students to take more challenging classes while also offering them the support and understanding they will need as they face those difficulties. The ongoing conversation about the importance of failure and risk should also become about supporting students as risk takers and mistake makers.
	Here, the writer is able to combine a discussion about the bigger ideas related to the prompt with a call for everyone to better support students as they take those challenging classes and learn to accept risks and mistakes.

KEY POINT: Rhetorical moves can help you convey your argument with power and effectively engage your reader.

PRACTICE

Review Prompt A below.

> At a ceremony to recognize the academic achievements of middle school students, a speaker encouraged them to "take the hard classes; don't just chase A's and a high GPA — it will benefit you more later."
>
> Write an essay that argues your position on the value of students taking challenging classes.
>
> In your response you should do the following:
> - Respond to the prompt with a thesis that presents a defensible position.
> - Provide evidence to support your line of reasoning.
> - Explain how the evidence supports your line of reasoning.
> - Use appropriate grammar and punctuation in communicating your argument.

Look closely at essay ARG.3.B in the Appendix on page 281.

1. Choose one place in the essay where you could revise it using one of the techniques in this lesson. Draft that revised part and explain how it relates to and improves the argument.

WRITE

Review Prompt B below. Then complete the activity on the next page.

> Technology allows us to fill our free time in ways never before imagined. However, a recent study finds that the constant distractions we experience today "could be preventing our minds from settling into a deeper, more complete feeling of boredom. . . . [w]hich is a shame, given complete boredom can be fertile grounds for innovation."
>
> Write an essay that argues your position on the extent to which boredom is necessary for creativity and innovation.
>
> In your response you should do the following:
> - Respond to the prompt with a thesis that presents a defensible position.
> - Provide evidence to support your line of reasoning.
> - Explain how the evidence supports your line of reasoning.
> - Use appropriate grammar and punctuation in communicating your argument.

Make an initial claim for this prompt or revisit work you have already done with it from a previous lesson. Then write for 5–10 minutes justifying your initial claim with an example and using one strategy from this lesson. Be ready to explain how the example and strategy enhance the argument.

👆 Watch this video (tinyurl.com/3xcryj5u) from AP Teacher Beth Hall for another approach to improving writing style for the sophistication point.

What's the Point? In one sentence, explain how this lesson can help you on the AP English Language and Composition exam.

_____

_____

_____

TEAM UP

Work in small groups as your teacher directs to form **Peer Review Circles.** Each student should bring their work from the Write activity above. Before you begin, review the following.

Guidelines for Peer Review	
Focus on Constructive Feedback	Phrase your feedback positively, focusing on how the work can be improved rather than just pointing out flaws.
Use Specific Examples	Provide specific examples from the text when discussing aspects that need improvement. This practice makes feedback more concrete and helpful.
Balance Positives and Negatives	Balance criticism with praise. Identifying what works well in a piece can be as valuable as noting what doesn't.
Reflect After Review	Reflect on the feedback you received and how you plan to use it to improve your work. This reflection can deepen your learning and make the peer review process more meaningful.

Begin by exchanging papers within your group. Each student should read one peer's writing, focusing on the rhetorical moves covered in this lesson.

Next, discuss each piece of writing following these steps:

- The first writer reads his or her paper to the group.
- The peer who read this paper offers feedback on the effectiveness of the rhetorical strategy the writer used, beginning with the impact the strategy had on the reader and the argument.
- Others in the group add their feedback, addressing (1) what worked well, (2) what did not work very well, and (3) what other rhetorical strategy might also work.
- The writer replies to feedback, asking questions for clarification as needed and explaining what, if anything, will be revised based on the group's comments.

After all essays have been discussed, reflect on what you have learned about rhetorical moves and how you might incorporate them in your writing. Be ready to share your reflections.

LESSON ARG.18 Stylistic Moves

Eyes on the Exam

Another way to earn the sophistication point is to consistently make stylistic choices that strengthen your argument.

LEARN

Your goal in the Argument Free-Response Question is to respond to the prompt with a claim and examples that help you show your thinking and justify that claim. Exam readers understand that your essay is a first draft, not a polished piece of writing.

The chart below shows what to avoid and what to use to improve your writing style and strengthen your argument and essay even as a first draft. The strategies are grouped into three categories: words, sentences, and punctuation. Since you may not have time to revise on test day, practice these strategies before test day so you can use them naturally as you write. Try revising old essays with them.

For each strategy, the bulleted explanation includes "what" to clarify the focus, provide examples, or suggest strategies; "why" so you understand the reasoning behind the move; and "how" to explain what to do. It also includes an example of an original "draft" and a "revised" version using the advice.

Stylistic Moves	
Words	
1. **Limit *Be* Verbs**	• **What:** *am, is, are, was, were, be, being, been* • **Why:** They often weaken writing by hiding the verb that should do the work. • **How:** Look for the verb—or word that wants to be a verb (probably nearby)—and revise. • **Draft:** Signing up for Algebra I turned out *to be* the thing that scared me all summer. • **Revised:** Signing up for Algebra I *scared* me all summer. In the revised sentence, the number of words is cut nearly in half while still getting the same idea across. Also, the original sentence had three verbs (*turned out, to be,* and *scared*), but the revised one has only the most important one: *scared*.

2. **Avoid "Smart" Words**	• **What:** words used to try to sound smart
	• **Why:** Sometimes they get used incorrectly and interrupt the reader's thinking about your argument.
	• **How:** Focus on what you want to say and say it with the best words for *you*.
	• **Draft:** Signing up for Algebra I would probably pose a *plethora* of problems for me.
	• **Revised:** Signing up for Algebra I would probably pose several problems for me.
	Plethora is not a common word. Since the rest of the words in the sentence are common and reasonable, *plethora* may stick out and make the reader think you are trying too hard to sound smart. Don't. Just *be* smart and say what you mean.
3. **Replace Vague or Imprecise Words**	• **What:** *stuff, things, good, bad, nice, it, that, this, those, them, they, there are, it is*
	• **Why:** Some words are too general (and overused) to express exactly what you want to say. They can blur your argument.
	• **How:** Look for words that may not be clear to the reader and either change them or explain them.
	• **Draft:** *It* was *bad* for me all summer.
	• **Revised:** Signing up for Algebra I scared me all summer.
	Signing up for Algebra I replaces *It* to be specific about the topic of the discussion. Using the word *scared* instead of *was bad* specifies *why* it was bad.
Sentences	
4. **Vary Sentence Beginnings**	• **What:** Use different sentence patterns. The beginnings of sentences are especially noticeable, so variety is welcome.
	• **Why:** Even the best ideas can get buried in repetitive, boring sentences.
	• **How:** Look for other words or phrases in the sentences that make sense at the beginning of the sentence.
	• **Draft:** *I wasn't* sure about signing up for Algebra. *I was* overwhelmed with a fear that I would fail. *I couldn't* quit thinking about it all summer.
	• **Revised:** I wasn't sure about signing up for Algebra. Fear of failure overwhelmed me. All summer long, I couldn't quit thinking about it.
	Each of the three sentences still communicates the same thought, but in the two revised ones, the first words or phrases focus on the real point of the sentence.

5.	**Use Active Sentence Beginnings**	• **What:** Start sentences with an *-ing* form of a verb (either a present participle or gerund). • **Why:** These words bring a sense of action to the essay and engage the reader. • **How:** Look for other words or phrases in the sentences that make sense at the beginning of the sentence. • **Draft:** I wasn't sure about *signing up for Algebra*. Fear of failure overwhelmed me. All summer long, I couldn't quit thinking about it. • **Revised:** Signing up for Algebra made me uncomfortable. Fear of failure overwhelmed me. All summer long, I couldn't quit thinking about it. The first sentence now focuses on the act of signing up for Algebra.
6.	**Use Transitions**	• **What:** Guide the reader's thinking and sharpen your own reasoning with words and phrases between sentences. • **Why:** The ideas in the sentences then connect for a more cohesive line of reasoning in your essay. • **How:** Use transition words or phrases that signal a connection or repeat key words. • **Draft:** Signing up for Algebra made me uncomfortable. Fear of failure overwhelmed me. All summer long, I couldn't quit thinking about it. • **Revised:** Signing up for Algebra made me uncomfortable. That discomfort came from the fear of failure that overwhelmed me. In fact, all summer long, I couldn't quit thinking about it. The second sentence connects to the first with the word *discomfort*, showing that the second sentence will expand on that idea. The third sentence uses a transitional phrase (*In fact*) to explain that not being able to quit thinking about it all summer was a factual result of the fear and feeling overwhelmed. Both of those terms are in the previous sentence, so *In fact* connects the second and third sentences.
7.	**Combine Sentences**	• **What:** Sentences could combine to express a complex thought. • **Why:** Multiple sentences may be so close in their ideas that they can be combined. • **How:** Look at the shared ideas and words and put them into one sentence. • **Draft:** Signing up for Algebra I made me uncomfortable. Fear of failure overwhelmed me. All summer long, I couldn't quit thinking about it. • **Revised:** Signing up for Algebra I made me uncomfortable. Fear of failure overwhelmed me, *and* I couldn't quit thinking about it all summer long. Sentences two and three were about the same idea—how overwhelmed the writer felt—so combining them makes sense. Notice the detail and language generally remain the same.

8.	**Use Short Sentences for Emphasis**	• **What:** Sometimes an important idea gets buried in long sentences. • **Why:** A short sentence can emphasize a key idea. • **How:** Separate a key idea in a simple, short sentence (maybe even a fragment). • **Draft:** Signing up for Algebra made me uncomfortable because I had a fear of failure that overwhelmed me, and I couldn't quit thinking about it all summer long. • **Revised:** *Algebra made me uncomfortable.* I had a fear of failure that overwhelmed me, and I couldn't quit thinking about it all summer long. The short sentence focuses on Algebra specifically (not signing up for it, as in the previous examples). That discomfort almost gets lost in the longer draft sentence which focuses on fear of failure. The short sentence emphasizes the feelings of discomfort that then relate to the fear of failure in the next sentence.
Punctuation		
9.	**Use Semicolons Well**	• **What:** Complex ideas are sometimes broken into separate sentences. • **Why:** A semicolon combines two independent sentences into one larger, more complex thought. • **How:** Place the independent sentences in the order that the reader needs to understand, and possibly use a conjunction to guide the reader's thinking. • **Draft:** Algebra made me uncomfortable. I had a fear of failure that overwhelmed me, and I couldn't quit thinking about it all summer long. • **Revised:** Algebra made me uncomfortable; in fact, I had a fear of failure that overwhelmed me, and I couldn't quit thinking about it all summer long. When the short sentence at the beginning is linked to the longer second sentence with the semicolon and the transitional phrase *in fact*, it combines the ideas of discomfort and fear in a way that explains their source and then expands on them with connections to failure and being overwhelmed.

10. Use Parenthetical Statements for Interesting but Nonessential Information	• **What:** Sometimes a piece of information is not necessary but is interesting to the argument.
	• **Why:** A parenthetical statement may show the reader you are thinking about bigger issues related to the topic while allowing you to stay focused on the topic.
	• **How:** Use dashes or parentheses to insert that piece of information into the sentence.
	• **Draft:** Algebra made me uncomfortable. I had a fear of failure that overwhelmed me, and I couldn't quit thinking about it all summer long.
	• **Revised:** Algebra made me uncomfortable; in fact, I had a fear of failure—something I'm still trying to overcome—that overwhelmed me, and I couldn't quit thinking about it all summer long.
	In this case, the additional information may help the reader empathize with you, since fear of failure is very common. Use this strategy *only sparingly* and make sure what you add connects in some solid way to the argument.

KEY POINT: Make **stylistic moves** to improve *your argument*, not just your writing.

PRACTICE

Read sample essay ARG.3.A in the Appendix on page 280, which is based on Prompt A about challenging classes.

1. Identify where the essay makes any of the stylistic moves listed in this lesson, and explain how those moves relate to and even improve the argument.

2. Choose one place you could revise using one of the stylistic moves in this lesson. Draft that revised part and explain how it relates to and improves the argument.

WRITE

Review Prompt B below. Then complete the activity on the next page.

Technology allows us to fill our free time in ways never before imagined. However, a recent study finds that the constant distractions we experience today "could be preventing our minds from settling into a deeper, more complete feeling of boredom. . . . [w]hich is a shame, given complete boredom can be fertile grounds for innovation."

Write an essay that argues your position on the extent to which boredom is necessary for creativity and innovation.

In your response you should do the following:

• Respond to the prompt with a thesis that presents a defensible position.

• Provide evidence to support your line of reasoning.

• Explain how the evidence supports your line of reasoning.

• Use appropriate grammar and punctuation in communicating your argument.

Make an initial claim for this prompt or use work from a previous lesson. Then explain your initial claim with an example and reasoning that support it, using as many of the stylistic moves above as possible. Identify each one you used and explain how it enhances the argument.

 Watch this video (tinyurl.com/3wv88bdd) from AP Teacher Beth Hall for another approach to improving writing style for the sophistication point.

What's the Point? In one sentence, explain how this lesson can help you on the AP English Language and Composition exam.

_____

_____

_____

TEAM UP

Beth Hall mentions sentence combining in her video as one way to produce an advanced writing style. Regularly practicing sentence combining has been shown to enhance writing quality.

As your teacher directs, work in small groups to combine the following sentences about board games. Develop at least one compound, one complex, and one compound-complex sentence (a sentence that includes two independent clauses and at least one dependent or subordinate clause). Be sure to use correct punctuation in the combined sentences. Try using at least one semicolon.

1. Board games bring people together for hours of fun.
2. Many board games require strategic thinking and planning.
3. Players often learn important social skills through these games.
4. Board games can lead to frustration and conflict among players, especially in games that require competitive strategies.
5. Some board games are based on historical events or cultures.
6. Children and adults alike enjoy the challenge and excitement of board games.
7. While playing, participants can experience a wide range of emotions, from joy to frustration.

When all groups have finished, be ready to share your results with the other groups and discuss the stylistic effect of the combined sentences. Consider smoothness of reading and the relationship of ideas as you evaluate their effect.

LESSON ARG.19 Complexity and Tension in Argument

Eyes on the Exam

Exam readers will reward essays that notice **subtleties and nuances** that reveal complexities and tensions.

LEARN

By definition, arguments include complexity and tension because they are based on the assumption that differing perspectives are in conversation with one another. However, with careful thought, you may uncover shades of meaning, contradictions, and ideas that challenge commonly held beliefs.

Complexity in argument, the quality of being complicated, results from

- Engaging with differing viewpoints, not just presenting them.
- Recognizing subtle shades of differences.
- Reaching for bigger ideas, not just the first thoughts that comes to mind.
- Expressing original thoughts.
- Writing clearly and with style (see Lesson ARG.18).

Tension in argument, a somewhat uncomfortable awareness of conflict, results from

- Addressing conflict between ideas.
- Balancing contradictions.
- Engaging with counterarguments.
- Presenting "what ifs" to explore consequences.
- Using writing and rhetorical strategies that highlight differences.

You may not have time to develop all possible complexities and tensions on exam day, but if you train yourself to think about them as you plan your argument, you may be able to include some and develop a very strong essay. Recognize that readers have different experiences and perspectives, and show readers that you have taken different perspectives seriously. Simply including complexity at one point in the essay is not enough, though. You need to weave it through your whole essay.

One way to approach tensions and complexities between perspectives is to think of perspectives as either *idealistic* or *realistic*.

- **Idealistic:** optimistic and hopeful for a better outcome to something; progressive; romantic. Often seen as impractical by realists.
- **Realistic:** rational and practical perspective; conservative. Often seen as cynical by idealists.

The sentence frame on the next page may help you work these tensions and complexities into your argument essay.

Sentence Frame for Tension and Complexity	
Frame	**[Subordinating conjunction]** *it could/can/might be argued that* [opposing perspective with some detail to show how it relates to what you are discussing], [direct counter to that opposing perspective] *because* [explain why that counter makes sense].
Example (from essay ARG.3.C in Appendix)	**[While]** *it could be argued that* [such early difficulties force many people to just give up], [this actually shows the importance of persevering through those challenges] *because* [his refusal to give up has made him a billionaire].

KEY POINT: To earn the sophistication point, you need to weave exploration of **tension and complexity throughout your essay.**

PRACTICE

The chart below shows differing perspectives on the topic of challenging courses.

1. On separate paper, add two more items in each column.

2. Use the sentence frame above to write about the items you added.

Topic: Students Taking Challenging Classes.	
Idealist	**Realist**
1. What doesn't "kill" us makes us stronger.	1. It might just "kill" us.
2. Students will come to see challenges as opportunities.	2. Students will get discouraged by too much challenge.
3. Grades don't matter as much as learning does.	3. Grades affect our future more than a challenging class on a transcript.

WRITE

Review Prompt B below. Then complete one of the activities that follows it.

Technology allows us to fill our free time in ways never before imagined. However, a recent study finds that the constant distractions we experience today "could be preventing our minds from settling into a deeper, more complete feeling of boredom. . . . [w]hich is a shame, given complete boredom can be fertile grounds for innovation."

Write an essay that argues your position on the extent to which boredom is necessary for creativity and innovation.

In your response you should do the following:

• Respond to the prompt with a thesis that presents a defensible position.

• Provide evidence to support your line of reasoning.

• Explain how the evidence supports your line of reasoning.

• Use appropriate grammar and punctuation in communicating your argument.

Option 1

Make an initial claim for this prompt or use work from a previous lesson.

1. Make a short list of idealist and realistic perspectives on this topic as in the chart in the Practice section.

2. Use the sentence frame to write a few statements based on items in each column of your list.

Option 2

Reread essay ARG.3.A on page 280 in the Appendix or an essay you have completed on your own.

1. Make a short list of idealist and realistic perspectives on this topic as in the chart in the Practice section.

2. Revise current sentences or paragraphs to address the complexity and tension of these perspectives *throughout* the essay.

 Watch this video (tinyurl.com/bdfmuuk8) from AP Teacher Timm Freitas for other approaches for the sophistication point.

What's the Point? In one sentence, explain how this lesson can help you on the AP English Language and Composition exam.

_____

_____

_____

TEAM UP

Form small groups as your teacher directs for an activity to explore complications and perspectives. During the activity, one person in each group will take notes.

Start with this **thesis statement:** Free speech is essential for a healthy democracy.

Round 1—Identifying Complications

With your group members, discuss the thesis and identify potential complications or challenging factors related to free speech (hate speech, for example). The notetaker records these.

Round 2—Adding Perspectives

Now consider different perspectives that could affect or be affected by the thesis (perspectives of journalists, for example, or realists and idealists). Identify a number of different perspectives and what they might have to say about the thesis statement. The notetaker records these.

After Round 2, be ready to share and compare the complications and perspectives the groups identified. Discuss how your understanding of free speech has been complicated or enriched through the game. Also discuss how this activity might apply to your argument essays.

Eyes on the Exam

Whether you receive a point for sophistication depends on how well your essay meets the criteria in Row C of the rubric.

LEARN

Carefully read each section of Row C.

- The first row describes in general terms what the essay must demonstrate to earn the sophistication point.
- The second row describes characteristics of essays missing or earning the sophistication point. It also provides specific examples and criteria.
- The final row provides additional clarifications for earning the sophistication point.

Row C: Sophistication (0-1 points), Scoring Criteria [2.A, 4.C, 6.B, 8.A, 8.B, 8.C]	
0 points	**1 point**
Does not meet the criteria for one point.	Demonstrates sophistication of thought and/or develops a complex understanding of the rhetorical situation.
Decision Rules and Scoring Notes	
Responses that do not earn this point:	**Responses that earn this point may demonstrate sophistication of thought and/or a complex understanding of the rhetorical situation by doing any of the following:**
Attempt to contextualize their argument, but such attempts consist predominantly of sweeping generalizations ("All over the world, people have different ways of . . ." OR "Since the dawn of time, people have been changing . . .").	Crafting a nuanced argument by consistently identifying and exploring complexities or tensions.
Only hint at or suggest other arguments ("I once heard someone say . . ." OR "While some may argue disagree. . .").	Articulating the implications or limitations of an argument (either the student's argument or an argument related to the prompt) by acknowledging counterarguments.
Use complicated or complex sentences or language that are ineffective because they do not enhance the argument	Making effective rhetorical choices that consistently strengthen the force and impact of the student's argument.
	Employing a style that is consistently vivid and persuasive.
Additional Notes:	
This point should be awarded only if the sophistication of thought or complex understanding is part of the student's argument, not merely a phrase or reference.	

Following are the skills from the Course and Exam Description that are assessed in Row C.

2.A Write introductions and conclusions appropriate to the purpose and context of the rhetorical situation.

4.C Qualify a claim using modifiers, counterarguments, or alternative perspectives.

6.B Use transitional elements to guide the reader through the line of reasoning of an argument.

8.A Strategically use words, comparisons, and syntax to convey a specific tone or style in an argument.

8.B Write sentences that clearly convey ideas and arguments.

8.C Use established conventions of grammar and mechanics to communicate clearly and effectively.

PRACTICE

Complete the following activities and answer the questions about the Row C Sophistication rubric and scoring guide.

1. How many of the following do you need to do to earn the sophistication point?
   - Identify and explore complexities and tensions.
   - Explain the limitations of an argument.
   - Employ a style that is consistently vivid and persuasive.

2. What should you avoid when trying to contextualize a text?

3. What kind of language should you use for your best chance at earning the sophistication point?

4. Why might efforts to add complexities in a few places fail to earn the sophistication point?

5. How important is making rhetorical choices in earning the sophistication point?

You Be the Reader

Read sample essay ARG.3.D in the Appendix on page 283. Decide whether the essay earns a sophistication point. Explain your answer.

Watch this video (tinyurl.com/22wb982f) by Timm Freitas in which he offers advice for writing a conclusion that will help you earn the sophistication point.

Revise

Review the efforts you have made to achieve sophistication in your essay in response to Prompt B about boredom and creativity. Revise as needed to make sure your efforts are woven throughout your essay.

LESSON ARG.20 Sample Essay: From a 3 to a 4

Eyes on the Exam

Aim for an essay score of 4 or higher.

LEARN

Exam readers score essays on a standard rubric that allows each essay to earn up to 6 total points. Up to 1 point is awarded for a thesis that responds to the prompt. Up to 4 points are awarded for including evidence and commentary that supports a student's argument. Up to 1 point is awarded for producing a sophisticated argument.

The gap between an essay scoring a 3 and an essay scoring a 4 may feel wide. However, usually only a few features make the difference, probably one or two of the following:

1. You are not fully explaining how the **examples** relate to your argument.

   - **Fix:** Expand your commentary to help the reader see your thinking about how the examples relate to your argument.

2. You are not providing enough **specific details** in the examples.

   - **Fix:** Add enough specifics about the examples so the reader really understands why you are using them.

3. Too many of the details seem **unrelated to the claim**.

   - **Fix:** Tie the details directly to the argument and clearly explain how they relate.

4. Your explanation of how the **evidence** relates to the argument is unclear.

   - **Fix:** You may have summarized rather than explained the evidence. Make sure you clearly discuss both the example and the claim and topic.

> **KEY POINT:** The **harder the reader has to work** to understand the argument, **the lower the score** will be.

The following essay is a student draft in response to Prompt A on challenging classes ("Write an essay that argues your position on the value to students of taking challenging classes"). This student earned a total score of 3 out of 6 points based on the AP English Language and Composition argument scoring rubric. The score breakdown is shown below. The points awarded for each row are in bold type.

Row A: Thesis	0				**1**
Row B: Evidence and Commentary	0	1	**2**	3	4
Row C: Sophistication	**0**				1
Total	3/6				

PRACTICE

Look closely at the first two paragraphs of this essay below, which have been annotated. Text from the essay is in the middle column. The left column provides thoughts that an exam reader might have, and the right column provides suggestions for improving the essay. Read the comments and advice carefully to be sure you understand them. In the Write activity that follows, you will be asked to make changes based on the advice.

Comments	Essay	Advice
It earns the thesis point; there is a clear claim about the topic of the prompt. The example connects the topic and claim to the idea that "difficulties make people stronger." While it explains a difficulty, it provides details that do not relate to the claim. It seems like steps are missing between sentence 5 and sentence 6.	**(1)** The advice given by the speaker is right because taking challenging classes may not give you straight A's, but you learn to face difficulties as you are challenged in your learning. **(2)** These kinds of difficulties make people stronger. **(3)** One example of someone improving in the face of difficulties is the rapper Jay-Z. **(4)** When Hova (a nickname his friends gave him) first started rapping, no companies would listen to him. **(5)** His first self-made CD became wildly popular. **(6)** He eventually made enough money to start his own record label and is now a billionaire. **(7)** If he had just given up when faced with these problems, then he would not have gotten where he is today. **(8)** Difficulties have a way of changing people and helping them realize things about themselves that they may not have known before. **(9)** This example shows how facing difficulties makes people stronger.	Try using a thesis statement that includes the examples for the argument. That would help establish a line of reasoning throughout the essay. Provide enough details so it's clear how the example connects to the claim.

WRITE

Part 1: Read the full student draft below. Then respond to the questions provided so that you can help this draft increase in score by at least one point in the Evidence and Commentary row. The changes you are asked to make address words, phrases, and whole sentences.

[1] The advice given by the speaker is right because taking challenging classes may not give you straight A's, but you learn to face difficulties as you are challenged in your learning. [2] These kinds of difficulties make people stronger.

[3] One example of someone improving in the face of difficulties is the rapper Jay-Z. [4] When Hova (a nickname his friends gave him) first started rapping, no companies would listen to him. [5] His first self-made CD became wildly popular. [6] He eventually made enough money to start his own record label and is now a billionaire. [7] If he had just given up when faced with these problems then he would not have gotten where he is today. [8] Difficulties have a way of changing people and helping them realize things about themselves that they may not have known before. [9] This example shows how facing difficulties makes people stronger.

[10] Mistakes also strengthen people, like I learned in middle school. [11] As a 7th grader, I did well in math. [12] The teacher told me and my parents that I should take Algebra I as an 8th grader. [13] They signed me up for it. [14] I was afraid, but the class showed me that making mistakes helped me. [15] We can't always know what will be worth it and what could hurt us; sometimes we just have to take a chance, like I did with algebra. [16] It was worth it because now I'm going to major in math and engineering. [17] This example shows that everybody makes mistakes, but those mistakes and challenges will make us better.

[18] Overall, some people might argue that taking challenging classes is not worth the trouble and frustration, but those kinds of challenges make us all stronger.

Complete the following activities, focusing on providing specific and precise changes that consider the context of what is written in the essay so that your recommended changes can be substituted into the essay and it will read smoothly. You may try to make changes that will help this paper earn the sophistication point; however, your focus should be on making changes that will raise the score at least one point in Row B of the scoring rubric.

As you revise, you may either completely rewrite sentences or use the initial sentence forms as the foundation for your revisions. Some instructions will ask you to write entirely new sentences. If you need reminders for any of the issues addressed, you can review the lessons that cover them, which are included at the end of the questions.

1. The writer wants to revise the thesis statement (sentence 2) to include the examples that will be used to justify the claim. Rewrite the thesis to fulfill the writer's goals. **(Lessons ARG.4, 5, 8)**

2. To avoid confusion, the writer wants to delete details (sentence 4) that do not directly relate to the claim. Revise to eliminate unnecessary or unrelated details. **(Lesson ARG.9)**

3. To make the essay more cohesive, the writer wants to connect the example of Jay-Z to the idea that struggling can have positive results. Write or describe a sentence that could be put between sentences 4 and 5 that would accomplish this connection. **(Lesson ARG.12)**

4. Sentence 7 touches on how difficulties Jay-Z faced got him where he is, but the lack of details in the example and weak connection to the claim mean the reader has to take the writer's word for it. Add one or more sentences after sentence 7 that would provide necessary details and connect more clearly to the claim. **(Lessons ARG.9–10)**

5. Sentence 8 makes a reasonable point about difficulty as it is used in the thesis, but there is no clear connection to the claim. Revise that sentence to spell out the connection to the claim. **(Lesson ARG.10)**

6. Paragraph 2 does not address an alternative perspective. Revise the paragraph to introduce and then rebut an opposing view. **(Lesson ARG.15)**

7. Sentence 10 introduces an example relating to mistakes. Revise the thesis statement so the idea of mistakes can be included in the essay. **(Lesson ARG.5)**

8. Sentence 14 refers to the writer being afraid, but it is not clear what the fear is about. Revise sentence 14 to clarify *afraid* and connect it to the claim and example. **(Lesson ARG.12)**

9. Sentence 15 suggests an opposing viewpoint but does not make it clear. Revise that sentence using a subordinate clause to clarify a counterargument and show why it is weaker than the main claim. **(Lesson ARG.14)**

10. The writer wants to make the essay more cohesive by revising the conclusion to make references to the examples offered in the argument. Revise the conclusion accordingly. **(Lesson ARG.13)**

Part 2: Review Prompt B below. Then complete one of the activities that follow.

> Technology allows us to fill our free time in ways never before imagined. However, a recent study finds that the constant distractions we experience today "could be preventing our minds from settling into a deeper, more complete feeling of boredom. . . . [w]hich is a shame, given complete boredom can be fertile grounds for innovation."
>
> Write an essay that argues your position on the extent to which boredom is necessary for creativity and innovation.
>
> In your response you should do the following:
> - Respond to the prompt with a thesis that presents a defensible position.
> - Provide evidence to support your line of reasoning.
> - Explain how the evidence supports your line of reasoning.
> - Use appropriate grammar and punctuation in communicating your argument.

Option 1

Make an initial claim for this prompt or use work from a previous lesson.
- Write a paragraph you might use in an essay for this prompt. Then reread it and fix any of the four problems listed in the Learn section that you may have introduced.

Option 2

Revisit an essay you have already written.
- Choose a paragraph you know could be improved and revise it based on the fixes listed in the Learn section.

 Read this blog (tinyurl.com/yesmanat) to see another sample essay with comments showing its strengths and weaknesses.

What's the Point? In one sentence, explain how this lesson can help you on the AP English Language and Composition exam.

_____

_____

_____

LESSON ARG.21 Sample Essay: From a 4 to 5

Eyes on the Exam

While the score of 4 is considered well-qualified, moving that 4 to a 5 can be easier than you think.

LEARN

The line between an essay scoring a 4 and an essay scoring a 5 (1-4-0) really comes down to one quality: **consistent explanation in your commentary.**

You may have written some outstanding explanations in your commentary of one or two of your examples, but if the commentary on the others is not consistent, then you will struggle to score higher than a 1-3-0.

Make sure you provide enough explanation of your thinking for each example for your audience to see how the details of the example relate to your argument.

KEY POINT: **Consistent commentary** for each example will help you earn a higher score.

The following essay is a student draft in response to Prompt A on challenging classes ("Write an essay that argues your position on the value to students of taking challenging classes"). This student earned a total score of 4 out of 6 points based on the AP English Language and Composition argument scoring rubric. The score breakdown is shown below. The points awarded for each row are in bold type.

Row A: Thesis	0				**1**
Row B: Evidence and Commentary	0	1	2	**3**	4
Row C: Sophistication	**0**				1
Total	4/6				

PRACTICE

Look closely at the first two paragraphs of this essay on the next page. Text from the essay is in the middle column. The left column provides comments that explain why the essay earned a 4, and the right column provides general suggestions and advice for writing good essays. Read the comments and suggestions carefully to be sure you understand them. In the Write activity that follows, you will be asked to revise or comment on parts of the essay.

Comments	Essay	Advice
It earns the thesis point; there is a clear claim about the topic of the prompt. It connects the topic and claim to the idea that "fear can actually strengthen people" and then provides examples that suggest a line of reasoning for the essay. It offers an example as evidence of what it is saying about fear and failure. Specific details it provides all relate to fear of failure in the life of the example given. There is a comment about fear of failure and how it affected the example. This connects the details about the example to the claim. Links directly to failure one more time as it relates to the experiences of the example.	**(1)** People make mistakes and failure happens. **(2)** In schools, failure is almost always a bad word, but it doesn't have to be. **(3)** Taking challenging classes might cause a fear of failure, but that fear can actually strengthen people, as shown by the early failures of rapper Jay-Z and my own fears of taking Algebra in middle school. **(4)** Fear of failure can strengthen people, as shown by Jay-Z going from selling CDs from his trunk to becoming a billionaire. **(5)** When the rapper Jay-Z was first starting out, he couldn't get a record company to even listen to him. **(6)** His fear of failure led him to sell his own CDs and tapes out of his car. **(7)** He eventually made enough money to start his own record label and is now a billionaire. **(8)** He probably became more successful than if he had been signed to a record label early on because he learned how to work harder. **(9)** Those early failures could have made him just give up, but he worked harder and became successful. **(10)** If he had just been signed, he would not have learned the value of working as hard as he had to, because he would not have had to overcome that initial failure. **(11)** This shows how facing failure makes people stronger.	Make certain that the commentary links back to fear and/or failure because that is the established line of reasoning with these examples. When you are planning or writing the details for your example, make certain you can explain how each one relates to the claim you are making (and then do that in the essay). If you can't explain it, don't include it, no matter how interesting.

WRITE

Part 1: Read the full student draft below. Then answer the following questions and complete the activities that follow.

[1] People make mistakes and failure happens. [2] In schools, failure is almost always a bad word, but it doesn't have to be. [3] Taking challenging classes might cause a fear of failure but that fear can actually strengthen people as shown by the early failures of rapper Jay-Z and my own fears of taking Algebra in middle school.

[4] Fear of failure can strengthen people, as shown by Jay-Z going from selling CDs from his trunk to becoming a billionaire. [5] When the rapper Jay-Z was first starting out, he couldn't get a record company to even listen to him. [6] His fear of failure led him to sell his own CDs and tapes out of his car. [7] He eventually made enough money to start his own record label and is now a billionaire. [8] He probably became more successful than if had been signed to a record label early on because he learned how to work harder. [9] Those early failures could have made him just give up but he worked harder and became successful. [10] If he had just been signed, he would not have learned the value of working as hard as he had to because he would not have had to overcome that initial failure. [11] This shows how facing failure makes people stronger.

[12] Fear of failure includes fear of mistakes that could lead to failure. [13] This specific kind of failure can still strengthen people, like I learned in middle school. [14] In 7th grade I did well in math. [15] The teacher told me and my parents that I should take Algebra I in 8th grade. [16] They signed me up for it and I was afraid all summer. [17] Once I was in the class I saw that making mistakes helped me to think different. [18] This example shows how accepting my mistakes made me stronger. [19] Though someone could argue that I was too young to see how these things really affected me, it's been three years and that is enough time to think about that experience and how it changed me. [20] Everybody makes mistakes, but those mistakes and challenges will make us better.

[21] Some people might argue that fear of making mistakes or failing are too painful and doing something like taking challenging classes is not worth it because of that. [22] However, these examples show, they can actually make us grow stronger from these painful events.

1. Revise the introduction to align more closely with the structure of the essay.
   (Lesson ARG.13)

2. The writer would like to revise sentence 10 to make it more clear. Revise it by reducing the number of words to achieve that goal.

3. The writer wants to revise sentence 11 to eliminate vagueness. Revise that sentence to avoid vague words. **(Lesson ARG.17)**

4. The writer is considering revising the sentences that create the transition between paragraphs 2 and 3. Explain why the writer should *not* do this and what makes the current transition cohesive. **(Lesson ARG. 17)**

5. The writer has noticed that the commentary in paragraph 3 is inconsistent and prevents the essay from being cohesive and coherent. Revise paragraph 3 to make the commentary more effective and consistent with the whole essay.

6. Add or revise one sentence in each paragraph to address a counterargument. Use a subordinate clause to introduce it. **(Lessons ARG.4, 13–15)**

7. The writer has recognized an opportunity to broaden the significance of the argument. Add a final sentence that broadens the argument more universally. **(Lesson ARG.13)**

Part 2: Review an essay you have already written. Choose a paragraph that you know could be improved with more consistent commentary (maybe more than one paragraph) and revise it/them based on the advice from this lesson. Note where you made specific revisions.

Watch this video (tinyurl.com/58zcztwm) by AP teacher Beth Hall, which includes valuable information on commentary, including suggestions for strong verbs. After watching, make additional revisions to your paragraph using those suggestions.

What's the Point? In one sentence, explain how this lesson can help you on the AP English Language and Composition exam.

_____

_____

_____

TEAM UP

Work in small groups as your teacher directs to review what you have learned about the argument essay.

Using the **Argument Key Point Review** on the next two pages, collaborate with your group members and briefly talk through each lesson's Key Point. Try to say as many things as you remember about each point. If you need a refresher, refer back to the page number indicated after the key point to review the lesson.

After you talk through each section (Prompt, Thesis, Evidence and Commentary, and Sophistication), pause and as a group try to come up with the single most important thing you should remember about that section. Then move on to the next section.

After you complete the Argument Key Point Review, complete the self-evaluation that follows it. When everyone has finished, regroup and share your evaluations. Ask for feedback on areas that concern you, and give feedback when you can to help others.

* * * * * * * * * *

After completing the Free-Response Practice Question: Argument on page 270, and if your teachers directs, meet with your group and read your responses to the argument prompt. Then partner up and use the rubrics for Row A (page 215), Row B (page 237), and Row C (page 258) to evaluate your partner's essay. Discuss the evaluations and articulate what you learned that will help you when exam day comes.

ARGUMENT Key Point Review

PROMPT

ARG.1 An argument prompt contains three main parts: the **introduction** of a topic and situation to give you context to consider, the **task** explains the topic for your argument, and the **directions** provide essential specific guidance for your essay. (page 193)

ARG.2 The first step in responding to the prompt is **identifying key words and the questions they might raise**. Your response must be reasonable based on possible understandings of the key words. (page 196)

ARG.3 Considering **big ideas** related to the topic of the prompt can deepen your understanding of that topic and lead to a better argument. (page 198)

ARG.4 Connecting to worlds or domains beyond the prompt will give you a chance to **tap into your knowledge** and find interesting examples to support your argument. (page 200)

THESIS

ARG.5 Your thesis must have a **defensible claim** and should **suggest a line of reasoning** that shows your thinking about the topic and claim. (page 203)

ARG.6 An **introduction,** though not required, may help focus your argument and also help the reader connect to it. (page 207)

ARG.7 Effective arguments address **alternative perspectives** without taking the focus away from the main perspective. (page 209)

ARG.8 Topic sentences **aligned with the thesis** unify your essay and create clarity. (page 212)

EVIDENCE AND COMMENTARY

ARG.9 Supporting examples need **specific details** that help the reader understand why each example helps support your argument. (page 218)

ARG.10 Commentary is your **analysis, interpretation, or explanation of the examples** you have chosen as evidence and how those examples support your reasoning and claim. (page 221)

ARG.11 Use words and phrases that **guide your reader's understanding** of how your examples relate to your thesis. (page 224)

ARG.12 For a reliable way to organize your paragraphs, follow the **I** (identify), **E** (explain), and **L** (link) pattern. (page 227)

ARG.13 Knowing a structure for your essay before the exam will help save you time. **Practice writing essays in one of these patterns often** so that it will be natural to you on exam day. (page 230)

ARG.14 You are always arguing with an alternative perspective. Introduce specific opposing views in a subordinate clause using a **subordinating conjunction**. (page 233)

ARG.15 **Rebuttal** and **refutation** show thinking about alternative perspectives in relation to your claim and may elevate the quality of your essay. (page 235)

SOPHISTICATION

ARG.16 Every argument enters a **broader, ongoing conversation** about a topic and other related topics, and each argument has both strengths and limitations. Pointing those out will show you are thinking critically about the topic. (page 240)

ARG.17 Rhetorical moves can help you convey your argument with power and effectively engage your reader. (page 242)

ARG.18 Make **stylistic moves** to improve *your argument*, not just your writing. (page 249)

ARG.19 To earn the sophistication point, you need to weave exploration of **tension and complexity throughout your essay.** (page 255)

SAMPLE ESSAYS

ARG.20 The **harder the reader has to work** to understand the argument, **the lower the score** will be. (page 260)

ARG.21 Consistent commentary for each example will help you earn a higher score. (page 264)

SELF-EVALUATION

In the spaces below, evaluate your readiness for answering the Argument Free-Response Question.

1. **What are your strengths? What part(s) of the argument essay do you feel confident about?**

2. **In what aspects of writing the argument essay do you need more practice and guidance?**

3. **What are three steps you can take for getting that additional practice and guidance?**

Free-Response Practice Question: Argument

Suggested time—40 minutes
(This question counts as one-third of the total essay section score.)

In a collection of lectures written in the 1st century, Greek philosopher Epictetus stated: "Be silent for the most part, or, if you speak, say only what is necessary and in a few words. Talk, but rarely, if the occasion calls you [to speak]."

Write an essay that argues your position on the value of being silent and/or using a few words.

In your response you should do the following:

• Respond to the prompt with a thesis that presents a defensible position.
• Provide evidence to support your line of reasoning.
• Explain how the evidence supports your line of reasoning.
• Use appropriate grammar and punctuation in communicating your argument.

Appendix

Sample Essays

Sample Essay SYN.1.A

[1] Sea-life attractions should be regarded as positive contributors in education and conservation efforts.

[2] Marine exhibitions have been found to create natural atmospheres that engage guests. [3] For instance, aquariums have become the birthplace of many young visitors' "most authentic [. . .] moments" with sea life (Source C). [4] The establishments' promotion of connections between knowledge and actuality highlights how they deliver enriching educational opportunities because visitors gain a real experience and can interact with the marine life they are learning about, rather than just reading about them in a textbook.

[5] Aquariums have demonstrated their significant financial support directed towards the wellbeing of wild and captive animals, showcasing their widespread and essential roles as positive contributors to preservation. [6] Take, for example, how zoos and aquariums "spend $230 million on field conservation" (Source E) every year, and that the average longevity of the mammals in enclosures is actually 6 years longer (Source D) compared to those in the wild. [7] These impressive donations, along with the health of the animals in their care, emphasize animal and sea-life establishments' positive essential roles in wildlife conservation. [8] Since a vast majority of people would choose to believe fact rather than opinion, aquariums should then be considered as a positive contributor to wildlife conservation as they have a track record for maximizing the life expectancy, particularly the lives of mammals. [9] Instead of generalizing the industry's motives and impacts based on immediate observations taken from mostly unregulated institutions, individuals must educate themselves about what aquariums really do.

[10] Aquariums may seem to promote over consumerism, but this isn't true. [11] For instance, though it may be true that marketing strategists encourage brands to partner with marine-life institutions since consumers "feel better about a brand" that "focus[es] on an environmental or social cause," this doesn't mean that the partner benefits actually lead to any unethical behaviors on the part of the business or institution (Source C).

(12) Aquariums contribute more to conservation and education than just about any other business. (13) Because of this, they should be heavily supported and visited.

Sample Essay SYN.1.B

[1] Meet Luna. [2] Soft eyes, chubby, fluffy face: she is the youngest of three puppies, born under a wild moon on the sea-green coast of Biscayne Bay. [3] It used to be that, come June, with those thick swarms of mosquitoes nose diving into window screens, you might have seen her. [4] If you caught the right breeze or turned just as the little yips hit your ear, Luna would rocket past—hair whipping around her cheeks as she yanked on the leash,

dashing toward the beach, riding her own gentle wind toward eternity. [5] But then one day, Luna was dragged from her mother and left on the concrete floor of the garage. [6] Her brother had been sold to nearby Jimmy Hartford, and both her sisters were packed up and moved to the farm upstate. [7] Luna, on the other hand, was to remain in this lonely garage. [8] Meals were given through the door; perhaps there was a ball or two to keep her busy. [9] Each day she watched the sun through a high window, and sometimes people came by and looked down at her through the glass, silent and amused before passing on. [10] Certainly, such conditions would draw the attention of the ASPCA or maybe even the local police: no living thing should ever have to endure that kind of treatment. [11] Yet, in thousands of facilities across the United States alone, marine animals experience remarkably similar circumstances—they are stripped of their vast, wild ocean and confined to a tank, forced to circle the same stretch of water again and again for the entertainment of some paying customers. [12] While it's true that conservation efforts have saved certain marine species from extinction and often extended their longevity, the poor, cramped quality of life animals have in many aquariums—along with the downplayed, money making motives behind many of these organizations—minimize the educational and ecological impacts that sea life attractions have, especially in comparison to organizations that do not keep creatures in captivity.

[13] Primarily, despite extending the lifespan of marine animals, many aquariums do not provide adequate living situations—a paramount issue for ocean conservation—which is why so many of these sea life attractions do not have the proper official accreditations. [14] For instance, aquariums fall under the scrutiny of the Association of Zoos and Aquariums which, in the past, has focused solely on the "absence of illness, successful reproduction and longevity" of animals, but now has become concerned with maintaining the "behavior typical of [different] species" (Source B). [15] Marine wildlife confined in aquariums and similar facilities often display "repetitive, purposeless habits such as constantly bobbing their heads [or] swaying incessantly" (Source A) which may be the reason that "less than 10 percent of the 2,800 wildlife exhibitors [. . .] meet the more comprehensive standards of AZA accreditation" (Source E). [16] Aquariums and other similar organizations have lost much of the conservation credit gained through prolonging marine life, because the very act of captivity creates damaging and unusual habits in these animals that prevents these institutions from even receiving necessary accreditations. [17] If proper accreditation is not achieved—which is the case for a vast majority of aquariums around the country—these conditions can cause far worse than uncharacteristic behavior since such businesses are hardly attempting to adhere to proper guidelines. [18] As for the other 10% of organizations that have received AZA certification, the possibility still remains that behavioral anomalies can appear because of captivity, thus objectifying the beings that many institutions claim to be protecting so they can thrive.

[19] Furthermore, though "repetitive habits" (Source A) that result from inadequate conditions may seem harmless to the masses, the actual neurochemistry of captive animals is seriously damaged—a side effect that stands in direct contrast to the conservation of a species. [20] As marine animals engage in these "purposeless habits" (Source A), coping with the stress and confusion of captivity, the "environment physically damages [their] brain" resulting in a suboptimal existence due to "compromised brain function" (Source A) that would not occur in a wild ecosystem. [21] Since captivity psychologically distorts an animal, any organization that perpetuates this neurological rot would be neglecting its duties as conservationist, since

the very definition of conservation deals in protecting species from harm, not knowingly damaging them on a cognitive level. [22] These neurological degradations could potentially create imbalances in the natural systems working within marine life—such as wither the appetite of a captive seal, or interfere with the reproduction of angelfish—which could actually injure the wellbeing of animals, and even their populations. [23] Stress can damage healthy biological functions, even for animals, and stress from captivity can be the most detrimental, despite being perpetuated by organizations that claim to do nothing but help.

[24] Finally, while being able to engage adults and children alike with oceanographic knowledge, the compiling of various marine species into a single, tight facility is often done in order to better promote brand partnership and interaction—rather than the pure education and real world conservation that could be better implemented in simply protecting the wild. [25] Take, for example, how in recent years, companies have discovered what they believe is a neglected gem for marketing sectors, and have decided to "inves[t] in US Zoos and Aquariums" (Source C). [26] Furthermore, the reason these facilities are becoming "ideal locations" for corporations seems to exist within the fact that studies have shown "Nine out of ten people feel better about a brand if [it] focus[es] on an environment[al] or social cause" (Source C). [27] Because of this growing brand focus, the question can certainly be posed if the consolidation of marine species into a single tourist destination is done not solely for the purpose of "education, conservation, and research" (Source B), but rather to promote attractions and increase revenue for businesses and "non-profit" organizations like the Association of Zoos and Aquariums. [28] Sea life attractions draw customers in through various exhibits, and they often do so with brand interaction in mind: a potentially harmful situation because as organizations cater to the whims of high paying partnerships, they may create programs and policies that benefit their pockets rather than education and conservation. [29] Similarly, while the idea of associating money-making with honorable causes may sound good on paper, it is often a cleverly disguised marketing tool—preying upon customer empathy while driving up profits. [30] Bringing animals into one designated location misleads curious visitors, because it allows the aquarium to congregate customers instead of learners who, while partly being engaged with marine knowledge, are also pushed toward branding snares and spending traps. [31]This scenario could be avoided if, instead, the aquarium brought visitors out to the animals in their natural environment, educating them on the true lifestyles of species and cutting out profiteering and clouded intentions.

[32] A great wave is breaking: a rising understanding about why it is important to protect the natural lives of sea creatures. [33] Despite having to deal with dangerous predators, coexisting within an untouched animal kingdom strengthens the wellbeing of wildlife. [34] It allows them to exist without restraint, with power and natural beauty—rather than just for amusement or profit. [35] Aquariums would be far better off focusing their efforts on revitalizing the ocean, rather than simply placing their animals in spoonfuls of it. [36] Out there, the sea rolls on, drawing into its mystery a vast abundance of life that deserves, if nothing else, to be free.

Sample Essay SYN.1.C

[1] Few things are as exciting for a child as taking a field trip to the local aquarium to watch live dolphins perform tricks, and then move to touching turtles, starfish, sharks, and stingrays in open tanks. [2] When choosing to spend the day at an aquarium or other sea-life attraction, individuals must consider the personal fun and bonding that these institutions offer.

[3] Any trip to an aquarium should be centered on group fun and experiential learning. [4] An analysis from Allionce Group—a company that specializes in marketing to families—reveals that the whole point of a such an attraction is to encapsulate its guests in an experience that is "in the moment" (Source C). [5] Aquariums can provide these moments as they are places where children and parents are "free from many distractions" that may "compete for their attention" (Source C). [6] The feeling of being in an open environment with loved ones, friends, or classmates and teachers, especially when connected to nature, can not only offer adult caretakers "a respite from the chaos of everyday life," but also heavily boost the "emotional connection" children experience when they engage their surroundings with a sense of "discovery, curiosity, health, and wellness" (Source C). [7] These magical and sentimental features of sea-life attractions are essential for individuals to take into account when considering journeying to the aquarium because education and caring for the environment become more meaningful as they are tied to the positivity of the experience.

[8] When choosing to visit a sea-life attraction, individuals must consider how animals are cared for. [9] Source B states that The Association of Zoos and Aquariums (AZA) has developed an "accreditation" process that requires institutions that want to be certified by AZA, to "demonstrate alignment with [the AZA] mission" by showing "significant activity in areas of education, conservation, and research" in regard to its animals (Source B). [10] Most importantly, as of 2018, any accredited aquarium must demonstrate it has achieved "animal welfare" (Source B). [11] All of this is important to consider because people don't want to support institutions that are hurting animals more than helping them. [12] So, visitors need to focus on finding institutions that meet the minimum standards for AZA care.

[13] People should also consider the neurological effects that living in captivity can have on marine life, especially when selecting which institutions to support. [14] For example, Bob Jacobs, a professor of neuroscience, explains the development of "stereotypies or purposeless, repetitive actions" within certain caged animals, demonstrated by how they "pace their enclosures" as a coping mechanism for battling living in captivity (Source A). [15] Jacob's article then includes an illustration comparing the thinned cerebral cortex and capillaries of animals existing in an impoverished environment (captivity) to the typical, healthy cortex and capillaries of those residing in an environment filled with enrichment, such as a natural environment. [16] These images prove that an animal's health and happiness can exponentially decline if it does not have the needed enrichment it may find on its own out in the natural habitat within which it would typically reside. [17] However, with a general understanding of this truth, employees and visitors alike can work to support establishments that do their best to provide the greatest care, particularly those endorsed by the AZA.

[18] Without a doubt, well-run and maintained aquariums can be fun, educational, and inspiring.

Sample Essay SYN.1.D

[1] In an era where the concepts of business and entertainment have resulted in the marketing of marine wildlife to the masses, it becomes increasingly difficult for individuals to make a decision on whether or not to visit aquatic-based attractions. [2] When choosing to do so, it is essential that people understand the neurological wellbeing of animals in captivity, the moral and philanthropic natures of the institutions, and the unique experiences each offers before concluding which to attend.

[3] Individuals should consider the potential negative effects that domestication has on wildlife when removed from their natural habitats so they can make an informed choice about supporting or shunning particular establishments within the aquarium industry. [4]It's a well-established fact that many sea creatures "try to cope with captivity by adopting abnormal behaviors," and studies have shown that "impoverished, stressful" environments "physically [damage] the [brains]" of animals via the "thinning of the cortex," (Source A). [5] The effect that harsh living conditions could potentially have should impact an individual's decision to visit aquariums because the known and forced deterioration of mental capabilities of any form of life is unethical. [6] Yet, though neurodegeneration may happen, the "quality of life for animals under human care" has become "formally [embraced]" by many aquariums striving to provide "a higher standard of care" to combat the negative "effects on both" the "brain and behavior" of wildlife in captivity. [7] Therefore, newly regulated responses promoting the greater "understanding of animals' cognitive abilities" (Source B) are now being commonly put into place by many aquariums. [8] Thus, when deciding which institutions to support, individuals must conduct significant research into the facility and its governing practices so that unethical business are not praised or supported.

[9] When conducting research about an institution's ability to care for different marine species, individuals should look no further than any aquarium's independent credentials. [10] The formal process of accreditation ensures that zoos and aquariums are "maintaining and pioneering [the] best practices" by requiring that such facilities "demonstrate [they have] achieved animal welfare" (Source B). [11] The Association of Zoos and Aquariums (AZA) promote and certify wildlife exhibits. [12] When it comes to protecting "threatened and endangered species," these are the institutions "saving species in the wild" (Source E). [13] The process of accreditation reflects the moral values of a zoo or aquarium because the licensing process—especially by an independent, non-profit organization such as the Association of Zoos and Aquariums—confirms that an establishment is maintaining the highest quality of life for its collected species. [14] Since each species of marine creature requires its own unique care, the accreditation also confirms that institutions are conducting research so as to ensure that the environment provided is similar to that of an animal's natural conditions in the wild. [15] These factors should positively influence the decision by individuals to visit aquariums due to the fact that an accredited exhibit can be more trustworthy than others.

[16] Individuals should also consider the personal benefits of going to aquariums. [17] Families that attend "aquariums are uniquely 'in the moment'" and are actively engaged with several "core themes like discovery, curiosity, health, and wellness" (Source C) that are increasingly difficult to find in this contemporary era. [18] Such "fun, safe, and educational . . . experience[s]" are a perfect outlet for "essential . . . science and environment education" with "hands-on opportunities" suited for families or "students who might otherwise have no firsthand experience" with marine life (Source E). [19] The chances offered to develop one's mind by aquariums should be considered because the type of learning environment offered

is unique—fit for all ages while promoting essential skills such as curiosity and discovery.

[20] Currents of knowledge flow from beneficial, research-based, accredited facilities that work to recreate natural habitats for their captive marine life. [21] Any aquarium's willingness to defend threatened species completely justifies consistent visits and support. [22] In a world where standards are often overlooked in order to make a quick buck, the existence of non-profit organizations that ensure an optimum quality of life for its creatures provides little room for concern or qualm when deciding to visit an aquarium. [23] By attending such institutions, the mind is enveloped in a metaphorical tide of curiosity, awe, and revelation indiscriminate of an individual's age, resulting in a priceless takeaway: being able to consider the majesty and wonders of the ocean.

Sample Essay RA.2.A

[1] In his 1986 speech at the Statue of Liberty torch-lighting ceremony, Ronald Reagan not only acknowledges the contributions of immigrants but also underscores the importance of liberty. [2] In doing so, he conveys the continued significance of both freedom and the American Dream.

[3] In order to ultimately convey that the U.S. remains a beacon of hope, Reagan begins his speech applauding the often under-acknowledged hard work of those who immigrated to America. [4] He states, "They worked in our factories, on ships and railroads, in stores, and on road construction crews." [5] He also states that "they were teachers, lumberjacks, seamstresses, and journalists" who "came from every land." [6] By listing the roles of these immigrants, Reagan emphasizes how important these men and women were to society: they filled important jobs that helped society function and grow. [7] As Reagan notes, these men and women left their lives behind and worked diligently so that "their children would be well fed, clothed, and educated." [8] By paying homage to the immigrants who passaged through Ellis Island—the ones whose first sight of the U.S. was likely the very statue at which Reagan is delivering his speech—Reagan underscores the vale of the American Dream: it drew people to America, and without their efforts, our country would not be what it is today.

[9] Next, Reagan expounds upon the importance of liberty. [10] To show the importance of liberty in American history, Reagan references several key events. [11] These examples prove that liberty is not a new concept. [12] It's a core ideal of the nation that has been of the utmost importance for generations. [13] He also quotes Thomas Jefferson, one of the nation's founding fathers, to support his message about the importance of liberty. [14] Jefferson referred to liberty as a God-given gift, implying that it is precious. [15] For this reason, Reagan claims that "liberty must not be taken for granted." [16] Given that he is speaking during the 1980s, amidst the end of the Cold War and rise of communism, his American audience would likely find his message important. [17] Therefore, they'd be more receptive to his call for America to continue to be a "beacon of hope" that will "never be extinguished."

[18] In conclusion, Ronald Reagan acknowledges the immigrants' hard work and examines the role of liberty throughout American history to convey the value of the American Dream. [19] While the American Dream drove thousands of people to start a new life in America, for many, it was just that: a dream.

Sample Essay RA.2.B

[1] Since its beginning, America has prided itself on being a place where people could get a fresh start. [2] During the late 1800s and early 1900s, the American Dream was alive and well. [3] Thousands of people immigrated to the U.S. in hopes of a better life. [4] For many, seeing the Statue of Liberty was a sign they'd made it. [5] Because of this, Lady Liberty has come to symbolize freedom. [6] In his 1986 speech at the Statue of Liberty torch-lighting ceremony, Ronald Reagan uses repetition, questions, and unifying diction to convey his message about the importance of liberty in American history.

[7] Reagan begins his speech by repeating "they" when talking about the immigrants. [8] For example, he says "they were the men and women who labored all their lives" so that their children would have better lives. [9] This quote shows that the immigrants worked hard. [10] This is important because America wouldn't be what it is today without their hard work. [11] Reagan also says that "they worked in factories, on ships and railroads, in stores, and on road construction crews." [12] He then adds that "they were teachers, lumberjacks, seamstresses, and journalists." [13] By saying "they," he emphasizes that we owe a lot of gratitude to the people who immigrated here and worked hard because they are a huge part of the reason why America is what it is today. [14] This repetition is important to help Reagan convey his message.

[15] Reagan also poses questions. [16] "What was it that tied these profoundly different people together?" [17] He does this to show that liberty has always been important to U.S. citizens: it's an ideal the country was founded on. [18] This question helps further his message and is important because he is at the Statue of Liberty.

[19] Reagan concludes his speech by repeating the word "we" to unite Americans. [20] By saying "we are the keepers of the flame of liberty" and "we hold it high for the world to see," Reagan invigorates a sense of pride in his American audience. [21] This leads to his call to action. [22] He asks the audience to join him in the symbolic lighting of the torch. [23] This act will remind people that the ideal of freedom is alive and well in the United States.

[24] When considering the topic of liberty in the United States, it is clear that freedom has been important since the country's beginning and remains important today, decades after Reagan's 1986 speech.

Sample Essay RA.2.C *(This essay was written by Ellie Dishington.)*

[1] For centuries, immigrants arriving in America were greeted at Ellis Island by a towering woman that the country has come to recognize as a symbol of freedom, or in other words, a Statue of Liberty. [2] In Ronald Reagan's 1986 speech, commencing the centennial celebration of this Statue of Liberty, the president leaned on the history of immigrants' trials and unique stories, applauded those who fought for the nation's freedom and founding, and emphasized America's position as a role model to other countries in order to demonstrate that the greatness of the United States is largely due to its diverse people who value hard work, perseverance, and hope. [3] These traits were evident in the country's founders and remained central to all who subsequently sought, and still seek today, to immigrate to America, drawn to the nation's shores by their shared "love of liberty."

[4] Reagan begins his speech by recognizing the dedication of American immigrants and the perilous trials they experienced both before entering the country and after their arrival,

highlighting the fact that the journey these multitudes embarked on was tumultuous but created perseverant heroes. Immigrants were fleeing civil wars, famine, rising taxes, or religious persecution in their home countries. [5] Many had no money to their name, yet they "labored all their lives so that their children would be well fed, clothed, and educated." [6] America, considered the land of opportunity, gave these struggling families a glimmer of hope for the future, yet they had to fight and toil to achieve this liberating future. [7] Reagan applauds those who arrived in the country willing to put in hours of labor to assure a better life for their children, ordinary men and women who "worked in factories, on ships and railroads, in stores, and on road construction crews" to feed their families and find refuge from their past lives. [8] These stories of hardship and dedication remind Reagan's audience that the backbone of America—the working class—values perseverance even when it involves sacrifice and hard work. [9] If immigrants had not been willing to fight for what they wanted, a chance to live in America, they never would have fled their homes, boarded ships, and embarked on perilous journeys across the ocean. [10] These determined people filled each and every state, bringing with them their values of freedom and dedication and passing them down into the melting pot of what would become modern American society.

[11] In addition to telling the stories of America's immigrants, whom he names as heroes, Reagan illustrates the commitment of the nation's forefathers in fighting the Revolutionary War, further emphasizing the American values of perseverance and liberty. [12] The brave men and women who traveled to the New World in the 17th century not only faced bitter cold and famine but the oppression and restraint of their foreign British rulers. [13] Although the colonists were "few in number and [had] little to defend themselves," they were committed to fight, and win "a war for independence with what was then the world's most powerful empire." [14] The colonists' low chance of success and lack of military and financial reinforcements emphasize just how dedicated they were to their pursuit; against all odds, ordinary men and women came together to defend what they held sacred and to found a nation on the principle of mere freedom. [15] Reagan's recollection of the nation's earliest rebels is not an archaic history lesson: the values of the colonists were written into the Constitution, a document that still governs the American people under the same principles and emphasizes that independence has held central to the nation's identity since its founding.

[16] To demonstrate this continual focus on liberty in the present as well as the past, Reagan concludes his speech by recognizing the United States as a role model for nations that do not uphold the same values, thus reiterating the importance of freedom on a global level as well as the American value of hope. [17] Lady Liberty holds her torch high in the air, symbolizing the nation's high regard for freedom and calling in immigrants who seek to experience it for themselves. [18] However, Reagan recognizes that freedom is a universal human right, and that the Statue of Liberty should point other nations towards liberation as well. [19] Therefore, he asks his citizens to " hold [the flame of liberty] high for the world to see" as "a beacon of hope, a light unto the nations." [20] The president recognizes that injustices exist worldwide in places where millions of individuals are not yet free from oppressive regimes, yet he hopes for a day where the ideals that his nation so strongly esteems will be experienced by all people, no matter where they live. [21 Reagan's urge to his people to be "a beacon of hope" demonstrates that freedom cannot be a value of complacency, since it motivates his listeners to take action both in and out of America's borders, fueled by the hope that liberty may spread to surrounding nations and all oppressed people. [22] Without hope as a core value, colonists wouldn't have fought for freedom against a global empire,

immigrants wouldn't have left their homes, and America wouldn't have intervened in foreign affairs to uphold the freedom of others overseas. [23] Therefore, hope is required to continue the pursuit of liberty worldwide, with the history of the American people demonstrating just how powerful of an ideal it can be.

[24] No historian would say that America in the 19th and 20th centuries (and still today) was a land of justice and freedom for all; there were major issues that prevented vast majorities of people such as women or people of color from basic rights for centuries. [25] The Statue of Liberty was likely scoffed at by women, Native Americans, and people of color who lived under her gaze yet could not vote, attend college, or drink from the same water fountain as other fellow "free" citizens. [26] America was and is a flawed nation, but the value of perseverance is evident in the history of its hundreds of heroes that recognized their nation's flaws and sought to resolve them for the betterment of the entire country. [27] The civil rights movement, the women's suffrage movement, and dozens of conventions, marches, and petitions were led by dedicated American heroes that would not settle for partial independence but sought to carry on in their battle, looking forward to a day when all people will be able to look up at the Statue of Liberty "with joy and celebration" of their freedom at last.

Sample Essay RA.2.D

[1] For centuries, the Statue of Liberty greeted immigrants arriving in America at Ellis Island. [2] In Ronald Reagan's 1986 speech, the president leaned on the history of immigrants' trials and unique stories, applauded those who fought for the nation's freedom and founding, and emphasized America's position as a role model to other countries in order to demonstrate that the greatness of the United States is largely due to its diverse people who value hard work, perseverance, and hope.

[3] Given that he is speaking at a landmark that quickly came to symbolize the American Dream to those who passed through Ellis Island, Reagan begins his speech by honoring the tireless dedication the immigrants exhibited for the betterment of their families. [4] Reagan recognizes that these men and women faced hardships on their tumultuous journey to the U.S. and after they settled in. Consequently, he highlights the fact that the journey these people embarked on was tumultuous, yet it created persistent heroes. [5] Many immigrants had no money to their name, yet they "labored all their lives so that their children would be well fed, clothed, and educated." [6] America offered these struggling families a glimmer of hope for the future. However, the immigrants had to toil to achieve this liberating future. [7] Reagan applauds those who arrived in the country willing to put in hours of labor to assure a better life for their children. [8] By noting that they were ordinary men and women who "worked in factories, on ships and railroads, in stores, and on road construction crews," he underscores the tremendous adversity the immigrants faced. [9] Their hard work and dedication not only helped their families find refuge in this new country, but also their efforts helped shape America. [10] These people showed up to work each day and got the job done. [11] Knowing that these men and women were regular people, not celebrities, Reagan honors their memories so that they won't become a forgotten part of American history. [12] Given that Reagan's audience is likely composed of hard working Americans, some of whom possibly descendants of immigrants themselves, they'd likely appreciate these stories of hardship and dedication, as the stories would remind them of the value of perseverance, even when it involves sacrifice and hard work.

[13] In addition to telling the stories of America's immigrants, whom he names as heroes, Reagan illustrates the commitment of the nation's forefathers in fighting the Revolutionary War, further emphasizing the American values of perseverance and liberty. [14] Although the colonists were "few in number and [had] little to defend themselves," they were committed to fight, and win "a war for independence with what was then the world's most powerful empire." [15] The colonists' low chance of success and lack of military and financial reinforcements emphasize just how dedicated they were to their pursuit. [16] They came together to defend their values and to found a nation on the principle of mere freedom. [17] Reagan's patriotic recollection of the nation's earliest rebels is not an archaic history lesson. [18] It was prevalent in 1986, as America was in the final bouts of the Cold War. [19] Thus, by referencing Thomas Jefferson in his speech, Reagan reminds his audience that liberty has been at the core of American ideals since the country's beginning. [20] This reminder showcases the notion that America was built on liberty and thus liberty must remain one of the nation's core values.

[21] To demonstrate how much freedom matters, Reagan wraps up his speech by recognizing that the United States has the power to be a role model to other countries. [22] Reagan recognizes that freedom is a universal human right and that the Statue of Liberty should point other nations towards liberation as well. [23] Therefore, he asks his citizens to "hold [the flame of liberty] high for the world to see" as "a beacon of hope, a light unto the nations." [24] This is an important message given that in 1986 the U.S. was in the tail end of the Cold War. [25] Reagan is no stranger to the fact that injustices exist worldwide, yet he hopes for a better world—one where other countries get to enjoy the freedoms America has. [26] Reagan's urge to his people to be "a beacon of hope" demonstrates that freedom cannot be a value of complacency, since it motivates his listeners to take action both in and out of America's borders. [27] If the American people do not unite, the flame of democracy will grow dim. [28] Therefore, hope is required to continue the pursuit of liberty worldwide, with the history of the American people demonstrating just how powerful of an ideal it can be.

[29] America isn't a perfect country. [30] In fact, some may say the American Dream does not exist. [31] That being said, it is important to remember those who paved the way for our country to become what it is today. [32] Reagan hopes that his words will resonate with the modern generation—that they will look up at the relit torch and be proud of where they came from and part of helping to create a brighter future for the country.

Sample Essay ARG.3.A

[1] Throughout history, the most successful people have often been those who also failed at something. [2] But in schools, failure is almost always a bad word. [3] Even though the pain of failure and difficulty prevent many people from taking risks, intentionally facing difficult situations, like taking challenging classes, strengthens people, as shown by the failure of young Jay-Z to get a record contract and my own experience with Algebra I, ultimately proving that accepting challenges helps us begin to see difficulty as opportunity.

[4] Difficult situations strengthen people, as demonstrated by Jay-Z going from selling CDs from his trunk to becoming a billionaire. [5] When the rapper Jay-Z was first starting out, he couldn't get a record company to even listen to him, so he sold his own CDs and tapes out of his car until he got so popular he couldn't be ignored. [6] He eventually made enough money to start his own record label and is now a billionaire. [7] Because he faced these challenges, he probably became more successful than if had been signed to a record label early on.